SEND GUNS AND MONEY

Security Assistance and U.S. Foreign Policy

Duncan L. Clarke,
Daniel B. O'Connor, and
Jason D. Ellis

PRAEGER

Westport, Connecticut
London

Library of Congress Cataloging-in-Publication Data

Clarke, Duncan L.
    Send guns and money : security assistance and U.S. foreign policy
  / Duncan L. Clarke, Daniel B. O'Connor, and Jason D. Ellis.
        p.   cm.
    Includes bibliographical references and index.
    ISBN 0–275–95991–0 (alk. paper).—ISBN 0–275–95992–9 (pbk. :
alk. paper)
    1. Security Assistance Program.   2. United States—Foreign
relations—20th century.   I. O'Connor, Daniel B.   II. Ellis, Jason
D.   III. Title.
UA12.C53   1997
355'.032'0973—dc21   97–5885

British Library Cataloguing in Publication Data is available.

Library of Congress Catalog Card Number: 97–5885
ISBN: 0–275–95991–0 (hc)
        0–275–95992–9 (pb)

First published in 1997

Praeger Publishers, 88 Post Road West, Westport, CT 06881
An imprint of Greenwood Publishing Group, Inc.

Printed in the United States of America

The paper used in this book complies with the
Permanent Paper Standard issued by the National
Information Standards Organization (Z39.48–1984).

10 9 8 7 6 5 4 3 2 1

To Our Parents

Contents

Tables

Acknowledgments

An outstanding study in February 1989 by the Committee on Foreign Affairs of the House of Representatives offered convincing evidence that U.S. foreign assistance legislation was "strewn with obsolete, ambiguous and contradictory policies, restrictions and conditions." A lengthy conversation in 1990 by one of us (Duncan Clarke) with the principal drafter of the study, which was informally titled the Hamilton-Gilman Report, provided the catalyst for this book. The early assistance of this staff person was the first of countless debts we were to incur before completing our treatment of a subject that, to the surprise of many, including ourselves, retains as much importance today as it did in 1990 as the Cold War wound down and the conflict in the Persian Gulf escalated.

The project would not have been undertaken without the active support of Dean Louis W. Goodman, Associate Dean Nanette Levinson, and Professor John Richardson of American University's School of International Service. They were rightly convinced of the value of encouraging intensive, protracted research collaboration between a senior member of the faculty and two doctoral candidates. Many others were also supportive, including Professors Philip Brenner and Renée Marlin-Bennett. Each of us benefited from various research grants and, especially, from the school's commitment to policy research and to spirited intellectual engagement. Of particular importance was the research assistance given at various stages of the project by master's-level graduate students Jennyfer Jones, Steven Woehrel, and Nicole Lewis—all of whom are now talented foreign policy analysts in government.

Of course, our gratitude extends to many other individuals as well. This book would not have been possible without numerous confidential interviews with past and present U.S. government officials, several of whom read and commented on portions of the manuscript. Throughout the research and writing processes, we spoke—often repeatedly—with officials from various offices at the State Department, several units of the Department of Defense (including the Defense Security Assistance Agency and individuals at Wright-Patterson Air Force Base), the Agency for International Development, the National Security Council, and the Office of Management and Budget.

Similarly, several offices and staff members of committees and subcommittees in the House of Representatives and the Senate provided invaluable assistance. So, too, did analysts with the General Accounting Office, the Congressional Budget Office, the United States Institute of Peace, and especially, the Congressional Research Service. Washington, D.C.'s nongovernmental policy community also contributed to this endeavor.

The dozens of people who were so vital to this study did not always agree with one another or with the authors. We always adjusted our findings in the face of telling commentary or criticism from those who worked the issues on a daily basis. When criticism was unpersuasive, we did not alter our views. Clearly, these fine people share none of the blame for whatever flawed judgments may appear in these pages.

Abbreviations

ACDA	Arms Control and Disarmament Agency
AECA	Arms Export Control Act
AHEPA	American Hellenic Educational Progressive Association
AHI	American Hellenic Institute
AIA	Aerospace Industries Association
AID	Agency for International Development
AIPAC	American Israel Public Affairs Committee
ALESA	American League for Exports and Security Assistance
ATA	Anti-Terrorism Assistance
AWACS	Airborne Warning and Control System
CATT	Conventional Arms Transfer Talks
CEEC	Central and East European Coalition
CENTO	Central Treaty Organization
CIA	Central Intelligence Agency
CIP	Commodity Import Program
CPD	*Congressional Presentation Document*
CR	Continuing resolution
CRS	Congressional Research Service
CTR	Cooperative Threat Reduction
DOD	Department of Defense
DSAA	Defense Security Assistance Agency
EDA	Excess defense article

ESF	Economic Support Fund
FAA	Foreign Assistance Act
FMF	Foreign Military Financing
FMLN	Farabundo Marti National Liberation Front
FMS	Foreign Military Sales
FY	Fiscal year
GAO	General Accounting Office
GNP	Gross national product
ICA	International Cooperation Administration
IMET	International Military Education and Training
INL	International Narcotics and Law Enforcement Affairs
KEDO	Korean Energy Development Organization
MAAG	Military Assistance Advisory Group
MAP	Military Assistance Program
MASF	Military Assistance Service Fund
MDAA	Mutual Defense Assistance Act
MFO	Multilateral Force and Observers
NAAA	National Association of Arab Americans
NATO	North Atlantic Treaty Organization
NDF	Nonproliferation and Disarmament Fund
NIS	New Independent States
NSC	National Security Council
ODC	Overseas Development Council
PAC	Political action committee
PD	Presidential Directive
PFP	Partnership for Peace
PKO	Peacekeeping operation
PL	Public Law
PLO	Palestine Liberation Organization
SDAF	Special Defense Acquisition Fund
SEATO	Southeast Asia Treaty Organization
SEED	Support for East European Democracy
SSA	Security Supporting Assistance

Introduction

American foreign policy since 1947 cannot be understood apart from the U.S. security assistance* program. Beginning with President Harry S. Truman, every president has considered security assistance programs important means for furthering U.S. national interests. Security assistance has been used to support a wide variety of policies, including, to name only a few, the Truman Doctrine and containment; rebuilding the defenses of postwar Western Europe and, later, South Korea; underwriting the Camp David Accords between Egypt and Israel; assisting Israel and Turkey during the 1990–1991 Gulf War; and channeling aid to the newly democratic countries of Central and Eastern Europe and the New Independent States of the former Soviet Union.

From its inception until well into the Bush administration, a primary rationale behind security assistance was to counter communism worldwide. The early Bush administration, like previous administrations, adopted most of the tradi-

---

Security assistance defined: Approximately 95 percent of the U.S. security assistance program has consisted of (1) military assistance—grants and some low-interest loans to friendly countries for military equipment and training; and (2) economic assistance for special political-strategic purposes under the Economic Support Fund (ESF). The ESF is the single largest U.S. economic aid program. The State Department's annual *Congressional Presentation for Foreign Operations* includes two other programs: U.S. support for international peacekeeping operations (PKOs) and the education and training of foreign military personnel. Some U.S.-funded international narcotics control and anti-terrorist activities are often considered security assistance, as is the State Department's Non-proliferation and Disarmament Fund (NDF). Finally, the Foreign Assistance Act of 1961 defines security assistance to include even cash (commercial) arms sales, but we exclude this since foreign aid is our subject. The elements of security assistance are discussed in detail in Chapter 1. Unless otherwise noted, information in the text and the tables on funding levels by program, by country, and by year is expressed in *current-year* dollars as reported by the U.S. Agency for International Development.

tionally declared goals for, and arguments in support of, security assistance: It
helps friendly countries defend themselves against external and internal threats;
it strengthens the economies of friendly nations and advances U.S. economic
interests; and it promotes regional stability and maintains the cohesion of U.S.
alliances. Administrations have also maintained that, inter alia, security assistance secures U.S. access to overseas military bases and facilities; increases
Washington's influence with recipient states; and furthers understanding of
American values, institutions, and policies by educating military and civilian
personnel.[1] The collapse of the Soviet Union obviously eroded the original core
rationale for the security assistance program, but the late Bush administration
and the Clinton administration continued to justify security assistance by using
many of the other above-declared objectives, as well as by emphasizing the
democracy promotion, counternarcotics, and nuclear nonproliferation aspects of
the program.

None of these goals or rationales were ever unchallengeable or self-evident
truths. For instance, security assistance can certainly strengthen indigenous military capabilities, but it does not invariably promote regional political and military stability or deter threats to the recipient state. Indeed, U.S. security
assistance has arguably contributed to ongoing, potentially destabilizing situa-
tions in areas like the Middle East, where deterrence has failed repeatedly. Security assistance in the past has also gone to repressive, unpopular, and
undemocratic regimes in Iran, the Philippines, Guatemala, and elsewhere. Similarly, the correlation between aid and influence is imperfect at best. While
security assistance has clearly given the United States a lever for significantly
affecting the policies and practices of some recipient states, it has also sometimes
bred resentment, particularly when prolonged aid has contributed to a dependency relationship, as in the case of the Philippines, Honduras, and even Egypt.

If it was important in the past to question the official goals of security assistance, it is imperative to do so today. A central purpose of security assistance
until at least 1989 was to contain and counter the Soviet Union and other communist forces on a global scale. But by 1989, and certainly by 1991, this justification largely had evaporated. The upheaval in the Soviet Union,
disintegration of the Warsaw Pact, collapse of communism in all but a few hard-
core states, rise of democracy or democratic movements throughout much of
the world, and end of the Cold War swept away much of the old geopolitical
playing field. New political, economic, and security systems were and are evolving in Europe and in other regions. In addition, the U.S. foreign assistance
program is beset by several long-standing problems that the changing international system and competing claims on a fiscally constrained foreign aid budget
make much harder to ignore.

Dissatisfaction with the foreign assistance program is widespread, even among
its advocates. There is a growing consensus that there must be a substantial
reexamination and rethinking of its goals and purposes. In 1989, Congress,
through the Hamilton Task Force, recommended a sweeping overhaul of the

program. By early 1991 the Bush administration, albeit haphazardly, began to articulate additional, somewhat different, themes for security assistance. Security assistance, said administration officials, should help consolidate democracy through the rule of law, free elections, and respect for human rights; support arms control and nonproliferation initiatives and regional conflict resolution; foster free market economic forces; and counter transnational dangers such as environmental degradation.[2] But these themes were intended to complement, not replace, most of the traditional goals.

Even the Clinton administration's attempt in 1994 to offer a new comprehensive vision for foreign aid in the post–Cold War era—the proposed Peace, Prosperity, and Democracy Act—largely restated most of the program's traditional objectives. Indeed, most primary elements of the Clinton national security strategy rested, in part, on security assistance programs: enlarging the community of free market democracies, maintaining strong military forces with peacetime forward presence commitments, sustaining other political-military elements such as multilateral peace operations, and responding to such global threats as those posed by terrorists, nuclear proliferation, and narcotics traffickers.[3] At least in declaratory policy, security assistance figured as prominently in the Clinton foreign policy calculus as it did in many administrations during the Cold War.

A major difficulty with security assistance, and foreign aid generally, concerns expectations. What is security assistance expected to do for the United States and for recipient countries? Presently, security assistance is overburdened with multiple expectations and goals that often reflect a bygone era, are inherently contradictory, or simply cannot be met. While many argue that security assistance can continue to serve U.S. interests in a changed and still rapidly evolving world, popular and congressional support for foreign aid—especially military assistance—is tentative and fragmented. Some argue that, absent a redefinition of U.S. policy goals and a reconsideration of how all foreign assistance programs serve these goals, it is an open question whether the contribution that security assistance might make to U.S. policy will be deemed sufficient to outweigh the political problems it causes for the executive branch and, especially, Congress in managing and funding the program.[4]

While there is a growing chorus of those who assert that security assistance must adapt to new international security and domestic political environments, this is perhaps the sole area in which there is total agreement. Questions about how, where, and sometimes even *whether* security assistance can and should serve U.S. interests spark considerable controversy. We argue for significant changes in the security assistance program, yet we also recognize that a number of seemingly advisable changes are unlikely to be made—at least in the near term. Programmatic adjustments will occur, some recipient nations will come and go, and funding levels will rise and fall, but truly important programs— that is, those with domestic political support—are unlikely to be eliminated entirely in the near term. A conceptually satisfying harmonization of U.S. policy goals with security assistance and other foreign assistance programs will inevitably go substantially unrealized. This is because foreign assistance is infused with domestic as well as international political considerations. Foreign assistance straddles one of the busiest intersections of executive-legislative relations, an intersection where institutional, interest group, liberal-conservative, and individual goals and interests meet and regularly collide. This does not imply that security assistance cannot adjust to a new environment, but it does mean that this adjustment will inevitably be imperfect.

In some form, by whatever name, security assistance will almost certainly continue to play a role in U.S. foreign policy. Even in a post–Cold War international system, security assistance remains by far the largest component of the overall U.S. foreign assistance budget (almost 48 percent in fiscal year 1996). Today, Israel and Egypt routinely receive more than 90 percent of all security assistance, although aid levels to these two countries, especially Egypt, may not be quite as secure as generally assumed. Aid to Turkey and Greece is now almost entirely on a loan basis, but Turkey is widely considered to be important to U.S. interests, and Greece still commands substantial political backing in Congress. Moreover, regional conflict, terrorism, the proliferation of weapons of mass destruction, and illicit transborder narcotics trafficking will continue into the foreseeable future. Finally, the multinational peacekeeping forces in the Middle East and elsewhere will continue to require American political, military, and financial support.

Our treatment of the security assistance program through fiscal year 1996 is comprehensive, but the depth and breadth of coverage varies from topic to topic. Chapter 1 presents the ''basics'' of security assistance: its legal foundations and formal and informal components. There are also statistical data and analyses showing how aid levels and regional recipients of aid have changed over time. Chapter 2 is a historical survey of the program from 1946 through the Ford administration, and Chapter 3 continues this survey into the Clinton administration. Chapter 4 details congressional involvement in the security assistance program. Particular attention is given to the various legislative and budgetary levers that Congress employs to influence and, often, control the program.

In Chapter 5 we speculate about the role of elite and mass-based public opinion on the security assistance program. This chapter assesses the polling data and survey research concerning the American public's attitudes toward security assistance, and foreign assistance generally. It also delineates various schools of thought concerning the effectiveness and advisability of the program and examines the role of special interest groups in security assistance decisionmaking. Chapters 6 and 7 deal, respectively, with the primary recipients of security assistance funds: first, the so-called base-rights countries such as Turkey and Greece, then Egypt and Israel. The major focus of both chapters is on the recent past, the present, and the future. Finally, Chapter 8 reviews why the old consensus behind security assistance has changed and suggests what a new, workable consensus might look like. Above all, we underscore that even with the sweeping changes in the international geopolitical landscape over the past few years, there remain persuasive rationales for a continued security assistance program—albeit in altered form.

This first book on security assistance[5] would not have been possible without the cooperation and assistance of scores of present and former officials from the national security bureaucracy, Congress, and various congressional agencies. These dedicated people, of course, have no culpability for whatever misjudgments may appear in these pages.

NOTES

1. *Congressional Presentation Document for Security Assistance Programs, Fiscal Year 1991* (Washington, D.C.: Government Printing Office [hereafter, GPO], 1990), pp. 2–3; Craig M. Brandt, ed., *Military Assistance and Foreign Policy* (Wright-Patterson Air Force Base, Ohio: Air Force Institute of Technology, 1990), pp. 1–3.

2. *Congressional Presentation Document for Security Assistance Programs, Fiscal Year 1992* (Washington, D.C.: GPO, 1991), pp. 3–10.

3. White House, *National Security Strategy of the United States* (Washington, D.C.: GPO, February 1995).

4. See U.S. Congress, House, Committee on Foreign Affairs, *Report: U.S. Foreign Aid in a Changing World: Options for New Priorities*, 102d Cong., 1st sess., 1991, pp. 20–21.

5. There are many works that deal with elements of the program, significant Congressional Research Service reports, and several government-sanctioned commission studies. But there are only two (edited) books that attempt coverage of some aspects of the larger program: Ernest Graves and Steven A. Hildreth, eds., *U.S. Security Assistance: The Political Process* (Lexington, Mass.: Lexington Books, 1985); Brandt, *Military Assistance and Foreign Policy*.

1

Dimensions and Elements of Security Assistance

Every American administration throughout the Cold War period employed security assistance to support the overriding policy objective of containing the Soviet Union and its allies. As originally outlined by George Kennan in his famous "long telegram" and subsequent 1947 *Foreign Affairs* article "The Sources of Soviet Conduct," the containment doctrine called for stopping Soviet expansion at the periphery of the Soviet Union. While the doctrine envisaged a variety of nonmilitary means for achieving this objective, military means had clearly become paramount by at least the time of the Korean War.[1]

Two key postwar components of U.S. military strategy were forward defense and collective security. Under the concept of forward defense, American air, land, and naval forces were stationed overseas in allied and friendly nations, especially those in proximity to the Soviet Union or its allies. These forces were to deter aggression; fight, should deterrence fail; and demonstrate the credibility of America's commitment to its allies through their physical presence. The collective security concept encompassed both mutual defense treaties with individual countries, like Japan, and formal regional alliances such as the North Atlantic Treaty Organization (NATO), the Southeast Asia Treaty Organization (SEATO), and others.

Security assistance was a critical tool for supporting forward defense and collective security. For instance, concerning forward defense, the United States signed executive agreements with the Philippines, Spain, Portugal, Turkey, and Greece whereby Washington offered security assistance in exchange for the use of military bases and facilities within those countries. Likewise, the collective security objective was furthered when U.S. security aid enabled allied nations to better defend themselves from external or, sometimes, internal threats. Security assistance often reduced the need for committing U.S. troops to the defense of allies, and it funded several programs designed to facilitate political-military coordination between the United States and its allies.

Just as every president implements national security policy differently, the use of security assistance varies with the administration in office. For example, although President Dwight D. Eisenhower sought to constrain growth in the defense budget and U.S. conventional forces, he, nonetheless, employed security assistance assertively for the purpose of strengthening the network of U.S. alliances. The Kennedy and first Reagan administrations expanded security assistance and used it to complement global reassertions of American military power. Under the Nixon Doctrine, however, security assistance was seen as a partial substitute for the direct employment of American forces.

Security assistance policy, of course, is hardly the sole prerogative of the executive. Foreign aid is authorized and appropriated by a Congress that takes a keen, critical interest in the subject (see Chapter 4). It is with foreign assistance, perhaps more than any other area, where Congress can affect foreign policy most directly. As security assistance involves the transfer of American tax dollars to nonvoting foreigners, Congress also has a political incentive—albeit a highly selective one—to oversee the executive's expenditure of these funds. Moreover, legislators know that foreign aid, while often supported by elite opinion, has never been popular with Joe Sixpack and the American public (see Chapter 5). There are few political costs for voting to cut foreign aid, except from highly specific constituencies like wheat farmers, many Jewish Americans, and defense firms that stand to profit from a particular arms transfer.

Over the years, Congress has expressed several concerns about security assistance, including its negative impact on the U.S. balance of payments and its diversion of resources away from domestic priorities. Congress also has worried that security assistance might entangle the United States in ill-considered commitments. This fear is rooted partly in a conviction by some that U.S. aid to the Saigon government, beginning in the 1950s, contributed to the subsequent large-scale commitment of U.S. troops to South Vietnam in the 1960s. Two other categories of concerns are commonly expressed: that security assistance has sometimes buttressed repressive undemocratic governments that abuse their citizens' human rights and that it has been a force for regional instability by contributing to arms races and military coups.

Because of these misgivings and the political volatility of foreign aid, Congress has restricted the president's flexibility to dispense security assistance. The original Greek-Turkish Aid Act of 1947 had comparatively few constraints on the president, but subsequent legislation embodied increasingly more stringent requirements for the allocation and receipt of such aid. Nor has Congress hesitated to exercise its budgetary prerogatives. Long before the post–Cold War, budget-cutting, Republican 104th Congress in 1995, the president's security assistance request was often reduced by 10 percent or more. Similarly, Congress has earmarked ever larger portions of the security assistance budget for favored nations and programs since the 1970s.

American security assistance policy is ultimately the product of bargaining and compromise between the president and Congress. The usual pattern has been for the president to propose and present a program he believes meets both national security requirements and at least some major congressional concerns. However, especially since the mid-1970s, Congress has often determined significant security assistance policies, even over executive branch opposition.

It is necessary at the outset to move beyond the summary definition of *security assistance* provided in the introduction. This chapter first gives a condensed overview of the major legislation that has governed the security assistance program since the 1940s. The principal formal elements of the program and their respective legal underpinnings are then detailed, although more attention is given to the broader foreign policy and geopolitical context of successive pieces of legislation in Chapters 2 and 3. Also addressed here, if briefly, are some smaller security assistance programs. The chapter's essential purpose is to provide a foundation for understanding the larger subject.

OVERVIEW OF MAJOR LEGISLATION

The first significant security assistance legislation was enacted in 1946. It authorized $20 million to train and equip the armed forces of the Philippines. In exchange, the United States gained access to 23 air and naval bases in that country for 99 years.[2] But 1947 marked the real beginning of the program. That year, President Truman issued a dramatic announcement that U.S. arms and advisers would be sent to Greece and Turkey to assist those countries resist communist insurgencies and threats. Toward this end, Congress enacted the Greek-Turkish Aid Act of 1947 (Public Law [PL] 80–75).

Much more comprehensive legislation was passed in 1949. The Mutual Defense Assistance Act (PL 81–329) was a security complement to the Marshall Plan's economic aid to Western Europe. It created what was to become a central element of U.S. foreign aid, the Military Assistance Program (MAP), discussed below. The Mutual Defense Assistance Act provided a statutory basis both for military aid to the new North Atlantic Treaty Organization and for cash Foreign Military Sales (FMS). It was followed by the Mutual Security Act of 1951 (PL 82–165), which consolidated the authorization for military and economic aid into one statute and established a Mutual Security Agency to administer the distribution of military and economic assistance. By authorizing the disbursement of economic assistance for the purpose of sustaining the military capabilities of friendly and allied nations, this legislation also created an early basis for what was to become the Economic Support Fund (ESF) in fiscal year (FY) 1979. Moreover, the act consolidated several prior statutes authorizing military aid to Greece, Turkey, the Philippines, Iran, and South Korea under this one legal umbrella.

Finally, still in this early postwar period, the cornerstone of the Eisenhower administration's aid program was the Mutual Security Act of 1954 (PL 83–665).

This act repealed all prior legislation. It authorized (section 131) one of several forerunners to the ESF, the Defense Support Program, for the purpose of channeling to friendly countries "commodities, services and financial . . . assistance designed to sustain . . . military effort." The act also authorized the FMS credit program and allowed the extension of security assistance to U.S. alliance partners.[3]

In 1961 the entire foreign aid system was reorganized. Congress consolidated major aid programs—including FMS, MAP, and security assistance for economic support—into the Foreign Assistance Act of 1961 (PL 87–185). The act created the Agency for International Development (AID), authorized peacekeeping operations, and for the first time, permitted the use of economic support funds for political purposes (instead of solely for sustaining military capabilities). All security assistance legislation since 1961 has been in the form of an amendment to the 1961 Foreign Assistance Act. As amended, the Foreign Assistance Act remains the principal legal foundation for U.S. foreign aid, including security assistance.[4]

The first major amendment to the 1961 legislation was the Foreign Military Sales Act of 1968 (PL 90–629), which provided separate authorizations for the FMS cash and FMS credit programs. Congressional concern about the levels and purposes of arms transfers was clearly manifested by the mid-1970s. The Foreign Assistance Act of 1973 (PL 93–189) mandated a reduction in the role of the U.S. government "in the furnishing of defense articles and defense services to foreign countries" and a "return . . . to commercial channels." Foreign aid legislation in 1974 forbade the use of security assistance to train police in foreign countries. It also contained the Nelson Amendment (PL 93–559, sections 36 [4] [b], 660), requiring that Congress be notified before the president offered to sell defense articles or services worth $25 million or more. Under this provision, Congress could, within twenty days of receiving such notification, pass a concurrent resolution overriding the proposed sale unless the president declared that an "emergency" existed.

Amid continuing concern about the utility of arms sales and military assistance generally, Congress passed the International Security and Arms Export Control Act of 1976 (PL 94–329). The Arms Export Control Act (AECA) again consolidated the laws governing U.S. arms sales. It covered both cash and credit sales and sales by both the U.S. government and private commercial contractors. The AECA separated the International Military Education and Training (IMET) program (discussed below) from the larger MAP program and mandated a phaseout of the latter.[5] Section 104 of the act also extended the time under the Nelson Amendment in which Congress could disapprove an arms sale from 20 to 30 days. Finally, while allowing for exceptions, section 502(b) incorporated a strong human rights provision: "[N]o security assistance may be provided to any country [whose] government engages in gross consistent violation of internationally recognized human rights."

The AECA represented a sweeping revision of those articles of the Foreign

Assistance Act of 1961 governing arms transfers, and it superseded outright the Foreign Military Sales Act.[6] Other important legislation is mentioned below. However, while there is considerable sentiment for changing the present statutory framework, the Foreign Assistance Act and the AECA continue to guide the security assistance program. Despite calls for wide-ranging reform during the Bush and first Clinton administrations, the program was revised only marginally.

OVERALL LEVELS OF SECURITY ASSISTANCE

Approximately one half of all U.S. foreign aid since 1946 has been security assistance. Only about 10 percent of foreign aid in the 1946–1950 period was security assistance, but with the outbreak of the Korean War in 1950 and the proliferation of postwar U.S. alliances, military assistance rose to 50 percent of the foreign aid budget. Military assistance plus the ESF constituted about two thirds of all foreign aid during the decade of the 1950s. Security assistance declined as a percentage of the foreign aid budget in the 1960s because military aid to Southeast Asia was moved out of this budget into a special Department of Defense (DOD) account—the Military Assistance Service Fund (MASF)—and because Presidents John Kennedy and Lyndon Johnson placed relatively greater emphasis on food and development aid. Much security aid during this period was channeled through a precursor of the ESF, the Security Supporting Assistance Fund.

During the Nixon administration, security assistance rose to more than 60 percent of the foreign assistance budget, primarily because of a sharp rise in military aid to the Middle East and East Asia. In the first two years of the Carter administration, security assistance dipped to 51 percent of overall U.S. aid allocations. Following a somewhat erratic transition in the second half of the Carter administration in which military aid first jumped to 48 percent of all U.S. aid in 1979 and then dropped to 22 percent in 1980, the Reagan administration established a steady new aid pattern in which development aid hovered around 40 percent of U.S. aid, the ESF ranged from 20 to 29 percent, and military aid constituted 30 to 39 percent of total assistance. Security assistance in the Bush administration declined gradually from 60 percent of the foreign assistance budget at the outset to about 50 percent of the $15.9 billion FY 1992 foreign aid budget.[7] Under Clinton, as overall foreign aid levels fell sharply, the percentage of aid going to security assistance fluctuated between 42 and 48 percent (see Table 1.1).

The data on the regional distribution of security assistance are also instructive (see tables in Chapters 2 and 3). In the early postwar period, security aid went primarily for rearming Western Europe. The expanding American commitment in East Asia is reflected clearly in the data for the 1953–1961 period. While some of the assistance to East Asia during this period went to Japan, most went to Vietnam to support the French and, later, the Saigon government. The data

Table 1.1
Post–Cold War Security Assistance Allocations by Program, FY 1992–FY 1996 (in millions of dollars)

PROGRAM	FY 92	FY 93	FY 94	FY 95	FY 96
ESF	3045.9	2857.3	2166.9	2368.6	2346.4
Int'l. Narcotics Control	147.8	147.8	100.0	105.0	150.0
Anti-Terrorism	11.8	15.6	15.2	15.2	15.0
Nonproliferation	--	--	10.0	10.0	20.0
FMF Grants	3992.3	3300.0	3149.3	3151.3	3207.5
FMF Loan Subsidy	50.1	149.0	46.5	47.9	64.4
IMET	44.6	42.5	21.3	25.5	19.0
Military-Military Contact	--	--	10.0	12.0	--
PKOs	27.6	27.2	75.6	75.0	72.0
TOTALS	7320.1	6539.4	5594.8	5810.5	5894.3
% Total Foreign Aid	48.9%	40.0%	41.9%	42.3%	47.8%

FMF = Foreign Military Financing.
PKOs = Peacekeeping operations.
Notes: Numbers rounded to nearest hundred thousand dollars. Dashes (--) indicate no funding for that fiscal year. Percentage calculations made
   by the authors.
Sources: Congressional Research Service; House Committee on Appropriations, Subcommittee on Foreign Operations (H.R. 104–143); U.S.
   Agency for International Development.

for the years 1962–1976 indicate the impact of the Vietnam War on the program as well as the growing assistance to regional allies like Thailand, South Korea, and the Philippines. The Near (Middle) East region also rose to prominence during this period after the 1967 and, especially, 1973 Arab-Israeli wars. In both the East Asian and Near Eastern cases, Security Supporting Assistance (SSA) comprised about 25 percent of the regional aid allocations.[8] Although a multi-billion-dollar aid program to Pakistan began in 1981, the Near East has dominated the security assistance program since the late 1970s—one tangible result of the 1979 peace treaty between Israel and Egypt (see Table 1.2). Israel and Egypt are the largest two recipients of foreign aid. From FY 1977 to the present, these two countries have accounted for an approximate aggregate 40 percent of all U.S. foreign aid and at least 60 percent of all security assistance funds.[9] Beyond this, the data reveal an expanded, global utilization of security assistance from the mid-1970s through the mid-1980s. Under Reagan, for example, Latin America became a significant recipient of security aid, although funds for this region leveled off in the Bush years and declined precipitously in the Clinton administration.

Given a steadily shrinking foreign aid pie, and continued actual or de facto congressional earmarking of large annual allocations to Israel and Egypt (see Chapter 7), there is an ever smaller pool of funds available for other countries. Even with aid to the so-called base-rights countries (see Chapter 6) in substantial decline during the Bush and Clinton eras, the end of the Cold War brought new programs in Eastern Europe and elsewhere to the foreign assistance table in their stead. Doing more with less became the catch phrase of the 1990s, as funds continued to decline and program responsibilities expanded.

ELEMENTS OF SECURITY ASSISTANCE

Security assistance has several components, the most significant of which are the Foreign Military Financing (FMF) and ESF programs and the former MAP program. Smaller program elements and security assistance–related endeavors include the IMET program, select peacekeeping operations, the Special Defense Acquisition Fund (SDAF), defense articles transfer and stockpiling, anti-terrorism assistance, the Nonproliferation and Disarmament Fund (NDF), and international narcotics control aid.

Military Assistance Program

Until phased out in FY 1989, the Military Assistance Program—which dated from the 1949 Mutual Defense Assistance Act—was the oldest U.S. security assistance program. MAP armed allied and friendly governments through direct grants for U.S. military equipment, services, and training. These grants were valued at more than $54 billion by FY 1982. Most of the military equipment transferred during the program's earlier years represented surplus World War II

Table 1.2
Post–Cold War Security Assistance Allocations by Region, FY 1992–FY 1996 (total military and economic aid in millions of dollars)

REGION	FY 92	FY 93	FY 94	FY 95	FY 96
Africa	54.7	35.8	19.8	12.1	31.0
Europe	1199.7	1232.0	851.1	809.5	926.9
Near East	5326.3	5341.2	4951.1	5527.3	5235.8
Asia	1437.0	126.6	44.6	44.9	101.1
Latin America	674.4	704.3	303.1	256.3	287.5

Notes: Figures for FY 1996 allocations are the administration's request, and percentage calculations are based on H.R. 1561 (House foreign aid authorization level of $11.3 billion); neither represents a final dollar amount. Numbers rounded to nearest hundred thousand dollars. In this table, military and economic aid include ESF, counternarcotic, FMF, and IMET funds.

Source: Congressional Research Service.

and Korean War defense articles that were no longer essential to U.S. defense requirements.

The MAP was initially intended to aid countries deemed important to the United States for collective security purposes, particularly NATO nations that could not afford costly military equipment. Indeed, the program was directed primarily toward Europe until about 1962. Thereafter, MAP grants went principally to the developing world. As industrial countries became able to pay for this equipment, and as the stocks of surplus defense articles began to dwindle, many foreign governments turned to commercial purchases of U.S. military equipment. Not surprisingly, therefore, MAP appropriations fell from $4.3 billion in FY 1952, to $1.7 billion in FY 1968, to $176 million in FY 1979.[10]

The Foreign Assistance Act of 1961 reauthorized MAP and governed the program until the AECA of 1976 changed it in important respects. Most notably, the AECA provided for the gradual elimination of the program. But in FY 1982 the MAP and FMS credit programs were merged, and the former was given new life with an appropriation of $171 million. Funding for MAP continued to rise during the Reagan administration to a high of $906 million in FY 1987, before dropping in FY 1988 and ending altogether the next year.[11] Nations receiving MAP funds could use them to purchase military goods, training, and services only from the United States. DOD regulations regarding pricing, delivery, inventory, and disposal of military equipment had to be followed by the recipients of MAP grants, and DOD was charged with monitoring the grants. The United States retained reversionary rights on all equipment provided under the MAP program; that is, Washington could reclaim the items provided. This reversionary rights stipulation, however, was eliminated with the FY 1982 incorporation of MAP into the FMS program.[12]

Foreign Military Financing Program

A clarification of terminology is necessary here. The FMS credit program became the Foreign Military Financing program in FY 1989. Both are central to any examination of security assistance. The FMS cash and Direct Commercial Sales programs are also formally classified as security assistance, but because they involve cash purchases of arms instead of U.S. government–funded purchases, they are *not* foreign aid programs and are beyond the scope of this book. Unless otherwise indicated, *FMS* refers to the FMS credit program. The acronyms FMS and FMF will sometimes be used interchangeably.

The FMS credit program dates from 1954 and was designed to permit allies and friends of the United States to purchase American military equipment and services on a credit basis. Most FMS participants were Third World countries. Prior to FY 1969, FMS was an element of MAP. Since then, FMS/FMF has been an independent program, and since FY 1976, it has been the largest U.S. military assistance program. All FMF loans come through the normal appropriations process, although before FY 1985 they were a combination of appropriated funds and "off-budget" lending. By the 1980s, the overall national debt burdens of many of the countries that were receiving these loans were staggering. Their FMS debts to the United States contributed, significantly in some cases, to the financial plight of these nations. In response, beginning in FY 1985 with Egypt and Israel, the U.S. government shifted the program's focus from loans to "forgiven loans" (grants) and concessional (low-interest) loans. In recent years, about 95 percent of the entire military aid package has been in the form of outright grants.[13]

The two primary components of security assistance, military aid and the Economic Support Fund (discussed next), composed approximately 33 percent and 27 percent, respectively, of all foreign aid in FY 1990. By FY 1995, the amount allocated for military aid had fallen to 24 percent, and the ESF allocation fell to 17 percent. Between FY 1985 and FY 1995, Congress appropriated $85.1 billion in FMF grants and loans, of which Israel received $38.4 billion and Egypt $19.8 billion. From FY 1977 through FY 1995, these two countries received more than 60 percent of all U.S. military aid, and their slice of a shrinking military assistance pie has been much greater than 60 percent since the end of the Cold War. Since FY 1987 the annual FMF allocation for Israel and Egypt, respectively, has been $1.8 billion and $1.3 billion. Turkey and Greece have also usually ranked among the top five recipients of FMF since the late 1970s. Of all countries receiving assistance in FY 1991, four accounted for 84 percent of the FMF program: Israel, Egypt, Turkey, and Greece.[14] Nor did this decrease with the end of the Cold War. By FY 1995, these four received almost all (98.7 percent) of allocated FMF funds.

Economic Support Fund

Background. The first of several forerunners to the ESF was a 1951 program called Economic Support of Defense (or Defense Support) that was authorized by the Mutual Security Act of that year. The program's purpose was to provide economic assistance for budget support so as to enable recipient countries to channel more resources toward building up their defense infrastructures. Defense Support financed the importation of raw materials, commodities, equipment, and military-related supplies. Between 1951 and 1961, Southeast Asia and South Korea received about 65 percent of this aid. Taiwan and Western Europe were also major beneficiaries. Defense Support was not development assistance, although it did underwrite some long-term development projects, especially in Pakistan and the Philippines.[15]

The 1961 Foreign Assistance Act changed the name of Defense Support to Supporting Assistance and expanded its scope. In addition to helping countries sustain their defense capabilities, the act now permitted Supporting Assistance to be used for the general objective of promoting political or economic stability. From 1964 through 1974, over 72 percent of Supporting Assistance went to Southeast Asia, primarily South Vietnam. Most of the aid supported commodity imports to assist the Saigon government's war effort, but a small portion did fund economic development projects. During this period the program again changed its name, this time to Security Supporting Assistance.

In 1971 Congress shifted authority for SSA from the economic to the military side of the Foreign Assistance Act in order to distinguish it from development aid. The program's purpose, however, remained the same.[16] Following the 1973 Arab-Israeli war, the thrust of SSA shifted toward the Middle East. Between FY 1975 and FY 1981, Israel and Egypt received nearly $10 billion in SSA, or 75 percent of all SSA disbursements. SSA increasingly moved away from direct support for U.S. overseas military interests and toward more "political" objectives in the Middle East. In 1973, in what became known as the New Directions Policy, Congress required that development aid be focused more directly on well-defined projects for the poorest populations of developing nations.

This relative emphasis on long-term economic projects, rather than on the rapidly disbursing budget support character of SSA, thereafter found its way into security assistance legislation. But a 1978 amendment to the Foreign Assistance Act (PL 95–384) merely urged the president to program economic security assistance consistent with the conditions for development assistance "to the maximum extent possible." While Congress changed the name of SSA to the Economic Support Fund that year, economic project aid has composed only a minority portion of the ESF since 1978. PL 95–384, the relevant sections of which remain in effect today, permitted the program to retain its most prominent features: immediate impact and flexible political or security-related application. The report accompanying this legislation states that the new program name, ESF, "reflects more accurately the actual use of these funds: to provide *budget support* and development assistance to countries of *political* importance to the United States" (emphasis added).[17]

Following the Soviet Union's invasion of Afghanistan in 1979, and particularly after the assertively anti-communist Reagan administration took office in 1981, the ESF grew dramatically. It increased from $2.2 billion in FY 1981 to $5.2 billion in FY 1985. The number of nations receiving ESF aid jumped from 20 in 1979 to 60 in 1985. Since FY 1986, while ESF has remained the largest single U.S. economic aid program, it has been affected by several factors, including budgetary pressures, congressional earmarking (discussed below), and by 1991, the substantial collapse of world communism.[18]

Purpose and Recipients. While the broad purpose of ESF since 1951 has been to promote U.S. political and security interests, economic security aid has never been defined precisely. Said a former U.S. ambassador in 1958: The category of U.S. aid "capable of creating the most confusion is 'defense support' [ESF]. One wonders whether this was . . . one motive in coining the phrase."[19] Stated differently, a congressional staff member found that ESF has a "constructive ambiguity" that is encouraged by the executive branch and is usually acceptable to a majority of Congress.[20]

Prior to 1990–1991, the most commonly cited objective of ESF was to thwart communist or communist-inspired aggression. Indeed, Larry Nowels rightly observes that during the Cold War, when international affairs were viewed largely in East-West terms, "virtually any country became a security asset if policymakers could show that the ESF program would exert pressure on Soviet or Soviet-client interests, or that it would bring the recipient into a closer relationship with the West."[21] Four other purposes of the ESF are commonly given: to maintain and promote Middle East peace, to facilitate U.S. access to overseas military bases, to foster political and economic stability, and since 1989, to assist newly emerging democracies.

The State Department directs the program, and AID administers it. From FY 1987 to the winding down of the Cold War in FY 1991, the annual ESF budget fluctuated between $3 and $4 billion. It fell to $2.4 billion by FY 1995. During the Reagan and early Bush administrations, countries like El Salvador, Pakistan, and the Philippines were often major recipients. But by FY 1995 Egypt and Israel received 85 percent of all ESF aid. Indeed, as of 1995, Israel and Egypt together accounted for 64 percent ($49.5 billion) of *all* U.S. economic security assistance distributed since the program's inception in 1951 ($77.4 billion).[22] Moreover, unlike any other ESF recipient, Israel, since 1985 (PL 99–83), has received all of its ESF aid as a lump-sum cash payment within the first 30 days of the fiscal year. These funds are then invested in U.S. Treasury notes until used. Annual interest paid on the notes—usually ranging from $50 million to $86 million—constitute substantial additional costs to the U.S. government.[23] This privilege was extended to FMF grants in FY 1991 (PL 101–513).

Components of ESF. There are three types of ESF aid: funds for the Commodity Import Program (CIP), development aid programmed for specific projects, and by far the largest, balance of payments support in the form of cash payments. Virtually all ESF funds are grants.

The CIP helps nations finance the importation of commodities. As Table 1.3 indicates, it now comprises less than 10 percent of the ESF. Congress has generally supported the CIP because the commodities must be purchased in the United States, and at least one half of these commodities must be shipped aboard U.S.-flagged vessels.[24] Project aid (discussed below) is the most developmental element of ESF, but cash transfers constitute the lion's share of the program. With cash transfers, the U.S. government simply writes a check to the recipient government for the authorized amount. Officially, cash transfers further four objectives: meeting U.S. political commitments to Egypt and Israel, securing U.S. access to overseas bases, assisting economic stabilization in friendly nations with serious balance of payments problems, and promoting economic policy reform.[25] As a rule, cash transfers may not be used for military purposes, although exceptions have been made for Israel.[26]

During the Cold War, presidents generally favored ESF because it afforded a degree of flexibility largely unrestricted by conditions that apply to other economic aid programs. It could facilitate relatively timely aid disbursements because a higher percentage of ESF goes for budget outlays in the first fiscal

Table 1.3
ESF Program Distribution, FY 1981–FY 1995 (in thousands of dollars)

FISCAL YEAR	CASH	CIP	PROJECT	TOTAL
1981	1,173,180	370,500	655,615	2,199,295
1982	1,470,714	597,500	702,050	2,770,264
1983	1,587,685	502,250	881,527	2,971,462
1984	1,011,894	301,055	1,833,217	3,146,166
1985	3,534,280	625,700	1,087,404	5,247,384
1986	3,477,580	446,149	989,267	4,912,996
1987	2,319,194	356,145	1,236,913	3,912,252
1988	1,793,211	357,278	869,766	3,020,255
1989	2,074,450	341,900	995,329	3,411,679
1990	2,510,652	227,241	1,272,964	4,010,857
1991	2,900,713	227,503	989,237	4,117,453
1992	1,806,916	202,000	1,036,980	3,045,896
1993	1,854,200	200,000	803,075	2,857,275
1994	1,419,000	200,000	547,906	2,166,906
1995 (est.)	1,655,328	200,000	513,272	2,368,600

Note: Since 1985, cash transfers include at least $1.2 billion for Israel; also $200 million for Egypt (appropriated but sometimes not obligated in the same year) is cash transfer. At least $200 million annually is for a CIP in Egypt.

Source: U.S. Agency for International Development.

year than does any other component of the foreign aid budget. Furthermore, unlike other aid accounts, ESF could be programmed in several ways so as to afford executive branch policymakers options in using the money. And some of the cash transfer account, unlike project aid, could be quickly reprogrammed to meet new requirements. However, heavy congressional earmarking of the ESF account by the 1980s, particularly in order to protect Israel and Egypt, greatly reduced presidential flexibility and, as a consequence, the appeal of ESF. Although many executive branch officials have long considered Israel's large portion of ESF to be unwarranted, Congress continues to shield Israel and, because of Israel, Egypt.[27]

A major problem with cash transfers is the issue of accountability. Recipient governments are required to maintain cash transfers in a separate account, but cash is fungible. It is, therefore, particularly vulnerable to unauthorized diversions, including from economic to military uses.[28]

ESF as Development Assistance? Although the ESF is economic assistance, it is classified as "security assistance" in the president's budget and grouped with military aid. This classification causes some confusion as to precisely what should constitute development assistance within the foreign aid budget. Coupling ESF with military aid makes security assistance the largest single element of the total budget. Alternatively, if the ESF is included with multilateral and bilateral development assistance, economic aid becomes the largest component.

Some security advocates, for various reasons, have argued that Congress should regard ESF as development aid.[29] However, while the ESF does fit somewhat uncomfortably with military aid, it is even less compatible with development aid. Congress allocates less than one-third of ESF for development, and this allocation has gone to further high-priority political-strategic interests, such as promoting Middle Eastern and Central American peace. Sound, self-sustaining, long-term development has consistently been a secondary objective. ESF, in fact, often hinders effective economic and political development.[30] As Bush administration AID administrator Alan Woods commented, "[S]trategic aid, sometimes in the form of direct payment transfers, has little bearing on development."[31] Furthermore, administrations regularly use a portion of the ESF as "political assistance" or "walking around money." For example, when Vice President Dan Quayle visited Jamaica and Nicaragua in 1990, he took several million dollars from the ESF to disperse locally. Indeed, virtually all U.S. foreign aid, including military and most development and humanitarian assistance, is designed to meet political-strategic objectives.[32] This is why the State Department, not DOD or AID, generally leads the interagency process for allocating ESF funds unless the White House intervenes.

International Military Education and Training Program

The U.S. military began to train and educate members of the armed forces of foreign countries in 1947. These functions were then transferred to the MAP program, where they remained until the AECA of 1976 placed them in a distinct and separate military assistance program—the International Military Education and Training program. All IMET aid is in grant form. DOD's Defense Security Assistance Agency (DSAA) manages the program, with the participation of the military departments and the unified military commands. The State Department determines the political advisability of instituting or continuing IMET in a particular country and also recommends country funding levels to Congress.

IMET has two broad missions. The first is to provide professional military education and technical training for allied or friendly armed forces. The training may be in the use and maintenance of American weapons and equipment or in a wide variety of other activities. In 1990 the U.S. military offered 2,000 courses at over 150 military schools in the United States and abroad. Foreign students who come to the United States receive English-language instruction and are offered DOD's "Instructional Program," a curriculum that furthers IMET's second mission: to expose foreign military personnel to democratic values, respect for individual and human rights, and belief in the rule of law. The Instructional Program is not designed to change behavior, but it may have affected the attitudes of some participants.[33]

A 1990 General Accounting Office (GAO) review of IMET stated that it was established to create skills necessary for the effective operation and maintenance of equipment provided by the United States; assist foreign countries in developing the expertise and systems needed for the effective management of their defense establishments; foster foreign countries' development of their own training capabilities; provide an alternative to Soviet military training; promote military rapport between the United States and foreign countries; and promote a better understanding of the United States, including its people, political system, and other institutions, showing how they reflect the U.S. commitment to and respect for human rights.[34] According to DOD, emphasis on these objectives should shift progressively from operations and maintenance, to management of in-country capabilities, and finally, to preserving military rapport with and understanding of the United States. The "ultimate objective is to limit programs to the latter and should be pursued as rapidly as possible, consistent with the achievement of overall objectives."[35]

The IMET program was expanded in FY 1991 (PL 101–513) to permit, in the case of existing and newly emerging democratic nations, the training of *civilian* as well as military officials in managing military establishments and budgets and in creating effective military codes of conduct and military judicial systems. IMET subsequently expanded rapidly into virtually all East European countries, including even Albania. Finally, while IMET is not concerned primarily with what is sometimes awkwardly called "nation- building" in developing countries (i.e., strengthening national infrastructures), some nation-building skills are offered, such as training in communications, health care, electronics, and management. Some U.S. officials in AID and elsewhere favor selective, case-by-case expansion of IMET into this area.[36] It has also drawn bipartisan support from many members of Congress, with Senator Alan Cranston (D-Calif.) even recommending in 1991 changing the name of the program from IMET to the Democratic Military Education and Training program, since this "best puts the program's title in sync with its purpose."[37]

IMET is a relatively low-cost program. Between 1950 and 1995 the United States spent $2.6 billion on IMET—roughly equivalent to recent annual allocations for ESF—to train approximately 585,000 personnel from about 140 countries worldwide. Since the mid-1980s, the largest number of foreign officers in the program have been from Latin America, especially Central America and such illicit drug–producing nations as Colombia and Bolivia. Other countries well represented in recent years include Thailand, Turkey, the Philippines, Egypt, and former East bloc nations.[38] While the program consistently received between $45 and $50 million annually during the Reagan and Bush administrations, in the post–Cold War Clinton years program funding declined substantially (see Table 1.1). Despite lower program funding, however, there were numerous military-to-military contacts with, especially, the former Soviet Union and Eastern Europe after 1992. Thus, although IMET has suffered, many of its missions have carried forward.

Criticisms have been leveled against training and education programs such as IMET for, among other things, fostering a potentially unhealthy dependence on the supplier nation.[39] However, IMET has broad support, not only within the U.S. national security bureaucracy and Congress but from many foreign governments. For example, former President of Argentina Raul Alfonsin remarked: "Joint training of military officers and civilians from the political community and from parliament is essential for the strengthening of our democratic governments."[40] IMET is commonly lauded as one of the "most cost-effective components"[41] of U.S. security assistance and is, arguably, among the most widely supported of American foreign aid programs. What is "dependence" from one perspective is much-needed training, cooperation, and potentially useful influence from another. While neither DOD nor State has an effective system for evaluating IMET training to assess its success in satisfying program objectives,[42] the GAO found—after interviewing U.S. and foreign government officials and former students—that there was "unanimous agreement that the program provides numerous advantages" to both the United States and the participating countries.[43] The GAO cited several specific instances where IMET graduates were instrumental in, for example, assisting U.S. counternarcotics efforts in Guatemala, Haiti, and Peru; facilitating U.S. military overflights of Austrian territory; (surprisingly) helping to maintain a fragile democracy in Guatemala; inducing Spain to purchase billions of dollars worth of U.S. military equipment; and improving interoperability between South Korean and American forces.[44]

Peacekeeping Operations

The Foreign Assistance Act of 1961 authorizes aid to friendly countries and international organizations for peacekeeping operations (PKOs) that further U.S. interests. PKOs funded by the security assistance account are *voluntary* U.S. contributions to various peacekeeping activities, not the much larger assessed contributions for United Nations PKOs. Peacekeeping (a subset of the broader term *peace operations*) involves, among other things, sanctions enforcement, multilateral maintenance of peace agreements, and active support of conflict resolution measures.

The Multilateral Force and Observers (MFO) in the Sinai Peninsula, one third of the cost of which is paid by the United States, has long been funded by security assistance. Over the years, security assistance has also supported PKOs in Central America, Somalia, Cambodia, Cyprus, and elsewhere. By 1995, Africa, Central Europe (including the Organization for Security and Cooperation in Europe), Haiti, and the MFO were major recipients.

From the early 1980s through FY 1993, annual funding for voluntary PKOs averaged about $30 million. This account rose to about $75 million in the mid-1990s as the Clinton administration opted for multilateral approaches to regional conflicts.[45] Although congressional and outside criticism of some international peace operations rose sharply after the Somalia debacle (1992–1994), PKOs are likely to remain important mechanisms for maintaining regional stability, particularly in the developing world.[46] Indeed, the Republican-controlled 104th Congress (1994–1995), while slashing the overall foreign aid budget and rejecting President Clinton's request for an increase in funding for PKOs, still authorized $72 million in FY 1996 for this account (see Table 1.1).

OTHER SECURITY ASSISTANCE PROGRAMS

The above programs compose the core of U.S. security assistance. However, there are several additional elements of security assistance, as well as programs in the nature of security assistance.

Special Defense Acquisition Fund

The massive U.S. resupply operation to Israel during the October 1973 Arab-Israeli conflict diverted stocks of U.S. military equipment, thereby downgrading the readiness of American forces. The SDAF was created in 1981 (PL 97–113) to address this kind of contingency. It afforded the United States the capability to provide large-scale defense supplies on an emergency basis to friends and allies. The SDAF was a vehicle for procuring defense equipment in anticipation of such crises; its utilization was intended to minimize potentially harmful, sudden withdrawals from U.S. defense stocks. The fund was used often, including during the Desert Shield/Desert Storm operations in the Persian Gulf in 1990–

1991. Congress initially capitalized the SDAF with $1.07 billion in FY 1982. Thereafter, the self-financing SDAF was funded through various charges on surplus sales of defense articles by the U.S. government and its contractors. No appropriations were ever requested for the fund, and all SDAF obligations were authorized by Congress.[47] Because of the end of the Cold War, the prepositioning of munitions overseas by the United States, and other factors, Congress authorized the gradual phasing out (decapitalization) of the SDAF over a period of several years in FY 1994 (PL 103–87).

Excess Defense Articles

Defense equipment no longer needed by the U.S. military is referred to as excess defense articles (EDAs).[48] Section 516 of the 1987 Foreign Assistance Act (PL 99–661), called the Southern Region Amendment, authorizes the transfer of EDAs to foreign nations on NATO's southern flank. Egypt, Greece, Israel, Portugal, and Turkey are among the major beneficiaries. In FY 1990, PL 101–167 (section 517) expanded eligibility to include major Latin American and Caribbean nations where illicit drugs were produced. Most EDAs transferred to foreign countries are outright grants, but foreign governments are charged for their packing, shipping, and related costs. DOD prices the items—for the purpose of congressional notification—at between 5 percent and 50 percent of their original acquisition value, but both the GAO and DOD agree that data on the actual value of EDAs transferred are unreliable and that the real value exceeds Pentagon estimates. It is clear that several billions of dollars of excess U.S. defense equipment have been transferred to various recipients since the late 1980s.[49]

The AECA limits the annual level of excess defense articles that may be transferred to a nation to $250 million (exclusive of ships). Israel, however, is a privileged recipient. For example, PL 101–513 (FY 1991) authorized the transfer of $700 million of U.S. military equipment in Western Europe to Israel.

Overseas Stockpiles of Defense Articles

Section 514(b)(c) of the Foreign Assistance Act authorizes the United States to maintain overseas military stocks as war reserves for possible use by NATO and major non-NATO allies. Japan, Australia, Korea, Israel, and Egypt are designated as non-NATO allies. The U.S. government controls these stocks, and they may be released to host nations only in accordance with U.S. law. The United States spent $3.7 billion between FY 1976 and FY 1991 stockpiling defense articles overseas.[50] These prepositioned supplies, of course, are supposed to further U.S. political and military interests. But there was considerable opposition in DOD and the State Department to the initial agreement in 1990 to stockpile $100 million of U.S. military equipment in Israel. Among several concerns was the stockpile's potential for involving the United States in Arab-

Israeli conflicts and for limiting U.S. leverage on Israel. Some officials in State and Defense continue to harbor many reservations.[51] Nevertheless, in FY 1991, Congress stipulated that $300 million of the $378 million appropriated for that year for all overseas stockpiles go to Israel (PL 101–513). From FY 1991 through FY 1995, Congress earmarked $1 billion for Israel of the total $1.6 billion appropriated for all overseas stockpiles.[52]

Other Defense Arrangements

The United States sometimes leases military equipment to allied and friendly nations and, under specific conditions, transfers U.S. Navy vessels to other countries. Generally, such arrangements are authorized under chapter 6 of the AECA when it is determined that there are compelling policy reasons for providing such articles on a lease, rather than a sales, basis.[53]

Anti-terrorism Assistance

In general, this program assumes that the U.S. government must rely on local law enforcement agencies overseas in order to counter terrorist activities that may affect U.S. interests. Accordingly, foreign police and security officials are presumed to be America's "first line of defense" against terrorism.[54]

Since 1983, Congress has authorized funds to train foreign police and security officials to deal with, among other things, hostage negotiations, airport and port security, and deactivation of explosive devices. The program, which is coordinated by the State Department's Bureau of Diplomatic Security, has a threefold approach: a seminar at American training facilities headquarters, a visit to participating nations by U.S. training delegations, and training and/or exchanges among professionals within the United States. The program's budget mushroomed from $971,000 at its inception in FY 1984 to $9.8 million in FY 1988. In FY 1995, $15.2 million was appropriated, and further increases were probable. By FY 1995, 16,500 students from 85 countries had participated in the program.[55]

The Nonproliferation and Disarmament Fund

The NDF is one of the newest elements of the security assistance program. It provides resources for the Freedom Support Act of 1992 (PL 102–511) in bilateral and multilateral efforts to stem the proliferation of weapons of mass destruction. Beginning in 1994, the NDF funded a variety of initiatives, including strengthening export controls and countering nuclear smuggling efforts in the former Soviet Union. The Clinton administration initially requested $50 million for the NDF, but Congress appropriated just $10 million in FY 1994 and in FY 1995. Funding for the NDF rose to $20 million in FY 1996 as certain elements of the Nunn-Lugar, or Cooperative Threat Reduction (CTR), program

(Chapter 3) were shifted from DOD to State. CTR is the primary vehicle for U.S. denuclearization efforts in the former Soviet Union and, as such, should be considered a security assistance–related program.[56]

International Narcotics Control

When President Reagan signed National Security Decision Directive 221 in 1986 designating illegal drugs as a national security issue, he said that illicit narcotics trafficking presented a greater threat to U.S. national security than any armed conflict except for war with a major power.[57] There followed a dramatic increase in expenditures to meet this threat. The U.S. military was initially reluctant to assume such a nontraditional mission as chasing drug traffickers. But the Pentagon's attitude changed by 1989–1990 with the end of the Cold War and the consequent reductions in DOD's budget. As General Maxwell Thurman, commander in chief of the U.S. Southern Command, remarked in 1990: The war on drugs in Latin America "is the only war we've got."[58]

The growth in security assistance expenditures for antinarcotics purposes paralleled the increasingly direct involvement of U.S. military forces in this area. A spate of legislation since 1987 has authorized, for example, the training and equipping of Latin American militaries and police forces to deal with illegal drugs; aid to Latin American countries contingent on their cooperation with U.S. antinarcotics efforts; the enlargement of U.S. military advisory groups in key Latin American countries, such as Colombia; and the use of economic incentives to induce these countries to comply with U.S. policy goals. The core objective is to stop or sharply curtail the flow of illicit narcotics coming into the United States. In FY 1991, more than $400 million of security assistance (ESF and FMF) went for this purpose, and the total annual U.S. government counternarcotics budget for international initiatives and interdiction was almost $3 billion. Despite this major undertaking, the GAO found that it had "not had a significant impact on . . . reducing drug supplies."[59] Moreover, criticisms of the overall U.S. approach to the problem, including the effectiveness of security assistance and DOD's interdiction operations, are widespread and come both from outside and from within the U.S. government.[60] By FY 1995, the security assistance element of a generally shrinking government-wide counternarcotics effort had fallen to just $105 million because Congress was reluctant to generously fund a program with such a mixed record. However, funding continued as the president and Congress were under domestic political pressure "to do something" about drugs.

NOTES

1. See George F. Kennan, "The Sources of Soviet Conduct," *Foreign Affairs* 25 (July 1947), pp. 566–82; Wilson D. Miscamble, *George F. Kennan and the Making of American Foreign Policy, 1947–1950* (Princeton, N.J.: Princeton University Press, 1992);

Terry L. Diebel and John Lewis Gaddis, eds., *Containment: Concept and Policy*, vol. 1 (Washington, D.C.: National Defense University Press, 1986); Giles D. Harlow and George C. Maerz, eds., *Measures Short of War: The George F. Kennan Lectures at the National War College, 1946–47* (Washington, D.C.: National Defense University Press, 1990).

2. William A. Brown and Redvers Opie, *American Foreign Assistance* (Washington, D.C.: Brookings Institution, 1953), p. 440.

3. See Richard F. Grimmett, "The Role of Security Assistance in Historical Perspective," in Ernest Graves and Steven A. Hildreth, eds., *U.S. Security Assistance: The Political Process* (Lexington, Mass.: Lexington Books, 1985), pp. 6, 10–12.

4. See Duncan L. Clarke and Steven Woehrel, "Reforming United States Security Assistance," *American University Journal of International Law and Policy* 6 (Winter 1991), p. 223.

5. See General Research Corporation, *U.S. Training of Foreign Military Personnel*, Department of Defense Rpt. No. 1088–01–79-CR, Washington, D.C., March 1979.

6. Because of congressional concerns over the role of Military Assistance Advisory Groups (MAAGs) in fostering arms sales, the AECA also required MAAGs to be specifically authorized by Congress.

7. Data are from U.S. Congress, House, Committee on Foreign Affairs [hereafter, HFAC], *Background Materials on Foreign Assistance*, Rpt. 94–080, 101st Cong., 1st sess., 1989, pp. 152–53; Larry Q. Nowels, *Foreign Aid: Budget, Policy, and Reform*, Congressional Research Service [hereafter, CRS] Issue Brief, Washington, D.C., August 1, 1991, p. 17. Overall levels of U.S. foreign aid as a percentage of gross national product (GNP) declined to less than 0.27 percent in the Bush years from a high of 3.21 percent in 1949. This declined even further under Clinton: FY 1996 levels represented approximately 0.15 percent of GNP.

8. See U.S. Agency for International Development [hereafter, AID], *U.S. Overseas Loans and Grants: 1945–1976*, Washington, D.C., 1977.

9. See HFAC, *Report of the Task Force on Foreign Assistance*, Rpt. 93–740, 101st Cong., 1st sess., 1989, pp. 10–12, 20–22; AID, *U.S. Overseas Loans and Grants: 1945–1993*, Washington, D.C., 1994.

10. Larry A. Mortsolf and Louis J. Samelson, "The Congress and U.S. Military Assistance," in Craig M. Brandt, ed., *Military Assistance and Foreign Policy* (Wright-Patterson Air Force Base, Ohio: Air Force Institute of Technology, 1990), pp. 149–50; U.S. Department of State, *Congressional Presentation for Security Assistance Programs* [hereafter, *Congressional Presentation*], *Fiscal Year 1989*, Washington, D.C., 1988, p. 20; Grimmett, "The Role of Security Assistance," p. 7.

11. U.S. Department of State, *Congressional Presentation, Fiscal Year 1991*, Washington, D.C., 1990, p. 10; Mortsolf and Samelson, "The Congress and U.S. Military Assistance," p. 150.

12. U.S. General Accounting Office [hereafter, GAO], *Security Assistance: Update of Programs and Related Activities*, NSIAD-89-78FS, Washington, D.C., December 1988, p. 23.

13. Mortsolf and Samelson, "The Congress and U.S. Military Assistance," pp. 148–49. Congress denied administration requests after FY 1989 to convert all military aid to grants, insisting instead on keeping some concessional and, later, market rate loans. For an assessment of the "off-budget" financing process used before FY 1985, see GAO,

Security Assistance: Update, pp. 9–10; "Foreign Military Sales Financing and the Guaranty Reserve Fund," *DISAM Journal* 8 (Winter 1985–1986), p. 58.

14. GAO, *Security Assistance: Update*, pp. 10–11; Clyde R. Mark, *Israel: U.S. Foreign Assistance Facts*, CRS Issue Brief, Washington, D.C., August 30, 1995; U.S. Department of State, *Congressional Presentation for Foreign Operations, Fiscal Year 1996*, Washington, D.C., 1995, pp. 202–3, 315, 364, 444–47; U.S. Congress, House, Committee on Appropriations, *Report: Foreign Operations, Export Financing, and Related Programs Appropriations Bills, 1996*, 104th Cong., 1st sess., 1995.

15. Larry Nowels, "An Overview of the Economic Support Fund," in HFAC, *Background Materials*, pp. 263–65; idem, "Economic Security Assistance as a Tool of American Foreign Policy," Research Report, National War College, Washington, D.C., February 1987, pp. 45–47.

16. Nowels, "An Overview," pp. 266–67; idem, "Economic Security Assistance," pp. 47–50.

17. See U.S. Congress, HFAC, *Report: International Security and Development Assistance Act of 1978*, Conf. Rpt., No. 95–1546, 95th Cong., 2d sess., 1978, p. 44; Nowels, "Economic Security Assistance," pp. 6, 50–52.

18. Nowels, "An Overview," pp. 268–70; U.S. Department of State, *Congressional Presentation . . . Fiscal Year 1996*, p. 102.

19. James Wiggins and Helmut Schoeck, *Foreign Aid Reexamined: A Critical Appraisal* (Washington, D.C.: Public Affairs Press, 1958), p. 31.

20. Interview by Duncan L. Clarke, congressional staff member, May 1990.

21. Nowels, "Economic Security Assistance," p. 28.

22. AID, *U.S. Overseas Loans and Grants: 1945–1993*; U.S. Department of State, *Congressional Presentation . . . Fiscal Year 1996*, pp. 100–102.

23. See Clyde Mark, *Israel: U.S. Foreign Assistance*, CRS Issue Brief, Washington, D.C., June 16, 1995, p. 6. A senior staff member of the House Appropriations Committee who is regularly supportive of aid to Israel used words more commonly heard in the executive branch when he characterized the payment of interest by American taxpayers on U.S. government grants in aid as "a financial outrage." Interview by Duncan L. Clarke, May 1990.

24. Indeed, language in committee reports effectively requires AID to allot a portion of ESF to CIP. See U.S. Congress, House, *Report: Foreign Operations . . . 1996*, p. 27. For criticism of the CIP, see Robert F. Zimmerman, *Dollars, Diplomacy, and Dependency: Dilemmas of U.S. Economic Aid* (Boulder, Colo.: Lynne Rienner, 1993), p. 62.

25. GAO, *Foreign Aid: Improving the Impact and Control of Economic Support Funds*, NSIAD-88–182, Washington, D.C., June 1988, p. 15.

26. In FY 1991, for instance, PL 101–513 authorized Israel to use up to $200 million of its ESF grant account as FMF grants.

27. Nowels, "Economic Supporting Assistance," p. 31.

28. GAO, *Potential for Diversion of Economic Support Funds to Unauthorized Use*, NSIAD-87–70, Washington, D.C., January 1987; GAO, *Foreign Aid*, pp. 42–43; Mark, *Israel: U.S. Foreign Assistance*, pp. 4–5.

29. Michael W. S. Ryan, "Foreign Assistance and Low-Intensity Conflict," in Loren B. Thompson, ed., *Low-Intensity Conflict* (Lexington, Mass.: Lexington Books, 1989), pp. 166–67.

30. John W. Sewell and Christine E. Contee, "Foreign Aid and Gramm-Rudman," *Foreign Affairs* 65 (Summer 1987), pp. 1021–22; Zimmerman, *Dollars, Diplomacy, and*

Dependency, pp. 1–4, 112, 145–46, 192–93; Stanton H. Burnett, *Investing in Security: Economic Aid for Non-Economic Purposes* (Washington, D.C.: Center for Strategic and International Studies, 1992), pp. 18, 42–43, 71; Nicholas Eberstadt, *Foreign Aid and American Purpose* (Washington, D.C.: American Enterprise Institute, 1988), p. 154.

31. AID, *Development and the National Interest: United States Economic Assistance into the 21st Century* (Washington, D.C.: GPO, 1989), p. 119.

32. Franklin Kramer, "The Government's Approach to Security Assistance Decisions," in Graves and Hildreth, *U.S. Security Assistance*, pp. 101–2.

33. There are conflicting accounts of IMET's ambiguous record on human rights. For instance, a GAO report, *Security Assistance: Observations on Post–Cold War Program Changes*, NSIAD-92–248, Washington, D.C., September 1992, pp. 33–35, argues that "IMET graduates are more likely than non-IMET graduates to realize that the United States places a high value on human rights," and even if a country's police force does "not actually see the need to improve human rights conditions," it often does so "to receive U.S. funding." However, this same report found (p. 37) that over one half of the students it contacted "could not recall receiving human rights training." Other reports argue that while "IMET offers no guarantee of far reaching capacity to alter recipient institutional values or governmental behavior" (p. 25), experience in the United States "changed [students'] thinking about democracy" (p. 35) and facilitated better understanding of the United States (p. 27). See John A. Cope, *International Military Education and Training: An Assessment*, McNair Paper 44 (Washington, D.C.: National Defense University, October 1995).

34. GAO, *Security Assistance: Observations on the International Military Education and Training Program*, NSIAD-90–215-BR, Washington, D.C., June 1990, p. 9.

35. DOD, Defense Security Assistance Agency (DSAA), *Security Assistance Management Manual*, DOD 5105.38-M, section 10–2, Washington, D.C., 1984.

36. GAO, *Security Assistance: Observations . . . Training Program*, pp. 9, 22–23, 25–27; Fred Coffey, Jr., *Best Dollar Spent: A Look at the International Program for Foreign Military Officers* (Washington, D.C.: National Defense University Press, 1985); U.S. Department of State, *Congressional Presentation, Fiscal Year 1992*, Washington, D.C., 1991; Lt. Gen. Teddy Allen, "Military Assistance in a Changing World Environment," *DISAM Journal* 13 (Spring 1991), pp. 46–47.

37. U.S. Congress, Senate, *Congressional Record*, vol. 137, January 14, 1991, p. S848.

38. U.S. Department of State, *Congressional Presentation . . . Fiscal Year 1996*, pp. 193–200.

39. See Christian Catrina, *Arms Transfers and Dependence* (New York: Taylor & Francis, 1988), pp. 228–29.

40. U.S. Congress, Senate, *Congressional Record*, vol. 137, May 21, 1991, p. 6258.

41. See, for instance, "Security Assistance Legislation and Policy: The FY 93 Assistance Budget Request," *DISAM Journal* 4 (Spring 1992), p. 11.

42. DSAA does report the number of IMET graduates who achieve prominent positions, but this has no necessary relationship to whether program objectives are being met. See GAO, *Security Assistance: Observations on . . . Training Program*, pp. 17–18. One recent estimate indicates that since 1957, 53 percent of international students at the Naval Command College (641 out of 1,219) from 77 different countries have risen to flag rank; 19 percent of these officers have become chiefs of service, and 5 percent held these positions in 1995. At the U.S. Army War College, 54 percent of its foreign grad-

uates (241 out of 449) from 85 different countries have attained general officer rank, and 3 percent (7 officers) held the highest position in their army or cabinet-level rank in 1995. See Cope, *International Military Education and Training*, pp. 24–25.

43. GAO, *Security Assistance: Observations on . . . Training Program*, p. 23. See also Captain Robert J. Kasper, Jr., USN, "Expanded International Military Education and Training: Matching Military Means to Policy Ends," *DISAM Journal* 16 (Summer 1994), pp. 77–86.

44. GAO, *Security Assistance: Observations on . . . Training Program*, pp. 23–25. See also Cope, *International Military Education and Training*, pp. 25–32.

45. U.S. Department of State, *Congressional Presentation . . . Fiscal Year 1996*, pp. 206–8; GAO, *Security Assistance: Update*, pp. 33–35.

46. See generally Steven R. Ratner, *The New UN Peacekeeping: Building Peace in Lands of Conflict* (New York: St. Martin's Press, 1995); Donald C. Daniel and Brad C. Hayes, *Beyond Traditional Peacekeeping* (New York: St. Martin's Press, 1995); Richard C. Haass, *Intervention: The Use of American Military Force in the Post–Cold War World* (Washington, D.C.: Carnegie Endowment for International Peace, 1994).

47. Thomas M. Meagher, "An Analysis of the Special Defense Acquisition Fund," *DISAM Journal* 13 (Winter 1990–1991), pp. 70–79; Bobby Davis, "The Special Defense Acquisition Fund at Ten Years," *DISAM Journal* 14 (Winter 1991–1992), pp. 73–87.

48. U.S. Department of State, *Congressional Presentation . . . Fiscal Year 1996*, p. 500.

49. GAO, *Security Assistance: Need for Improved Reporting on Excess Defense Article Transfers*, NSIAD-94–27, Washington, D.C., January 1994, esp. pp. 2–5; idem, *Security Assistance: Excess Defense Articles for Foreign Countries*, NSIAD-93–164FS, Washington, D.C., March 1993, esp. pp. 1–4.

50. U.S. Department of State, *Congressional Presentation . . . Fiscal Year 1996*, pp. 505–6.

51. See Colin Campbell, "Israel Seeks Ways to Squeeze More Benefit from U.S. Aid," *The Atlanta Constitution*, January 24, 1990, p. A1.

52. U.S. Department of State, *Congressional Presentation . . . Fiscal Year 1996*, p. 506; PL 101–513, PL 102–172, PL 102–391, PL 103–87.

53. See GAO, *Security Assistance: Update*, pp. 42–44.

54. U.S. Department of State, *Congressional Presentation . . . Fiscal Year 1996*, p. 181.

55. Ibid., pp. 181–89.

56. Ibid., 190–92; GAO, *Weapons of Mass Destruction: Reducing the Threat from the Former Soviet Union: An Update*, NSIAD-95-165, Washington, D.C., June 1995.

57. Mark P. Hertling, "Narcoterrorism: The New Unconventional War," *Military Review* (March 1990), p. 17.

58. Douglas Jehl, "GIs Escalate Attack on Drugs in South America," *Los Angeles Times*, July 2, 1990, p. 1.

59. GAO, *Drug Control: Impact of DOD's Detection and Monitoring on Cocaine Flow*, NSIAD-91–297, Washington, D.C., September 1991, p. 13.

60. For example, Col. August G. Jannarone, "Toward an Integrated United States Strategy for Counternarcotics and Counterinsurgency," *DISAM Journal* 13 (Winter 1990–1991), pp. 53–54; Peter Andreas, Eva Bertram, Morris Blackman, and Kenneth Sharpe, "Dead-End Drug Wars," *Foreign Policy* 85 (Winter 1991–1992), pp. 106–28;

U.S. Congress, House, Committee on Appropriations, *Report: Foreign Operations, Export Financing, and Related Programs Appropriations*, 103d Cong., 2nd sess., 1994, pp. 86–87; GAO, *Drug Control: Interdiction Efforts in Central America Have Had Little Impact on the Flow of Drugs*, NSIAD-94–233, Washington, D.C., August 1994.

2

U.S. Security Assistance Program: 1946–1977

Chapters 2 and 3 examine the security assistance program from the Truman administration through the Ford presidency and from the Carter years through the Clinton administration, respectively. These chapters offer a broad-based description and analysis of the role played by security assistance in U.S. foreign policy as underscored by the historical record of successive presidential administrations.

TRUMAN ADMINISTRATION: SECURITY ASSISTANCE IN THE FORMATIVE YEARS

Except for some military aid to various Latin American governments in the 1920s, American security assistance really began with Franklin D. Roosevelt. Fearing a German victory in Europe after the outbreak of World War II, Roosevelt circumvented a maze of legal barriers to transfer munitions and some old U.S. destroyers to Great Britain in 1940 in exchange for British bases in the Western hemisphere. But prior to the passage of lend-lease legislation in March 1941, congressional opposition to U.S. entry into the war prevented Roosevelt from providing Britain with the level of military assistance London required. That legislation gave the president extraordinary authority to transfer any item to any country deemed vital to U.S. security. After Japan's attack on Pearl Harbor, lend-lease became a massive foreign aid program and a formidable instrument of coalition warfare. The United States had provided $49.1 billion of lend-lease aid to 38 nations by the end of the war.[1]

Early Truman National Security Policies

Immediately after the war, in 1945 and 1946, U.S. national security policy rested heavily on the notion of collective security through the aegis of the United

Nations. The U.S. military was largely demobilized by 1946, and American economic aid was extended to Western Europe for reconstruction and to provide for basic necessities. In the Pacific, the United States adopted a forward defense posture and formally initiated its postwar security assistance program in 1946 by agreeing to train and equip the armed forces of the Philippines in exchange for the use of air and naval bases in that country.

Growing disillusionment with the Soviet Union led the Truman administration in 1946 to rethink its entire national security policy. Soviet actions in Eastern Europe and Iran and threats to Turkey were largely responsible for the policy shift. Hence, when Great Britain announced in February 1947 that it was withdrawing its economic and military support to Turkey and Greece, the administration asked Congress to authorize American aid to these countries.

President Truman appeared before Congress on March 12, 1947, to request $400 million in aid for Greece and Turkey. He declared, "It must be the policy of the United States to support free peoples who are resisting attempted subjugation by armed minorities and outside pressure." The long-term implications of the president's words for American foreign policy and for security assistance policy were enormous, particularly when he stated that "totalitarian regimes, imposed upon free peoples by direct and indirect aggression, undermine the foundations of international peace and hence the security of the United States."[2]

Although Congress was concerned that the country had limited resources to meet sweeping new commitments, the Greek-Turkish Aid Act of 1947 authorized the aid requested. Congress also authorized bilateral military aid to Iran, South Korea, and China. The Truman Doctrine was born. Active containment of Soviet power and other communist forces was to be at the core of American foreign policy for more than 40 years. America's conception of world order also now focused on the internal affairs of other nations as well as the threat posed by external aggression. And security assistance went hand in hand with containment. Without security assistance and mutual defense pacts, containment would have been toothless.[3]

Containment gave American foreign aid a focus. In Greece and Turkey that focus was on a perceived communist military threat. The primary threat to Western Europe in 1947, however, was thought to be economic chaos, which, it was feared, could foster communist takeovers. After Secretary of State George C. Marshall's commencement address at Harvard University in June 1947 calling for massive economic assistance to war-ravaged Europe, the Marshall Plan was submitted to Congress as the Economic Cooperation Act. Its easy passage in March 1948 was facilitated by the February communist coup against a democratically elected government in Czechoslovakia. This coup, and the Soviet blockade of Berlin in June, ushered in an acute security consciousness. The Brussels Treaty for mutual defense was concluded among five West European nations in 1948, and that year the U.S. Senate passed the Vandenberg Resolution expressing support for U.S. association with regional defense organizations. The military threat loomed large as NATO came into existence in 1949. Like the

Truman Doctrine, the Atlantic Alliance had profound significance for America. It demonstrated unmistakably the activist global role the United States had now assumed.

Mutual Defense Assistance Act (1949)

Prior to 1949 the United States provided only economic aid to Western Europe. But several considerations prompted President Truman to request a major military assistance appropriation from Congress that year, including a conviction that a new, still weak, European collective security system required U.S. military aid; Mao Zedong's rise to power in China; and the Soviet Union's acquisition of atomic weapons in 1949.

Enactment of the Mutual Defense Assistance Act (MDAA) of 1949 (PL 81–329), authorizing $1.3 billion in military aid, was a landmark event in the development of U.S. military assistance. This first truly global postwar military aid program directed funds primarily to NATO countries but also to Greece and Turkey (not yet NATO members), Iran, Korea, and the Philippines. It also allowed the president to sell military equipment to formal allies of the United States. In stipulating four types of aid—military equipment, training and technical assistance, military production projects, and military equipment transferred on a reimbursable basis—the Military Assistance Program (MAP) provided the initial legal foundation for major security assistance programs that continued, in some form, throughout the Cold War and beyond. Executive Order 10099 in January 1950 empowered the secretary of state to head the MAP. In general, State directed and oversaw the program, while the Department of Defense implemented it.[4]

Passage of the MDAA ended the piecemeal approach to military aid. Senior officials now had an instrument for implementing foreign policy that many had wanted since 1947. Congress raised questions about the level of aid and about which countries should receive assistance. Some legislators grumbled about excessive executive power and about the program's possible future cost. But Truman got almost everything he requested. Even a congressionally imposed provision to arm only those NATO forces that could contribute to a forthcoming European defense plan was in line with the administration's intentions. Members of Congress did not ask about the MAP's long-term goals or, indeed, how long it would last. "At a time when military assistance was still a secondary and even somewhat novel instrument of national policy," says Chester Pach, "Congress demanded from the Truman administration only a superficial justification . . . for large-scale arms aid to accomplish its foreign goals."[5] The worldwide U.S. security assistance program was really launched in 1949. Yet its destination and duration were unknown. Just as few, if any, U.S. senators who supported the NATO Treaty in 1949 ever would have dreamed that the Alliance would outlive the threat that brought it about, so, too, members of Congress never would have assumed that the security assistance program ushered in that year by the MDAA would continue to function long after the Cold War had ended.

A Framework for Security Assistance

The issuance of NSC-68 in early 1950 calling for sweeping countermeasures against a Soviet Union and communist world thought to be aggressive and expansionist and, especially, the outbreak of the Korean War in June—which seemed to confirm this view—elevated the role of security assistance. The military aid budget rose exponentially in this crisis atmosphere. By March 1951, just eighteen months after President Truman had signed the MDAA, a total of $6.5 billion had been appropriated by Congress for military aid (see Table 2.1).[6]

At the insistence of Congress, the three existing pieces of aid legislation—the MDAA, the Economic Cooperation Act of 1948, and the Act for International Development of 1950—were integrated into a single statute, the Mutual Security Act of 1951 (PL 82–165). All foreign assistance was now to be administered by a new Mutual Security Agency established by this legislation. The 1951 legislation also created a program called Economic Support of Defense, or simply Defense Support. This was the first of several predecessors to what, since 1978, has been the Economic Support Fund. The Truman administration had discovered that economic aid was more palatable to Congress if it was given a security flavor—hence, the label Defense Support.

The lion's share of aid still went to Western Europe in 1951 because, said Secretary of State Dean Acheson, "[w]e cannot scatter our shots equally all over the world. We just haven't got enough shots. . . . If anything happens in Western Europe the whole business goes to pieces."[7] But the Korean War now spotlighted Asia, and that region received about $800 million in military and economic aid in 1951. By 1952, the last year of the Truman administration, Congress was anxious to accelerate the gradual reduction of economic aid to a rapidly recovering Western Europe. Even in 1951, Congress had scaled back the president's request for $1.68 billion in economic aid for Europe to $1.02 billion. The focus of U.S. foreign aid was turning to other regions.[8]

As the Truman years drew to a close, the legal and political frameworks of the security assistance program were firmly in place. So, too, were alliance systems. Security aid was distributed principally within the network of defense agreements. By January 1953, President Truman had signed defense treaties with 41 nations. There was a direct relationship between formal defense agreements and the receipt of security assistance. The highest levels of aid went to nations linked to the United States by such accords.[9]

EISENHOWER ADMINISTRATION: SECURITY ASSISTANCE AND THE NEW LOOK

The incoming Eisenhower administration moved to end a costly Korean conflict without weakening containment in East Asia or elsewhere. President Eisenhower believed that military strength rested ultimately on a sound domestic economy. He insisted on fiscal responsibility and a constrained defense budget.

Table 2.1
Security Assistance, FY 1946–FY 1953 (in millions of dollars)

FISCAL YEAR	DEFENSE SUPPORT	MILITARY AID	ECONOMIC ASSISTANCE
1946	–	–	2317.0
1947	–	166.4	6388.7
1948	–	314.8	2632.9
1949	–	301.3	7799.8
1950	0.7	1170.5	4687.1
1951	155.6	4116.2	3365.8
1952	191.9	4299.7	2277.7
1953	435.7	2495.8	2166.0
TOTALS	783.9	12864.7	31635.0

Notes: Economic assistance encompasses Defense Support aid and includes both grants and loans. Military aid includes MAP grants, transfer of excess defense articles, and international military education and training. 1946–1948 was the postwar relief period, and 1949–1952 was the European Recovery Program (Marshall Plan) era. Dashes (–) indicate zero allocations for that year.

Source: U.S. Agency for International Development.

The New Look, Eisenhower's defense policy, therefore, was designed to protect American security interests while simultaneously meeting the criterion of affordability. This objective, "more bang for the buck," was achieved in major part through relatively greater reliance on nuclear weapons at the expense of the more costly conventional forces.[10]

Nuclear weapons were not the only partial substitute for American conventional forces. Security assistance played a vital role in the New Look. Indeed, President Eisenhower stated that overseas bases in Morocco, Spain, and elsewhere, which U.S. strategic nuclear forces relied on in the 1950s, were made available by host countries in "direct part" because of security assistance.[11] Moreover, following the drawdown of U.S. conventional forces from their Korean War levels, the Eisenhower administration indicated that while the United States would deter the Soviet Union, local forces of allied and friendly countries must bear the primary burden of their own defense. These local forces would also be de facto manpower reserves for the United States. That is, administration officials noted repeatedly that it was cheaper to maintain a foreign soldier than an American soldier. Security assistance financed the supply and training of these foreign soldiers. Even economic development aid to the Third World was motivated primarily by a security-grounded fear that poverty bred conditions conducive to communism.[12] And aid went overwhelmingly to U.S. allies. So, for instance, SEATO, which came into being in 1954, was an umbrella under which U.S. assistance went to countries like Pakistan and, via a protocol to SEATO, to others, including South Vietnam.

The Eisenhower administration found it somewhat easier to convince Congress to fund foreign aid requests for Third World nations after the Soviet bloc initiated its aid program in 1955 with Czechoslovakia's sale of arms to Egypt. U.S. officials asked themselves the following question: If our aid can influence the alignment and attitudes of foreign leaders and peoples and help keep otherwise fragile governments in power, why can't Soviet aid do the same?[13]

Aid Composition and Distribution

The focus of aid turned from Europe to the Third World, especially Asia. Military assistance was forthcoming, of course, but now security-oriented economic aid became more prominent. Two types of aid in this latter category were Defense Support, which helped defray some of the costs of a nation's military buildup, and Direct Forces Support, which provided various items needed for military development not covered by military assistance.

This shift toward the Third World coincided with a decline in overall aid levels, a trend that (in constant dollars) continues to the present day. Total U.S. foreign aid declined from over 2 percent of the GNP in the late 1940s, to 1 percent in the late 1950s, to less than 0.2 percent in 1996. From the end of the Korean War until 1964, military aid generally also declined, although Defense Support—mostly to Asia— increased throughout the mid-1950s (see Table 2.2).[14]

Table 2.2
Security Assistance Distribution by Program, FY 1954–FY 1961 (in millions of dollars)

FISCAL YEAR	DEFENSE SUPPORT	MILITARY AID	IMET	MAP
1954	1534.3	2237.3	55.8	2003.8
1955	1273.4	1545.0	54.4	1347.8
1956	1164.5	2140.8	51.1	1962.7
1957	1127.7	1759.5	61.0	1583.8
1958	777.1	1372.4	67.4	1036.2
1959	852.6	1760.7	79.8	1463.3
1960	819.7	2070.8	71.7	1640.9
1961	838.1	1813.7	83.8	1430.6
TOTALS	8387.4	14700.2	525.0	12469.1

Notes: Military assistance includes FMS credit, MAP, IMET, and other grants. During this period both IMET and the FMS credit programs were funded under MAP.

Source: U.S. Agency for International Development.

Western Europe had skilled workers and the sound political and economic institutions necessary for recovery. As U.S. security interests and assistance expanded to lesser developed countries, it became clear that prescriptions for Europe were inapplicable to the Third World. Some developing countries lacked the essential political and economic base to effectively absorb security assistance. Except for countries like Korea, Taiwan, and Japan, it was often difficult to define the threat or interests to be protected. Were the security threats from Soviet/Chinese supported insurgencies? economic deprivation? a spectrum of internal political, ethnic, and cultural forces? or some combination of these factors? Hence, by the late 1950s, U.S. foreign aid shifted from its heavy military focus toward development programs that policymakers saw as antidotes to communism and toward projects aimed at winning in-country support for sometimes shaky anti-communist regimes. From 1956 to 1964, military aid fell from about 49 percent to about 22 percent of the foreign aid budget.[15] This change was particularly evident during the Kennedy administration.

Europe. If it were not for continuing European defense requirements, U.S. foreign aid to Western Europe would have largely ended by 1953 because of the success of the Marshall Plan. However, except for Turkey, Greece, and Spain—which received substantial security assistance for their base agreements with the United States—both Defense Support and direct military aid to Western Europe were phased out in the mid-1950s (see Table 2.3). U.S. arms transfers to Western Europe then shifted from grants to sales since the Europeans could now afford to purchase military equipment.[16]

East/Southeast Asia. Continuing tension on the Korean peninsula after 1953, Communist China's threat to Taiwan (particularly evident in the clash over the offshore islands of Quemoy and Matsu), the French collapse in Indochina in 1954, and internal wars in countries like the Philippines meant that, by FY 1955, 50 percent of overall U.S. foreign aid, much of it Defense Support, was going to East and Southeast Asia. From FY 1954 through FY 1961, the United States provided more than $6.2 billion in military assistance grants to this region and $7.9 billion in economic assistance. Defense Support constituted $5.5 billion of the economic aid. Two-thirds of all economic and military aid to the region during this period went to Korea ($4.2 billion), Taiwan ($2.7 billion), and South Vietnam ($2.2 billion).[17] The overriding purpose of security assistance was to maintain regimes and nations friendly to the United States and to secure military bases and facilities in the region—from Japan to the Philippines—that could be used in a conflict with China or the Soviet Union.[18]

Near East/South Asia. The Near East and South Asia region received more than $1.3 billion in security assistance during the FY 1954–FY 1961 period. Excepting India, a major aid recipient that received no security assistance, the leading overall recipients of both U.S. development aid and security assistance were Pakistan ($1.8 billion) and Iran ($996 million).[19]

The United States supported, but did not join, the Baghdad Pact when it was created in 1955 by Great Britain, Iran, Iraq, Pakistan, and Turkey. The pact sought to form a geopolitical bridge between NATO and SEATO. In 1957, President Eisenhower sought, and Congress passed, a joint resolution authorizing military and economic aid to those Middle East nations requesting assistance to resist communist-supported aggression. The resolution also sanctioned deployment of U.S. armed forces to that region for the same purpose. The Eisenhower Doctrine, as it was called, was not embraced by most Middle East nations, but U.S. Marines were sent to Lebanon in 1958 at the request of that country's pro-Western government. This episode, various pressures on Jordan's King Hussein, and the successful 1958 Baathist revolt in Iraq moved the United States toward closer ties with some regional states. Through an executive agreement in 1958, the United States formally joined the Central Treaty Organization (CENTO), which, absent Iraq, was the successor to the Baghdad Pact. CENTO then became a vehicle for channeling security assistance to member states.[20]

Latin America/Africa. Neither Latin America nor Africa was yet on the front lines of the Cold War. Hence, they received very little foreign aid during the 1950s. Africa, in particular, was of tertiary importance to the United States. What scant aid it did receive was largely for economic development, food, and humanitarian purposes.

Latin America, however, began receiving modest levels of military aid in FY 1952 and Defense Support in FY 1956. From FY 1952 through FY 1961, $577 million in military assistance went to Latin America. Defense Support from FY 1956 through FY 1961 totaled $177 million.[21] Most military equipment transferred to Latin America came from excess U.S. defense stocks, but increasing attention was paid to the training of Latin American militaries. While internal security was an explicit goal of security assistance in most regions of the world, that was not yet the case in Latin America. Some members of Congress were concerned that security aid could buttress repressive governments in the region, especially when Assistant Secretary of Defense Mansfield Sprague acknowledged in 1958 that this did sometimes happen. The Mutual Security Act of 1954 was amended that year to stipulate that military aid was not "normally" to go to Latin America for internal security purposes.[22]

Congress and Foreign Assistance

Whether through its authorization and appropriation authority or through its oversight and constituency representation functions, Congress keeps a watchful eye on foreign aid expenditures. Congressional attention during the Eisenhower years focused particularly on executive branch administration of the aid program, the level and programmatic mix of aid, and generally keeping the executive on a short, tight budget and policy leash.

Administration of Aid. The administration of the aid program was criticized, partly because neither American nor foreign officials had professional experience or training in the area but even more so because there was little organizational constancy or central direction. The Mutual Security Agency (mentioned

Table 2.3
Security Assistance Distribution by Region, FY 1954–FY 1961 (in millions of dollars)

REGION	FISCAL YEAR	DEFENSE SUPPORT	MILITARY AID	IMET	MAP
Near East/South Asia	1954	–	25.6	1.1	13.7
	1955	–	26.0	0.8	21.3
	1956	57.5	29.0	1.2	27.2
	1957	45.0	113.2	2.8	103.9
	1958	6.5	170.4	8.3	121.7
	1959	3.0	105.0	7.7	79.4
	1960	32.0	96.2	4.1	86.1
	1961	22.0	84.7	4.5	68.8
Europe	1954	508.5	1544.2	42.8	1445.9
	1955	309.6	745.0	32.2	676.2
	1956	237.3	877.4	26.2	801.2
	1957	184.8	509.4	24.0	438.8
	1958	161.5	677.8	27.1	592.1
	1959	192.5	845.3	32.8	756.8
	1960	166.5	894.3	23.1	738.1
	1961	181.0	750.4	18.1	672.4
East Asia/Pacific	1954	1025.8	638.9	10.7	522.5
	1955	963.8	746.7	19.0	635.5
	1956	825.6	1193.4	20.5	1106.9
	1957	861.6	1065.5	30.2	1000.3

42

Year				
1958	588.1	468.1	28.3	292.9
1959	634.6	740.0	31.4	591.3
1960	602.6	1003.1	38.7	773.0
1961	536.0	842.1	52.3	624.2

Latin America/Caribbean

Year				
1954	–	23.5	1.1	16.7
1955	–	26.2	2.2	13.9
1956	44.1	35.3	2.7	22.8
1957	36.3	59.7	3.6	30.2
1958	21.0	47.1	3.2	22.1
1959	22.5	60.9	5.8	28.9
1960	18.6	69.3	4.5	38.6
1961	34.2	115.6	8.1	49.8

Africa (Sub-Saharan)

Year				
1954	–	5.1	0.1	5.0
1955	–	1.1	0.2	0.9
1956	–	5.7	0.5	4.6
1957	–	11.7	0.4	10.6
1958	–	9.0	0.5	7.4
1959	–	9.5	2.1	6.9
1960	–	7.9	1.3	5.1
1961	64.9	20.9	0.8	15.4

Notes: Military assistance includes FMS credit, MAP, IMET, and other grants. During this period, both IMET and the FMS credit programs were funded under MAP. Dashes (–) indicate no appropriations for that year. Greece and Turkey are included in the "Europe" category rather than the "Near East."

Source: U.S. Agency for International Development.

above) was replaced by, respectively, the Foreign Operations Administration in 1953 and, then, the International Cooperation Administration (ICA) in 1955. The ICA, however, did not coordinate all economic and humanitarian aid programs. Moreover, military assistance continued to be directed by the State Department and administered by the DOD. One reason why decentralization of authority and rapid organizational succession were tolerated for so long was that, well into the mid-1950s, most members of Congress assumed that foreign aid was a temporary program, one that would be phased out. If it was temporary, why concentrate on long-term management issues?[23]

By the late 1950s, several congressional committee reports had castigated the "maladministration" of foreign assistance. The Senate Special Committee to Study the Foreign Aid Program faulted the program's management in 1957, especially the ineffective coordination among government agencies.[24] Military and economic aid were criticized on both administrative and substantive grounds. Concerning military assistance, the House Committee on Government Operations stated:

We do not know what we are trying to accomplish through military aid. There is no comprehensive plan against which yearly progress can be measured. There is no way to relate program costs to yearly appropriation requests. Congressional appropriations are little better than blank checks. . . . There is large wastage of resources. Inordinate complexities of organization and serious deficiencies in planning and administration plague the program.[25]

President Eisenhower responded to the rising tide of congressional criticism by appointing a commission whose 1959 report, the Draper Report, had considerable impact. For instance, the report's recommendation that DOD continue to administer military assistance under guidance from both the National Security Council and the State Department has been followed over the years. The report also called for a new semi-independent agency under State's policy supervision to replace the several administrative units then responsible for economic assistance.[26] This prescription was effectuated when the Agency for International Development was created in 1961.

Authorizations and Appropriations. Between 1956 and 1959, President Eisenhower tried repeatedly to persuade Congress to give him more flexibility in implementing the security assistance program by granting him continuous multiyear authorizations. But Congress was not interested. "Flexibility" was seen as a code word for diminishing Congress's authority over the annual foreign aid budget. The House was particularly adamant in its opposition. Foreign aid critics such as the legendary chairman of the Foreign Operations Subcommittee of the House Appropriations Committee, Otto Passman (D-La.), were not to be denied their annual grilling of nervous aid administrators.[27]

Another issue was whether to fold the military aid program into the defense budget, as had been recommended by a 1957 presidential commission.[28] Many legislators were supportive of the idea; they argued that giving military aid to foreign nations to resist communism accomplished the same mission as stationing American troops overseas, but at less cost. House Minority Leader Joseph Martin (R-Mass.) asked, "Do we want to send more American boys abroad or spend $105 for a Turkish soldier?"[29] But the Pentagon predictably opposed the proposal, as did Otto Passman. Military assistance remained apart from the defense budget.

There was little public support for increasing foreign aid. A 1957 Roper Poll indicated that only 5 percent of the public would raise aid levels, while 61 percent would reduce or eliminate economic aid, and 36 percent would reduce or eliminate military aid.[30] After a sharp increase in aid brought on by a sense of urgency at the outset of the Korean War in 1950, Congress reduced administration requests for military aid by an average of 20 percent annually between FY 1953 and FY 1961. For example, $4.3 billion in military aid was requested for FY 1954, but $3.2 billion was appropriated; $1.9 billion was requested for FY 1958, and $1.3 billion was granted.[31]

By the late 1950s, many members of Congress blamed U.S. balance of payments problems on continuing foreign aid to an increasingly affluent Western Europe. In FY 1960 Congress cut off all security assistance to nations deemed able to provide for their own defense. Military aid was denied specifically to Germany, Great Britain, and Luxembourg.[32]

Congress, however, was not of one mind on aid. Opposition to the foreign assistance bill was usually assured, certainly from some powerful members of the House Appropriations Committee and many southern Democrats and midwestern Republicans. But the administration often found allies in Speaker of the House Sam Rayburn (D-Tex.), a majority of the Senate Appropriations Committee, Senate Majority Leader Lyndon B. Johnson (D-Tex.), a majority of members of both houses from the Northeast and Pacific states, and among midwestern Democrats. Four groups of legislators can be distinguished. Some, like Otto Passman, opposed or questioned virtually all foreign aid. Many conservatives favored military over economic aid. Moderate "Eisenhower Republicans" constituted a third group, one that generally backed the president's aid requests. The fourth group was composed primarily of liberal legislators, like Senators John F. Kennedy (D-Mass.) and Hubert H. Humphrey (D-Minn.), who urged that economic aid be given a higher priority than military aid.[33]

By the end of the Eisenhower administration, both Congress and the president were frustrated with the aid program—and with each other. The president resented what he considered to be Congress's interference in foreign policy and its refusal to grant him multiyear aid authorizations. Congress, on the other hand, wanted a complete overhaul of the program's administration and direction.

KENNEDY/JOHNSON YEARS: SECURITY ASSISTANCE ON THE NEW FRONTIER

In his inaugural address, President John F. Kennedy laid down a gauntlet:

Let every nation know, whether it wishes us well or ill that we shall pay any price, bear any burden, meet any hardship, support any friend, oppose any foe to assure the survival and success of liberty. We will do all this and more.[34]

Kennedy sought to *win* the Cold War. When he assumed office in 1961, there was a pervasive sense that the paramount position of the United States in the world was beginning to slip. Fidel Castro was offshore, there as a chronic balance of payments problem, and many newly emerging nations were opting for nonalignment instead of alliance with the West. Kennedy put the world on notice that the United States would defend and promote the interests of the noncommunist world. Security assistance was to be a major instrument in the promised reinvigoration of American foreign policy.

Whereas Eisenhower held that excessive defense spending could harm the domestic economy and, therefore, national security, Kennedy called for a greater investment in waging the Cold War. Kennedy was not reluctant, at least after the Bay of Pigs debacle in 1961, to employ military force. Defense expenditures rose by 13 percent during his tragically short administration; U.S. nuclear, conventional, and unconventional forces expanded; and the United States began to sink into the Vietnam quagmire. Indeed, the Third World was viewed as the crucial Cold War battleground. The rhetoric of the era called for winning the "hearts and minds" of the peoples of Asia, Africa, and Latin America in order to turn back revolutionary forces that were, or were thought to be, communist inspired and led.[35] Said Secretary of State Dean Rusk in 1961: "Communist aggression has taken a new form through . . . infiltration and guerrillas. These soldiers of subversion feed on discontent and the urge for revolution. There is a need for assistance from us to prevent a takeover from within, as has occurred in Cuba and has been attempted in Vietnam."[36]

President Kennedy, and President Johnson as well, believed in the "domino theory" and the necessity of stopping "wars of national liberation." If communism succeeded in Cuba or Vietnam, they thought, it would spread to other countries. To stop the virus from spreading, the United States should, among other things, engage in a process of "nation building" by increasing economic aid to developing nations, augmenting internal security and counterinsurgency capabilities through security assistance, and instituting cooperative endeavors between DOD and AID to professionalize and enlarge local military forces so they could advance economic development through various civic action programs.[37]

Aid Composition and Distribution

Between FY 1962 and FY 1969, there was a relative shift from the grant MAP program to credit and cash Foreign Military Sales programs, although a separate and very large military aid fund (discussed below) was set up for Vietnam (see Table 2.4). Congress made it clear that most major European allies

Table 2.4
Security Assistance Distribution by Program, FY 1962–FY 1969 (in millions of dollars)

FISCAL YEAR	MILITARY AID	IMET	SA	MAP
1962	1855.9	133.2	797.1	1187.4
1963	1663.8	67.3	610.1	1135.8
1964	1058.5	82.5	460.2	812.4
1965	1203.4	63.3	479.3	805.9
1966	2027.0	68.4	887.5	1428.2
1967	2027.2	72.8	751.3	1428.1
1968	2605.7	52.4	581.4	1735.1
1969	3061.2	50.1	421.0	2070.9
TOTALS	15502.7	590.0	4987.9	10603.8

Notes: Military assistance includes FMS credit, MAP, IMET, and other grants. Prior to 1977, IMET was funded under the MAP program, as was FMS credit from 1950 to 1969. SA is Supporting Assistance.

Source: U.S. Agency for International Development.

were expected to purchase their weapons. The only European countries receiving security assistance after 1966 were the base-rights countries of Spain, Portugal, Greece, and Turkey. Asian and Pacific countries like Japan, Australia, and Taiwan also turned increasingly to weapons purchases. Hence, FMS commercial sales rose from $646 million in FY 1962 to $1.2 billion in FY 1969.[38]

The Kennedy and Johnson administrations relied heavily on economic aid as a foreign policy tool. Levels of food and development aid to the Third World rose sharply. Development-type aid in the Eisenhower administration went from 18 percent of all foreign aid in FY 1954 to 41 percent in FY 1960. In the Kennedy/Johnson years, annual development aid averaged about 55 percent of the foreign aid budget; it rose as high as 68 percent in FY 1964 and FY 1965.[39]

After the passage of the Foreign Assistance Act of 1961, Defense Support was renamed Supporting Assistance. A few years later, it became Security Supporting Assistance. The lion's share of Supporting Assistance from the early 1960s until the end of the Vietnam War went to Southeast Asia. The cash transfer portion of Supporting Assistance increased markedly by the early 1960s.[40] While an outright cash transfer was the quickest way to help friendly nations with balance of payments problems, it was also the form of aid least susceptible to effective monitoring.

East Asia/Pacific. From FY 1963 through FY 1973 the East and Southeast Asia regions dominated the U.S. security assistance program (see Table 2.5). South Korea received $4.1 billion in military aid during this period, but the Vietnam War drove the allocation of security assistance. South Vietnam, Thailand, and Laos were primary aid recipients. South Vietnam was the leading recipient of both Supporting Assistance and military aid (mostly MAP grants), with $3.7 billion of the former and $14.2 billion of the latter during this period. In addition to established foreign aid programs, a special fund was created for Vietnam—the Military Assistance Service Fund. The MASF was part of DOD's authorization and appropriation between FY 1966 and FY 1975. Through its peak year of FY 1973, the MASF program distributed grant military aid and training in excess of $15 billion to South Vietnam and four other Asian countries. Despite its location in the DOD budget, the MASF was clearly a security assistance program. The size and visibility of the MASF, combined with the bitter aftermath of the Vietnam conflict, contributed substantially to diminished domestic political support for security assistance in the 1970s.[41]

Presidents Kennedy and Johnson saw Vietnam as a test case for defeating wars of national liberation. Until 1965 their principal weapons were security assistance and growing numbers of American military advisers. But this aid-and-advice strategy was bankrupt by 1965,[42] and that year saw an escalation in U.S. military involvement. Even such an ardent Vietnam hawk as Robert W. Komer says, in retrospect, that the "massive U.S. aid . . . ended up largely wasted," partly because there were no "visible indigenous institutions to carry out the programs."[43]

Aid certainly was wasted. The reasons for this go far beyond weak, corrupt indigenous institutions. They go to the Cold War context within which American leaders approached the developing world; to the conviction that America's ambitions had few limitations that a unified national will could not overcome; and to an insensitivity to competing international and, especially, domestic priorities.[44]

Near East/South Asia. Iran was the third largest recipient in this region, although after FY 1969 it purchased most of its military equipment. While the already high levels of economic development aid to India and Pakistan rose substantially, all MAP aid was suspended after the India-Pakistan War of 1965. And in the wake of the Arab-Israeli War of 1967, the Israeli camel began to poke its nose under the U.S. foreign aid tent. Lyndon Johnson, against the advice of almost all of his principal national security advisers, agreed in 1968 to sell F-4 Phantom fighter aircraft to Israel. U.S. military aid (FMS credits) to Israel went from $25 million in FY 1968, to $85 million in FY 1969, to $545 million in FY 1971.[45]

Latin America/Africa. Food and development aid to Africa rose in the 1960s, but Africa received little security assistance. However, countries like Morocco and Ethiopia received some security aid in exchange for permitting U.S. military bases and facilities in their territories.[46]

Latin America, on the other hand, was now in the spotlight. President Kennedy's dramatic speech in March 1961 announcing the Alliance for Progress promised a Marshall Plan for Latin America, a "decade of development."[47] Indeed, $7.6 billion of aid, mostly development assistance, flowed to the region during the Kennedy/Johnson years to underwrite a Cold War policy designed to foster constructive change that, supposedly, would thwart revolutionary forces symbolized by Fidel Castro's Cuba. Although Congress kept military aid to Latin America at relatively low levels, it did exceed the levels of the 1950s, and the U.S. military trained thousands of Latin American military personnel in counterinsurgency techniques. But the Alliance for Progress was a failure. Latin America was not Europe; it simply lacked the political and economic traits and historical experiences that made the Marshall Plan a success. Economic development was not advanced significantly, gross maldistribution of wealth continued, the Kennedy and Johnson administrations sometimes backed authoritarian regimes, and the specter of internal revolutionary war was not lifted.[48]

Congress and Foreign Assistance

Congress and the Kennedy administration cooperated to produce a new legal charter for foreign aid, the Foreign Assistance Act of 1961 (PL 95–384), to replace the Mutual Security Act of 1954 (as amended). But Congress grew more critical of foreign aid, especially military aid. Congressman Passman led the charge, and he had substantial liberal support for reducing military assistance. To strengthen his case for foreign aid, Kennedy appointed General Lucius Clay to head a presidential commission on foreign assistance. The Clay Commission,

Table 2.5
Security Assistance Distribution by Region, FY 1962–FY 1969 (in millions of dollars)

REGION	FISCAL YEAR	MILITARY AID	IMET	SA	MAP
Near East/South Asia	1962	82.0	8.5	152.8	50.7
	1963	92.1	6.4	81.2	59.6
	1964	48.5	7.1	65.1	35.9
	1965	119.4	6.4	48.5	37.5
	1966	352.2	7.8	34.8	64.1
	1967	331.1	5.6	34.0	50.7
	1968	182.8	4.7	10.2	22.6
	1969	242.7	5.3	–	22.8
Europe	1962	532.6	42.9	106.6	351.8
	1963	648.2	10.8	55.0	441.5
	1964	284.1	13.6	16.9	250.6
	1965	277.2	8.6	–	190.6
	1966	328.3	9.8	–	238.4
	1967	319.5	6.6	–	231.0
	1968	267.9	6.7	–	127.4
	1969	311.2	4.9	–	136.3
East Asia/Pacific	1962	1064.1	64.7	344.1	724.6
	1963	814.5	40.5	318.7	593.2
	1964	599.1	47.8	276.7	468.1
	1965	689.6	35.0	341.3	507.4

1966	1191.7	36.7	727.9	1043.1
1967	1260.4	46.7	648.3	1138.7
1968	2061.3	29.5	528.5	1556.3
1969	2445.5	29.6	388.7	1887.1

Latin America/Caribbean

1962	153.3	15.3	107.1	47.6
1963	96.7	8.4	104.3	33.4
1964	106.4	11.7	68.8	45.3
1965	95.4	10.0	62.5	54.0
1966	130.4	10.7	100.2	64.6
1967	89.9	10.9	50.3	42.2
1968	77.7	8.9	26.1	16.2
1969	45.7	7.9	2.3	12.1

Africa (Sub-Saharan)

1962	23.9	1.8	86.5	12.7
1963	12.3	1.2	50.9	8.1
1964	20.4	2.3	32.7	12.5
1965	21.8	3.3	27.0	16.4
1966	24.4	3.4	24.6	18.0
1967	26.3	3.0	18.7	19.5
1968	16.0	2.6	16.6	12.6
1969	16.1	2.4	30.0	12.6

Notes: Military assistance includes FMS credit, MAP, IMET, and other grants. Prior to 1977, IMET was funded under the MAP program, as was FMS credit from 1950 to 1969. SA is Supporting Assistance. Dashes (–) indicate no appropriations for that year. Greece and Turkey are included in the "Europe" category rather than the "Near East."

Source: U.S. Agency for International Development.

which issued its report in March 1963, found that foreign aid was essential for national security, yet it gave ammunition to the critics by recommending aid reductions. Shocked by this recommendation, Kennedy announced $400 million in program cuts that April. But Congress was not appeased. Armed with the Clay Report, Congress cut the president's foreign aid request by more than one-third in FY 1964, the largest cut in the program's history.[49]

Congressional criticism of grant military aid was instrumental in the relative shift from grants to commercial sales of military equipment in the 1960s. Sales of arms constituted almost 60 percent of arms transfers during the Kennedy/Johnson period, up from less than 20 percent in the Truman and Eisenhower years. By 1967, however, Congress was moving toward restricting certain arms sales, particularly those thought to be fueling arms races in the developing world.[50]

The next year Congress passed the Foreign Military Sales Act of 1968 (PL 90–629), which removed arms sales authorizations from the Foreign Assistance Act and created a separate authorization for such transactions. Section 4 of the act forbade the export of sophisticated weapons to "any underdeveloped country other than Greece, Turkey, Iran, Israel, the Republic of China, the Philippines, and Korea" unless the president deemed it necessary. Section 36 required the secretary of state to transmit periodic reports to Congress on recent past and anticipated future exports of defense articles, and section 32 prohibited the Export-Import Bank from extending "any credit to an 'economically less developed country' for military purposes." These new restrictive provisions reflected congressional concern about the role of arms transfers in American foreign policy.[51]

Congress's distaste for military aid led Lyndon Johnson to circumvent the established foreign aid authorization process, thereby avoiding the Senate Foreign Relations Committee and its chairman, Senator J. William Fulbright (D-Ark.), an outspoken critic of both the Vietnam War and military aid. The MASF was initiated in FY 1966 when Johnson asked for a $1.7 billion supplemental appropriation for Vietnam to be funded under the regular DOD budget. Thereafter, as MAP grants to Vietnam dwindled, the MASF soared.[52]

Senator Fulbright held that it was "not possible to talk about foreign aid, or indeed any problem of this country's foreign relations, without discussing the war in Vietnam."[53] Fulbright, Senator Frank Church (D-Idaho), and others argued that past U.S. military aid to the Saigon government was a major reason for America's involvement in Vietnam. Hearings on military aid before Fulbright's committee raised fundamental questions about U.S. policies in Southeast Asia and, for the first time since the late 1940s, challenged the rationale that had underpinned the military aid program.

Because of the MASF, ample funding for Vietnam continued well into the Nixon administration. But liberal critics—joined by some fiscal conservatives worried about inflation and budget deficits—mounted a formidable assault on grant military aid to countries outside the Southeast Asia region. Congress cut the FY 1968 foreign assistance appropriation to its lowest level ever and refused Johnson's request for advance authorization for FY 1969. The administration in FY 1969 then submitted the smallest security assistance request since the earliest years of the program.[54]

By the close of the decade, the bipartisan consensus on foreign policy that had held throughout the Cold War was disintegrating under the weight of a costly, frustrating war. This erosion of bipartisanship impacted heavily on the security assistance program.

NIXON/FORD ADMINISTRATIONS: SECURITY ASSISTANCE AND AMERICAN RETRENCHMENT

The Nixon/Ford years saw significant changes in American foreign policy. In 1969, by which time the Soviet Union had acquired strategic nuclear parity with the United States, the two superpowers began moving toward a general relaxation of tensions. This "era of détente" continued until about 1973. Key European allies, like West Germany, assumed a more independent stance from the United States on various international economic and East-West issues. The Sino-Soviet rift deteriorated into a Sino-Soviet clash, thereby making possible a dramatic rapprochement between Washington and Beijing. And while Latin America and most of Africa once again faded from America's strategic vision, U.S. involvement in the Middle East escalated sharply.

Nothing had more political salience, however, than Vietnam. U.S. troop withdrawals began in 1969, but the disengagement process dragged on until the American ambassador was helicoptered off the roof of the American embassy in the spring of 1975. The war was exceedingly divisive at home; bipartisan foreign policy was shaken to its core; and Congress belatedly reasserted itself in foreign policy. In striking contrast to John F. Kennedy's rhetoric about "paying any price, bearing any burden," the huge economic and human costs of the Vietnam conflict made it evident to many in government that even the United States had resource limitations. Presidents Richard Nixon and Gerald Ford were determined, however, that America would remain a world power. But Uncle Sam could no longer straddle the globe, relatively oblivious to costs. Henry Kissinger put it well: "The deepest cause of our national unease was the realization . . . that we were becoming like other nations in the need to recognize that our power, while vast, had limits."[55]

Security assistance—within the conceptual framework of the Nixon Doctrine—was presented as a low-cost mechanism permitting the United States to remain engaged in, especially, Third World affairs. The Nixon Doctrine was announced in November 1969 when the president pledged that the United States would continue to honor its commitments, furnish economic and military aid to friends and allies, and provide a nuclear shield. Nonetheless, said Nixon, primary responsibility for providing the manpower for self-defense must be with the allies themselves.[56] "Central" to the doctrine, declared Nixon in 1971, was the provision of "substantial assistance" to friends and allies.[57] So, too, were cash arms sales. Washington concentrated particular attention on bolstering regional surrogates like Iran and Saudi Arabia that were thought to be positioned to advance important American interests. Finally, while not related directly to the Nixon Doctrine, the first aid program for international narcotics control was initiated in FY 1973.

Aid Composition and Distribution

Especially after FY 1973, as the United States withdrew gradually from Vietnam, commercial Foreign Military Sales (FMS) far surpassed grant military aid in dollar amount (see Table 2.6).

Security Supporting Assistance remained an important policy tool. Most of it went to Vietnam and other countries in Indochina throughout the Southeast Asian conflict. But with the fall of Saigon in April 1975, the Middle East quickly and completely eclipsed East Asia and every other region. Indeed, SSA soon tripled in size as Israel and Egypt came to dominate the program.

Europe. The only European countries receiving security assistance in 1970 were the base-rights nations of Spain, Portugal, Greece, and Turkey (see Table 2.7). For the purpose of *presenting* the security assistance budget to Congress, Greece and Turkey were moved during the second Nixon administration (and in subsequent administrations) from the "Near East/South Asia" category to "Europe." Appearance was a factor in this move. Whether because of their military governments, human rights abuses, or the Cyprus dispute, Greece and Turkey were often the objects of congressional criticism. Placing these two NATO members in the Europe category, and thereby within the larger alliance, made it slightly easier to make the case for aid on national security grounds. Moreover, the shift diminished slightly the Near East's perennial post-Vietnam dominance of the security assistance budget.

East Asia/Pacific. Most military aid to this region went through the MASF account within DOD's budget until that account was finally terminated by Congress in the Foreign Assistance Act of 1973 (PL 93–189). In addition to Vietnam and (by 1971) Cambodia, South Korea received substantial MASF and MAP aid. The Nixon/Ford administrations held that South Korea presented the best case for demonstrating that generous U.S. security assistance grants could permit a reduction in U.S. troop levels and, consequently, cost savings. In fact, South Korea's growing economy and strong armed forces allowed it to be "graduated" entirely from security assistance grants by FY 1977.[58]

Near East/South Asia. By the late 1960s, Israel's major arms supplier, France, ceased all military sales to the Jewish state. Israel soon became virtually dependent on Washington for its military equipment. Early U.S. foreign aid to Israel had been modest. From FY 1949 through FY 1965 it averaged about $63 million annually, 95 percent of which was economic development and food aid. Aid to Israel rose to an average of about $102 million annually from FY 1966

Table 2.6
Security Assistance Distribution by Program, FY 1970–FY 1977 (in millions of dollars)

FISCAL YEAR	MILITARY AID	SSA	IMET	NARCOTICS	MAP
1970	2866.5	465.0	81.7	–	2153.0
1971	4672.7	538.7	68.7	–	2947.2
1972	5052.1	604.9	57.8	–	3270.3
1973	5327.1	603.9	46.1	–	4183.1
1974	4576.8	584.6	47.0	21.0	1503.3
1975	1981.8	1155.7	32.3	21.8	1050.3
1976	3155.4	2323.4	26.4	37.1	279.9
1977	2126.3	1756.3	24.7	27.1	159.6
TOTALS	29758.7	8032.5	384.7	107.0	15546.7

Notes: Military assistance includes FMS credit, MAP, IMET, and other grants. Prior to 1977, IMET was funded under the MAP program. Dashes (–) indicate no appropriations for that fiscal year. Figures for FY 1976 include appropriations for a transitional quarter as the U.S. government altered its accounting system.

Source: U.S. Agency for International Development.

Table 2.7
Security Assistance Distribution by Region, FY 1970–FY 1977 (in millions of dollars)

REGION	FISCAL YEAR	MILITARY AID	NARCOTICS	IMET	SSA	MAP
Near East/South Asia	1970	38.0	–	4.4	–	2.7
	1971	646.0	–	4.0	5.0	37.4
	1972	400.3	–	3.2	105.0	41.1
	1973	385.8	–	1.5	100.0	38.1
	1974	2536.7	*	1.8	103.5	41.5
	1975	426.7	0.2	2.4	748.8	70.6
	1976	1894.9	–	2.5	1794.5	54.9
	1977	1212.5	–	2.6	1600.3	54.4
Europe	1970	293.5	–	5.4	–	127.1
	1971	342.1	–	5.0	–	137.4
	1972	420.6	–	4.1	9.5	78.1
	1973	392.3	–	3.8	17.4	76.7
	1974	286.3	–	3.2	12.5	77.8
	1975	195.3	–	2.3	27.5	14.2
	1976	353.7	–	2.5	134.3	70.3
	1977	451.5	–	4.2	102.0	80.3
East Asia/Pacific	1970	2494.3	–	62.1	433.6	2003.2
	1971	3277.2	–	49.6	512.5	2755.8
	1972	4117.2	–	40.3	484.7	3135.7
	1973	4442.9	–	31.5	486.5	4054.0

	1585.9	14.1	32.3	468.6	1367.1
1974	1585.9	14.1	32.3	468.6	1367.1
1975	1149.7	2.9	17.7	379.3	946.6
1976	656.0	15.4	8.5	1.7	139.1
1977	353.7	8.3	7.4	–	19.2

Latin America/Caribbean

1970	26.1	–	7.6	3.4	9.2
1971	79.8	–	7.9	2.8	5.8
1972	96.9	–	8.2	2.0	5.9
1973	87.1	–	8.1	–	5.4
1974	140.5	6.9	8.4	–	6.1
1975	161.3	18.7	8.6	0.1	6.8
1976	179.3	21.7	10.3	–	9.4
1977	49.4	18.8	7.3	–	3.2

Africa (Sub-Saharan)

1970	14.6	–	2.2	28.0	10.8
1971	27.6	–	2.2	18.4	10.8
1972	17.1	–	2.0	3.7	9.5
1973	19.0	–	1.2	–	8.9
1974	27.4	–	1.3	–	10.8
1975	48.8	–	1.3	–	12.1
1976	71.5	–	2.6	15.3	6.2
1977	59.2	–	3.2	54.0	2.5

Notes: Military assistance includes FMS credit, MAP, IMET, and other grants. Prior to 1977, IMET was funded under the MAP program. Dashes (–) indicate no appropriations for that year. Asterisk (*) indicates less than $50,000. Figures for FY 1976 include appropriations for a transitional quarter as the U.S. government altered its accounting system.

Source: U.S. Agency for International Development.

through FY 1970. Loans for military equipment composed 47 percent of the aid during this period. Then, in FY 1971, total aid to Israel escalated by more than 600 percent to $634 million as Congress mandated the first in what has been an unbroken series of large, earmarked aid packages.[59]

Before FY 1974, all U.S. military aid to Israel was in loan form. That fiscal year, following the 1973 Arab-Israeli War and the subsequent U.S.-brokered search for peace between Israel and its neighbors, Israel received $2.65 billion in total aid. All but $164 million of this amount was military assistance, and for the first time, Israel received substantial ($1.5 billion) grant military aid.[60]

An astonishing 70 percent of all U.S. security assistance was going to the Middle East by the mid-1970s. Most of it went to Israel and Egypt, but Jordan, and for a time even Syria, were notable recipients. The primary rationale for this aid, said Secretary of State Henry Kissinger, was "to further the momentum [of] the peace process."[61] The United States also acquired a sweeping, costly, written security commitment to Israel through a 1975 executive agreement, one section of which obligated Washington to be "fully responsive to Israel's military equipment and other defense requirements, to its energy requirements and to its economic needs."[62]

Latin America/Africa. Africa was an inconsequential security assistance recipient in the Nixon/Ford years, receiving less than 1 percent of all U.S. military aid. Latin America fared only slightly better. The U.S. government saw little reason for sizable arms transfers to the region, but for commercial reasons, the Ford administration did persuade Congress to raise the $75 million ceiling that had been placed on arms sales to Latin America in 1968. FMS credits to Latin America then reached a high for the period of $158 million in FY 1976, one half of which went to Argentina and Brazil. Commercial arms sales to the region also rose during the Ford administration to an average yearly level of about $200 million.[63] Yet human rights considerations began to figure more prominently, as evidenced by the 1974 denial of military aid to the repressive Augusto Pinochet government in Chile.

Congress and Foreign Assistance

The 1970s witnessed a resurgence of Congress's role in foreign policy. This was nowhere more evident than with foreign aid. Congressional activism, however, did not manifest itself in reduced levels of aid; indeed, security assistance actually increased after the MASF was abolished in 1974. Rather, Congress moved to exercise tighter control over aid programs and, thereby, extend its influence into major substantive areas of foreign policy. Congress required a flood of informational reports from the executive, insisted on a timely say in significant arms sales, sought to end most grant military aid programs, exerted itself in the areas of human rights and nuclear proliferation, and heavily earmarked the foreign aid program. In addition to Vietnam and growing concern about regional arms races, human rights, and nuclear proliferation, Congress acquired a pervasive distrust of the Nixon administration. This distrust was grounded partly in the executive's frequent withholding or distortion of important information.

In 1971, for the first time in 24 years, Congress failed to pass a foreign assistance authorization act. Liberals and conservatives alike criticized foreign aid, albeit for different reasons. Continuing budget resolutions kept aid flowing, but it was clear that changes were imminent.[64]

The first wave of change came with two pieces of legislation in 1973. In special legislation (PL 93-199) Congress earmarked a huge security assistance allocation to Israel for FY 1974 (discussed above). Also, the Foreign Assistance Act of 1973 (PL 93-189) ended the MASF and required that all aid measures be authorized in the foreign assistance budget.

The next wave came with the Foreign Assistance Act of 1974 (PL 93-559). Congress tightened executive branch accountability and reporting requirements for military assistance, especially concerning excess defense articles and Military Assistance Advisory Groups (MAAGs). A "sense of the Congress" provision in this legislation asked the president to present a plan for reducing and eventually terminating the MAP (except for military education and training). And section 36(b), called the Nelson Amendment after its chief sponsor, Senator Gaylord Nelson (D-Wis.), gave Congress a legislative veto over foreign military sales in excess of $25 million. The Nelson Amendment gave Congress twenty days from the date of formal executive notification of a proposed arms sale to express its disapproval by means of a concurrent resolution, although the president could bypass this provision if he certified that an "emergency" jeopardized U.S. national security interests.

The 1974 legislation reflected congressional activism in other ways. For instance, all military aid to Chile was cut off because of that country's dismal human rights record. Virtually all funding for the training of foreign police forces was ended. In addition, over the protestations of the Ford administration, U.S. arms sales to Turkey were required to be ended in 1975. Turkey had invaded Cyprus in July 1974 with U.S.-provided weapons. While the Greek lobby in the United States influenced this congressional action, an equally crucial factor was Congress's lack of confidence in the executive branch and its concomitant determination to be a full partner in foreign policy formulation.[65]

In 1975 and 1976 Congress worked on a major overhaul of security assistance legislation. After President Ford vetoed a bill submitted to him in May 1976, Congress removed most of the objectionable language, and later that year, Ford signed the International Security and Arms Export Control Act of 1976 (PL 94-329). AECA's principal provisions include the following:

• The notion that arms transfers contribute to regional conflict was now stated as official policy. Therefore, the United States must "bring about arrangements for reducing the international trade in implements of war" (section 202).

- The notification requirement of the Nelson Amendment was extended from 20 to 30 days (section 204 [e]).

- Human rights considerations were elevated to new prominence, at least in law. Except in "extraordinary circumstances," as determined by the president, military assistance may not be given to nations engaged "in a consistent pattern of gross violations of internationally recognized human rights." The AECA also created a "Coordinator for Human Rights and Humanitarian Affairs" in the State Department for the purpose of gathering information about and reviewing human rights matters to assist in determining a country's eligibility for U.S. aid (section 502).

- Subject to a presidential waiver, foreign aid is to be denied countries that deliver or receive "nuclear reprocessing or enrichment equipment, materials, or technology" outside of accepted international regimes for the control of nuclear proliferation (section 669).

- Limits were imposed on the size of MAAGs and the number of military missions. Any U.S. organization performing a military advisory function must be specifically authorized by Congress before it may operate overseas (section 104).

- The military education and training function was separated from the MAP. A new International Military Education and Training program was created (sections 541–43).

The AECA was a bold statement of congressional concern about the direction and implementation of military assistance programs and arms transfers generally. It was a milestone of congressional activism in foreign policy that set the stage for the incoming Carter administration's goal of limiting arms transfers.

NOTES

1. Chester J. Pach, Jr., *Arming the Free World: The Origins of the United States Military Assistance Program, 1945–1950* (Chapel Hill: University of North Carolina Press, 1991), pp. 8–10.

2. *Congressional Record*, vol. 92, March 12, 1947, p. 1981.

3. Richard F. Grimmett, "The Role of Security Assistance in Historical Perspective," in Ernest Graves and Steven A. Hildreth, eds., *U.S. Security Assistance: The Political Process* (Lexington, Mass.: Lexington Books, 1985), pp. 3–4; John Lewis Gaddis, *Strategies of Containment* (New York: Oxford University Press, 1982), pp. 23, 58–59; Pach, *Arming the Free World*, pp. 88–129.

4. William A. Brown and Redvers Opie, *American Foreign Assistance* (Washington, D.C.: Brookings Institution, 1953), pp. 463–64; Pach, *Arming the Free World*, pp. 198–226; Robert H. Connery and Paul T. David, "The Mutual Defense Assistance Program," *American Political Science Review* 40 (June 1951), pp. 328, 330–32.

5. Pach, *Arming the Free World*, pp. 198, 225–26; Lawrence S. Kaplan, *A Community of Interests: NATO and the Military Assistance Program, 1948–1951* (Washington, D.C.: Office of the Secretary of Defense, Historical Office, 1980), pp. 48–49.

6. However, only $549 million had actually been expended. Brown and Opie, *American Foreign Assistance*, p. 483.

7. Quoted in Gaddis, *Strategies of Containment*, p. 114.

8. See Charles Wolf, *Foreign Aid: Theory and Practice in Southern Asia* (Princeton,

N.J.: Princeton University Press, 1960), p. 116; Brown and Opie, *American Foreign Assistance*, pp. 483ff.; Larry Nowels, "Economic Security Assistance as a Tool of American Foreign Policy," Research Report, National War College, Washington, D.C., February 1987, pp. 45–47.

9. Gaddis, *Strategies of Containment*, p. 152; Grimmett, "The Role of Security Assistance," p. 10.

10. Arnold Kanter, *Defense Politics: A Budgetary Perspective* (Chicago, Ill.: University of Chicago Press, 1975), p. 38; Samuel P. Huntington, *The Common Defense* (New York: Columbia University Press, 1961), pp. 64–113.

11. U.S. Congress, House Committee on Foreign Affairs, *Message from the President of the United States Relative to Our Mutual Security Program*, Doc. 338, 85th Cong., 2d sess., 1958, pp. 2–3.

12. See U.S. Department of State, *The Mutual Security Program, Fiscal Year 1961: A Summary Presentation*, Washington, D.C., March 1960; Gaddis, *Strategies of Containment*, pp. 119, 179.

13. Andrew W. Westwood, *Foreign Aid in a Foreign Policy Framework* (Washington, D.C.: Brookings Institution, 1966), pp. 48, 61.

14. Stanley J. Heginbotham and Larry Q. Nowels, *An Overview of U.S. Foreign Aid Programs*, Congressional Research Service [hereafter, CRS] Report for Congress, Washington, D.C., March 30, 1988, pp. 13, 17, 19.

15. Ibid., p. 18; Grimmett, "The Role of Security Assistance," pp. 14–21.

16. Harold Hovey, *United States Military Assistance: A Study of Policies and Practices* (New York: Praeger Publishers, 1966), pp. 76, 183.

17. U.S. Agency for International Development [hereafter, AID], *U.S. Overseas Loans and Grants, Volume III: East Asia—Obligations and Loan Authorizations, FY 1946–1990* [hereafter, *East Asia*], Washington, D.C., 1991 (not paginated).

18. Legislative Reference Service, U.S. Library of Congress, *U.S. Foreign Aid: Its Purposes, Scope, Administration, and Related Information*, H. Doc. 116, 86th Cong., 1st sess., 1959, p. 58.

19. AID, *U.S. Overseas Loans and Grants, Volume I: Near East and South Asia—Obligations and Loan Authorizations, FY 1946–1990* [hereafter, *Near East and South Asia*], Washington, D.C., 1991 (not paginated).

20. See generally William R. Polk, *The United States and the Arab World*, 4th ed. (Cambridge, Mass.: Harvard University Press, 1980), pp. 372–84; Grimmett, "The Role of Security Assistance," pp. 12–13.

21. AID, *U.S. Overseas Loans and Grants, Volume II: Latin America and Caribbean—Obligations and Loan Authorizations, FY 1946–1990* [hereafter, *Latin America and Caribbean*], Washington, D.C., 1991 (not paginated).

22. Legislative Reference Service, *U.S. Foreign Aid*, p. 60.

23. Ibid., pp. 69–70; Benjamin J. Williams and Harold Clem, *National Security Management: Mutual Security* (Washington, D.C.: Industrial College of the Armed Forces, 1964), p. 101; Westwood, *Foreign Aid*, pp. 48–50.

24. U.S. Congress, Senate, Special Committee to Study the Foreign Aid Program, *Report: Foreign Aid*, Rpt. 300, 85th Cong., 1st sess., 1957, esp. pp. 26–31.

25. U.S. Congress, House, Committee on Government Operations, *Report: United States Military Aid and Supply Programs in Western Europe*, Rpt. 1371, 85th Cong., 2d sess., 1958, p. 3. See also U.S. Congress, House, *Report: Mutual Security Act of 1959*, 86th Cong., 1st sess., 1959; Steven A. Hildreth, "Perceptions of U.S. Security Assistance,

1959–1983: The Public Record,'' in Graves and Hildreth, *U.S. Security Assistance*, pp. 47–49.

26. *The President's Committee to Study the United States Military Assistance Program: Composite Report* [Draper Report] (Washington, D.C.: Government Printing Office [hereafter, GPO], 1959), pp. 23, 37. Two 1957 presidential commission studies on foreign assistance, chaired, respectively, by Benjamin Fairless and Eric Johnston, had little impact.

27. U.S. Congress, House, *Conference Report: Mutual Security Act of 1957*, Rpt. 1042, 85th Cong., 1st sess., 1957, pp. 1–4; H. Field Haviland, Jr., "Foreign Aid and the Policy Process: 1957," *American Political Science Review* 52 (September 1958), pp. 706–22.

28. *Report to the President by the President's Citizen Advisers on the Mutual Security Program* [Fairless Report] (Washington, D.C.: GPO, 1957).

29. *Congressional Record*, 103, August 15, 1957, p. 13517. See also Haviland, "Foreign Aid," pp. 721–22.

30. Cited in Haviland, "Foreign Aid," p. 700.

31. Paul Hammond, David J. Louscher, Michael D. Salomone, and Norman A. Graham, *The Reluctant Supplier: U.S. Decisionmaking for Arms Sales* (Cambridge, Mass.: Oelgeschlager, Gunn & Hain, 1983), p. 46.

32. David J. Louscher, "The Rise of Military Sales as a U.S. Foreign Assistance Instrument," *Orbis* 20 (Winter 1977), p. 943; Hovey, *United States Military Assistance*, p. 77.

33. Haviland, "Foreign Aid," pp. 710–13, 718–20.

34. *Public Papers of the Presidents, John F. Kennedy, 1961* (Washington, D.C.: GPO, 1962).

35. Thomas G. Patterson, "John F. Kennedy's Quest for Victory and Global Crisis," in Thomas G. Patterson, ed., *Kennedy's Quest for Victory: American Foreign Policy, 1961–1963* (New York: Oxford University Press, 1989), pp. 5–14. See generally Roger Hilsman, *To Move a Nation* (New York: Delta, 1964).

36. Secretary of State Dean Rusk, "The Importance of Foreign Aid in Today's World," *Department of State Bulletin* [hereafter, *DOS Bulletin*] 45 (September 11, 1961), p. 454.

37. *The Foreign Assistance Program: Annual Report to the Congress, Fiscal Year 1963* (Washington, D.C.: GPO, 1963), p. 22; Harold J. Clem, *Collective Defense and Foreign Assistance* (Washington, D.C.: Industrial College of the Armed Forces, 1968), p. 39; Robert W. Komer, *Bureaucracy at War: U.S. Performance in the Vietnam Conflict* (Boulder, Colo.: Westview, 1986), p. 137.

38. Hammond et al., *The Reluctant Supplier*, pp. 131, 151; Grimmett, "The Role of Security Assistance," p. 22; AID and U.S. Department of Defense [hereafter, DOD], *Proposed Mutual Defense and Development Programs, FY 1966*, Washington, D.C., 1965, p. 196.

39. Heginbotham and Nowels, *An Overview of U.S. Foreign Aid Programs*, p. 19.

40. Westwood, *Foreign Aid*, p. 89.

41. AID, *East Asia*; Grimmett, "The Role of Security Assistance," pp. 23–24.

42. See Leslie H. Gelb and Richard K. Betts, *The Irony of Vietnam: The System Worked* (Washington, D.C.: Brookings Institution, 1979), p. 117.

43. Komer, *Bureaucracy at War*, p. 171.

44. See generally Gelb and Betts, *The Irony of Vietnam*; Stanley Karnow, *Vietnam:*

A History (New York: Viking Press, 1983); Larry Berman, *Planning a Tragedy* (New York: W. W. Norton & Co., 1982); David W. Levy, *The Debate over Vietnam* (Baltimore, Md.: Johns Hopkins University Press, 1991).

45. AID, *Near East and South Asia*; Steven L. Spiegel, *The Other Arab-Israeli Conflict* (Chicago, Ill.: University of Chicago Press, 1985), pp. 160–63.

46. AID, *U.S. Overseas Loans and Grants, Volume IV: Africa—Obligations and Loan Authorizations, FY 1949–1990*, Washington, D.C., 1991 (not paginated).

47. *DOS Bulletin* 44 (April 3, 1961), pp. 471–78.

48. Stephen G. Rabe, "Controlling Revolutions: Latin America, the Alliance for Progress, and Cold War Anti-Communism," in Patterson, *Kennedy's Quest for Victory*, pp. 105–22; Rich S. Thorn, "The Alliance for Progress: The Flickering Flame," in Cole Blasier, ed., *Constructive Change in Latin America* (Pittsburgh, Pa.: University of Pittsburgh Press, 1968), pp. 117–59; AID, *Latin America and Caribbean.*

49. Hilsman, *To Move a Nation*, pp. 394–95; Benjamin Williams and Harold Clem, *National Security Management: Mutual Security* (Washington, D.C.: Industrial College of the Armed Forces, 1964), pp. 92–93; Usha Mahajani, "Kennedy and the Strategy of Aid: The Clay Report and After," *Western Political Quarterly* 18 (September 1965), pp. 656–68.

50. U.S. Congress, Senate, Committee on Foreign Relations, *Report: Arms Sales and Foreign Policy*, 90th Cong., 1st sess., pp. 1–13; Chester J. Pach, Jr., "Military Assistance and American Foreign Policy: The Role of Congress," in Michael Barnhart, ed., *Congress and United States Foreign Policy* (Albany: State University of New York Press, 1987), pp. 144–45.

51. See Hildreth, "Perceptions of U.S. Security Assistance," pp. 61–64.

52. Ibid., p. 59.

53. *Congressional Quarterly Almanac*, vol. 24 (Washington, D.C.: Congressional Quarterly Service, 1969), p. 427.

54. Pach, "Military Assistance and American Foreign Policy," p. 145; Hildreth, "Perceptions of U.S. Security Assistance," pp. 60–61.

55. Henry Kissinger, *White House Years* (Boston: Little, Brown, 1979), pp. 57–58.

56. Richard M. Nixon, "U.S. Foreign Policy for the 1970s: Strategy for Peace," *DOS Bulletin* 62 (March 9, 1970), p. 294.

57. Richard M. Nixon, "U.S. Foreign Policy for the 1970s: Building for Peace," *DOS Bulletin* 64 (March 22, 1971), p. 413.

58. William Rogers, "The Fiscal 1972 Budget Request for Development Assistance and Security Assistance," *DOS Bulletin* 65 (September 27, 1971), p. 337; Henry Kissinger, "Security Assistance and Foreign Policy," *DOS Bulletin* 74 (April 19, 1976), p. 504; Steven Gilbert, "The Nixon Doctrine and Military Aid," *Orbis* 15 (Summer 1971), p. 676.

59. Clyde Mark, *Israel: U.S. Foreign Assistance*, CRS Issue Brief, Congressional Research Service, Washington, D.C., June 16, 1995, p. 14; Lewis Sorley, *Arms Transfers under Nixon* (Lexington: University of Kentucky Press, 1983), p. 79.

60. Mark, *Israel: U.S. Foreign Assistance*, pp. 14–15.

61. Henry Kissinger, "Foreign Assistance and America's Purposes in the World," *DOS Bulletin* 70 (June 24, 1974), p. 712. Kissinger later remarked, however: "I ask [Prime Minister] Rabin to make concessions, and he says he can't because Israel is weak. So I give him more arms, and he says he doesn't need to make concessions because

Israel is strong." Quoted in Richard R. F. Sheehan, *The Arabs, Israelis, and Kissinger* (New York: Reader's Digest Press, 1976), p. 199.

62. U.S. Congress, Senate, Committee on Foreign Relations, *Hearings: Early Warning System in Sinai*, 94th Cong., 1st sess., 1975, pp. 249–51. See also Duncan L. Clarke, "Entanglement: The Commitment to Israel," in Yehuda Lukacs and Abdalla Battah, eds., *The Arab-Israeli Conflict: Two Decades of Change* (Boulder, Colo.: Westview Press, 1988), pp. 219–23.

63. DOD, Defense Security Assistance Agency, *Foreign Military Sales Facts, 1977*, Washington, D.C., 1978.

64. Hildreth, "Perceptions of U.S. Security Assistance," pp. 65–67; Hammond et al., *The Reluctant Supplier*, p. 46.

65. See Thomas M. Franck and Edward Weisband, *Foreign Policy by Congress* (New York: Oxford University Press, 1979), p. 35.

3

U.S. Security Assistance Program: 1977–1995

CARTER ADMINISTRATION: ATTEMPTED RESTRAINT

On January 12, 1977, Jimmy Carter asked his soon-to-be national security assistant Zbigniew Brzezinski to coordinate a National Security Council (NSC) policy study to set forth fundamental foreign policy goals. The completed study was presented to President Carter on April 30; it resulted in the president's approving ten goals. They included a pronounced emphasis on human rights and moral considerations; a strong defense posture parallel with active arms control negotiations with the Soviet Union; normalization of relations with China; a Middle East peace settlement; closer cooperation among the world's advanced, industrialized democracies; and a more accommodating stance on North-South issues. The eighth goal was to "restrict the level of global armaments, unilaterally and through international agreements."[1]

The administration's policy on conventional arms transfers was formalized on May 13 when Carter signed Presidential Directive 13 (PD-13) (discussed below). Nine days later the president delivered his first major foreign policy address at Notre Dame University. That speech dedicated the country to a foreign policy with human rights at its core; it offered an olive branch to the Soviet Union; and it promised that American power and policy would "be rooted in our moral values" and "designed to serve mankind."[2] Jimmy Carter believed deeply that a demonstration of "idealism was a practical and realistic approach to foreign affairs" and that "moral principles were the best foundation" for American foreign policy.[3]

U.S. arms transfers were virtually suspended for the three months preceding the issuance of PD-13.[4] The new policy, formally announced on May 17, was the most restrictive of any post–World War II administration. Arms transfers were now to be "exceptional" tools of foreign policy, although major treaty partners—NATO, Japan, Australia, and New Zealand—were excluded from the new guidelines. So, too, was Israel after its supporters took their case to receptive members of Congress. Moreover, the president left himself the discretion to ignore the guidelines when he felt this was warranted. The guidelines included the following:

- A reduction in the MAP and FMS credit programs for FY 1978. Commercial sales and services were excluded from the restrictions.
- The United States would "not be the first supplier to introduce into a region newly developed advanced weapons systems which would create a new or significantly higher combat capability," and the development of "advanced weapons systems solely for export" was prohibited.
- Coproduction agreements for significant weapons were prohibited, as were retransfers of U.S. military equipment.[5]

The president further indicated that human rights considerations and the economic impact of arms transfers to developing nations would be important factors in security assistance decisions. Finally, Carter stated that while he recognized that reductions in the international arms trade required multilateral cooperation, the United States must take the first step.[6] An Arms Export Control Board, chaired by the undersecretary of state for security assistance, was created to implement the new policy. The State Department's Bureau of Human Rights and Humanitarian Affairs was also required to review proposed transfers to nations with human rights problems.[7]

The Carter policy was clearly rooted in the sentiment, and much of the substance, of the 1976 Arms Export Control Act. Carter's suspicion of military aid stood in marked contrast to his predecessors' embrace of this foreign policy implement. His policy was also unique in its detail and in its refusal to cooperate actively with U.S. defense firms seeking to expand their overseas business.[8] No other president took such a close interest in conventional arms transfers. In FY 1979 alone, President Carter personally reviewed 88 of 126 major proposed arms transactions.[9]

Yet partly because of Soviet assertiveness in places like the Horn of Africa and Afghanistan, arms transfers did not, in fact, become an exceptional tool of foreign policy in the Carter years. They, instead, served familiar American interests and actually increased in volume. Indeed, security assistance contributed importantly to the 1979 peace treaty between Egypt and Israel, and President Carter urged Congress to repeal the U.S. arms embargo on Turkey.

Storm of Criticism

Carter's policy was assailed from all sides.[10] Conservatives saw it as naive and unworkable. They attacked everything from the now closer linkage between arms transfers and human rights considerations to the very assumption that arms transfers are destabilizing.[11] Liberals denounced what they thought was a hypocritical gap between a declaratory policy of restraint and an operational policy of business as usual. They pointed out that egregious human rights violators, like South Korea and Iran, received "exceptions" from the Carter administration and that total arms transfers (military aid plus commercial sales) rose from $12.8 billion in 1977 to $17.1 billion in 1980.[12]

PD-13 certainly could be faulted for being excessively optimistic and overly ambitious. Its tone of restraint was not shared by major European arms suppliers or the Soviet Union. Absent multilateral cooperation among supplier nations, there was little hope of realizing key policy objectives. This, indeed, was a central reason for the failure of the U.S.-initiated Conventional Arms Transfer Talks (CATT) with the Soviet Union. Moreover, Carter soon concluded that military aid could be more useful than he assumed initially. Hard trade-offs were made between, for example, aiding strategically important countries and maintaining a spotless record on human rights; between promoting peace between Israel and Egypt and vastly augmenting the quantity and quality of armaments in the Middle East. Brzezinski acknowledged, retrospectively, the limitations of much of Carter's arms transfer policy and that "we attempted to do too much [in 1977]."[13] In the end, Carter's policy was in line with what Congress would permit under the AECA. It came to resemble fairly closely the general approach of the late Ford administration.

It would be wrong, however, to label this policy of attempted restraint an abject failure. First, U.S. arms transfer decisions were scrutinized far more rigorously than ever before. For the first time in its history, for example, the U.S. Arms Control and Disarmament Agency (ACDA) was actively involved in many major arms transfer decisions. ACDA's director, Paul Warnke, was sometimes instrumental in persuading the president to stop a proposed arms sale.[14] Second, the Carter administration rejected or deflected arms requests from over 60 countries for major weapons systems such as advanced fighter aircraft, armored vehicles, and air-to-air missiles. Carter said no to Iran, Pakistan, Taiwan, and others.[15] Moreover, denial of, or curbs on, security assistance, combined with other U.S. and, sometimes, international sanctions, did pressure some gross abusers of human rights in several relatively weak noncommunist states, including Argentina, Guatemala, and Uruguay.[16]

Aid Composition and Distribution

The general security assistance allocation pattern of the late Ford administration was firmly entrenched during the Carter administration and, with notable exceptions, continued until the Cold War ended. Aid to East Asia dropped; European security assistance focused almost exclusively on the base-rights nations; huge earmarks for Israel and Egypt, which seemed extraordinary in the Ford years, became commonplace and predictable; Africa rose somewhat in prominence; and Carter's human rights emphasis brought a marked decline in security aid to Latin America.

There were some significant changes in the composition of security assistance. MAP aid dwindled, and most of it went to base-rights countries. A second development was to put most military aid on a loan basis, which, ironically, resulted in smaller administration appropriations requests to support *larger* programs. As Secretary of State Cyrus Vance remarked in 1979, "FMS loans are eventually repaid and require only $1 of appropriations to guarantee each $10 of loans" made by the U.S. government.[17] This had the effect, however, of burdening poor countries, like Turkey and others, with high interest rate loans. A third change was the replacement in 1978 of Security Supporting Assistance (SSA) with the Economic Support Fund (ESF). Security-driven economic aid reached new heights in the Carter years, surpassing even the levels of the Vietnam era (see Table 3.1).

Europe. Once again, Greece, Turkey, Spain, and Portugal received almost all of the approximately $3.5 billion in total security assistance distributed to Europe during this four-year period (see Table 3.2). Turkey got one half of the $920 million in ESF aid and 38 percent of the $2.1 billion in military aid (mostly loans).[18] The Carter administration fought hard to persuade Congress to repeal the arms embargo on Turkey, arguing that it "was harmful to U.S. security . . . and to a Cyprus settlement."[19] The lifting of the embargo in FY 1979 allowed the resumption of ESF and MAP assistance to Ankara. Even during the embargo, however, Turkey continued to receive FMS loans for arms purchases.

East Asia/Pacific. With the Vietnam War over, total security assistance to this region plummeted to about $350 million annually during the Carter years. The region received very little ESF, and 50 percent of all military aid to Asia went to support South Korea's defense modernization plan.[20]

Near East. The Middle East dominated the security assistance program. Of the $23 billion in security assistance disbursed worldwide from FY 1978 through FY 1981, $17 billion went to the Middle East. Israel, alone, received $7.4 billion in military aid and $3.1 billion in ESF during this period. Israel and Egypt together accounted for $15.9 billion in security aid, or 70 percent of the entire program. Moreover, beginning in FY 1981, and for every year thereafter, all economic aid to Israel was in grant form. It was also during this period that Israel began to benefit from what was to become another customary practice: concessional financing of its FMF debts on exceedingly favorable terms and forgiveness of many of its outstanding FMF loans.[21]

The Carter administration's bitterly contested, narrow victory in the Senate (by a 54–44 vote) on the so-called package arms sale of fighter aircraft to Saudi Arabia, Egypt, and Israel resulted in a sharp increase in FMF aid to Israel and Egypt in FY 1979. It also helped facilitate a peace treaty between Egypt and Israel in 1979. Washington's interest in maintaining this peace, and domestic political realities in the U.S. Congress, effectively guaranteed large annual allotments of foreign aid for Israel and Egypt.[22]

Table 3.1
Security Assistance Distribution by Program, FY 1978–FY 1981 (in millions of dollars)

FISCAL YEAR	MILITARY AID	ESF	IMET	NARCOTICS	MAP
1978	2302.5	2204.3	31.3	31.3	170.2
1979	6672.8	1972.5	24.0	26.9	175.9
1980	2066.0	2173.9	20.8	32.6	95.1
1981	3181.4	2198.4	24.1	26.2	111.1
TOTALS	14222.7	8549.1	100.2	117.0	552.3

Note: Military assistance includes MAP, FMS credit, IMET, and other grants.
Source: U.S. Agency for International Development.

Table 3.2
Security Assistance Distribution by Region, FY 1978–FY 1981 (in millions of dollars)

REGION	FISCAL YEAR	MILITARY AID	NARCOTICS	IMET	ESE	MAP
Near East/South Asia	1978	1199.3	0.1	5.3	1750.5	55.0
	1979	5720.9	–	5.4	1829.3	41.0
	1980	1169.6	0.5	4.3	1744.0	28.3
	1981	2091.5	–	4.6	1614.0	1.4
Europe	1978	515.5	–	7.0	331.5	73.4
	1979	545.2	–	4.9	82.2	105.4
	1980	513.6	–	6.6	260.0	39.0
	1981	609.9	1.0	7.3	246.0	56.1
East Asia/Pacific	1978	453.4	6.3	8.9	0.6	41.6
	1979	346.3	6.9	7.1	–	29.1
	1980	284.3	7.0	4.7	22.0	27.6
	1981	335.7	8.1	4.9	32.0	25.9
Latin America/Caribbean	1978	79.2	24.4	7.0	11.0	0.2
	1979	30.9	20.0	3.3	8.0	0.4
	1980	21.2	25.1	2.5	15.2	0.2
	1981	59.6	17.1	3.3	143.4	25.0
Africa (Sub-Saharan)	1978	55.1	–	3.1	110.7	–
	1979	29.5	–	3.3	53.0	–
	1980	77.3	–	2.7	132.7	–
	1981	84.7	–	4.0	163.0	2.7

Notes: Military assistance includes MAP, FMS credit, IMET, and other grants. Dashes (–) indicate no appropriations for that year.
Source: U.S. Agency for International Development.

Latin America. Security assistance to Latin America nearly disappeared. Military aid never rose above the FY 1978 level of $79 million, and ESF was negligible until 1981. Latin America was the central focus of much of Carter's human rights campaign. Whether because U.S. criticism of the human rights practices of several Latin American nations inclined them to refuse U.S. military aid or because Washington curtailed this aid, countries such as Argentina, Brazil, Chile, El Salvador, and Guatemala stopped receiving military assistance.[23]

Africa. The Soviet Union's involvement in Angola and Ethiopia and its 1979 invasion of Afghanistan sparked an increase in U.S. security assistance to Africa. Kenya and Somalia, for example, were rewarded for allowing the U.S. Navy to use various facilities. Although human rights abuses were pervasive throughout the continent, they were overshadowed by strategic considerations. Some ESF was distributed in southern Africa to support a peaceful transition to majority rule in Zimbabwe.[24] Total military assistance to Africa from FY 1978 through FY 1981 averaged about $65 million annually. ESF averaged about $130 million annually.[25]

Congress and Foreign Assistance

The Carter White House does not get high marks for its overall handling of executive-legislative relations.[26] Moreover, the administration had major tiffs with Congress over the package arms sale to the Middle East and resumption of arms transfers to Turkey. Relations with Congress in the broad security assistance area, nonetheless, were notably less confrontational than during the Nixon-Ford era. Carter's handling of military aid, after all, was generally compatible with the approach that Congress itself took in enacting the AECA. The outpouring of aid to Israel and Egypt was not only supported by Congress; it was, in substantial part, driven by Congress. And when the Soviet invasion of Afghanistan altered the global security situation, Congress met the administration's request to loosen some of the AECA's restrictions. For example, in 1980 Congress exempted NATO members, Japan, Australia, and New Zealand from the section 36(b)(d) notification and waiting requirements.[27]

An important change in security assistance legislation appeared in the International Security Assistance Act of 1978 (PL 95–384). A new title program, the Economic Support Fund, was created to replace the SSA program. The ESF, like the SSA, was intended to advance various political and security interests, including Middle East peace. Section 531(c) specified that ESF could be used for "economic programs only and may not be used for military or paramilitary purposes." A report of the Senate Committee on Foreign Relations explained the rationale for renaming the program:

The name change . . . reflects more accurately the actual use of these funds: to provide budget support and development assistance to countries of political importance to the United States. The old name [SSA] indicated the close relationship between these funds

to military assistance efforts. . . . In general, the proximity of purposes between SSA and
military assistance no longer exists. . . . It is the intention of this committee that these
funds [ESF] shall be used to the maximum degree possible for development purposes.[28]

Most ESF disbursements since 1978, however, have been direct cash payments for budget support to select countries, especially Israel. The economic
development objective has not fared nearly as well as the committee intended.

Congress's extensive earmarking of PL 95–384 was indicative of future congressional behavior. Sections 531–34, for instance, earmarked 88 percent of the
$1.97 billion ESF authorization for FY 1979. Military aid was also earmarked
heavily. In addition to the primary recipients, Israel and Egypt, funds were
earmarked for Turkey, Jordan, and some other countries. This left presidents
little flexibility to adjust aid allocations.

REAGAN ADMINISTRATION: SECURITY ASSISTANCE IN A
RENEWED COLD WAR

President Carter's attempt to steer American foreign policy away from its
fixation on the Soviet Union ultimately failed, and the incoming Reagan administration soon placed the Soviet-American confrontation at the very core of
its foreign policy. Ronald Reagan had what his third national security assistant,
Robert McFarlane, called a visceral "disdain for Commies," and the president
himself portrayed the Soviet Union as "the focus of evil in the modern world."[29]
Senior officials in the new administration held that the Soviets had made significant advances at the expense of the West largely because of the weakness
and naïveté of Jimmy Carter and, according to some conservatives, because of
the misdirected policies of Henry Kissinger and the Nixon/Ford administrations.[30] The Reagan team was determined to meet the Soviet challenge. While
pragmatism was never absent from the Reagan White House, the hard-line, anti-
Soviet stance did not moderate appreciably until some time after Mikhail Gorbachev had initiated fundamental change in the Soviet Union. Also, by the late
1980s, some of the administration's more fervent anti-communists had either
died, resigned, or been caught up in the Iran-Contra affair.

To counter the Soviet Union, close an alleged "window of vulnerability" in
U.S. strategic nuclear posture, modernize American conventional forces, and
counter real or supposed Soviet proxies from Central America to Asia, Reagan's
first term witnessed the largest peacetime defense buildup in the country's history. And security assistance was seen as playing a vital role, not just as a
foreign policy implement but as a major factor in U.S. defense planning.

On July 8, 1981, President Reagan signed a directive that superseded PD-13.
The differences between the two directives were stark. The transfer of conventional arms by the United States was now an "indispensable," not exceptional,
component of foreign policy and an "essential element" of America's global
defense posture. Henceforth, Washington would assess arms transfer requests

"in terms of their contribution to enhanced deterrence and defense." The United States rejected "unilateral restraint" in arms exports; indeed, American officials overseas were directed to provide the same assistance to U.S. defense firms "marketing items on the U.S. munitions list as they would to those marketing other U.S. products."[31] Military aid was clearly slated for significant growth.

President Reagan went beyond the parameters of the Nixon Doctrine in helping allies and friends defend themselves. By 1984 the so-called Reagan Doctrine openly advocated assisting a spectrum of ideologically diverse groups resisting regimes backed by Moscow or its allies.[32] This introduced a new mission for security assistance. The repeal in 1985 of the Clark Amendment—which prohibited assistance for military or paramilitary operations in Angola—cleared the way for U.S. aid to Angolan rebels, and by at least 1986, Nicaraguan, Cambodian, and Afghan resistance movements were receiving humanitarian aid through the ESF.[33]

Aid Composition and Distribution

During the first term of an administration that made security assistance a cornerstone of the global contest with the Soviet Union, the program experienced explosive growth. In constant FY 1989 dollars, between FY 1981 and FY 1985 ESF doubled from $3 billion to $6 billion, and military assistance increased from $4.6 billion to about $6 billion. The composition of the overall foreign aid program also changed somewhat. Between FY 1978 and FY 1981, 47 percent of the entire aid budget went for developmental-type aid, 20 percent for the ESF, and 33 percent for military aid. Between FY 1982 and FY 1989 these figures were 40 percent, 23 percent, and 37 percent, respectively.[34] While security assistance continued to dominate U.S. foreign aid in the second Reagan term, Congress cut the program in reaction to growing federal deficits, uneasiness about the tilt away from development aid, and a gradual thawing in the Cold War (Table 3.3).

The foreign assistance program saw a dramatic shift from loans to grants in the 1980s. About one half of total foreign aid in the 1970s was composed of grants; the other half was loans. By 1989, more than 90 percent of all aid, and almost all military aid, was in grants.[35] The shift was made to provide recipients better "quality" assistance in recognition of declining U.S. aid budgets, a growing world debt crisis, and the large FMS debt burden of several nations—including Israel, Egypt, Turkey, and Pakistan.

Recipients of security assistance fell into four categories. Israel and Egypt consistently received more than one half of all security assistance; when aid to others fell in the late 1980s, their allotment remained intact. The base-rights nations of Greece, Turkey, Spain, Portugal, and the Philippines formed a second group. They received annually between 15 percent and 20 percent of U.S. security assistance. A third category, labeled "front line states" by the administration, bordered hostile nations backed by Moscow or its allies. South Korea,

Table 3.3
Security Assistance Distribution by Program, FY 1982–FY 1989 (in millions of dollars)

FISCAL YEAR	MILITARY AID	ESF	IMET	NARCOTICS	MAP
1982	4115.8	2769.8	37.3	27.6	195.0
1983	5545.6	2971.3	41.5	28.6	398.8
1984	6413.8	3181.3	45.9	32.5	651.7
1985	5743.0	5225.5	50.8	40.4	752.8
1986	5749.0	4909.2	51.8	53.5	750.4
1987	5013.7	3909.5	55.6	87.4	904.8
1988	4760.7	3010.4	47.2	73.8	664.6
1989	4746.4	3393.6	47.1	67.4	426.6
TOTALS	42088.0	29370.6	377.2	411.2	4744.7

Note: Military assistance includes FMS credit, MAP, IMET, and other grants.
Source: U.S. Agency for International Development.

Thailand, Pakistan, and the Sudan were among those in this group. The aid cuts of the late 1980s fell heavily on these states. Finally, and overlapping the third category, there was the Central American–Caribbean grouping. Here aid was requested to fight insurgency in El Salvador, counter the Sandinista regime in Nicaragua, and support weak local economies.

Although all aid accounts, including development assistance, increased during Reagan's first term, growth in the ESF and MAP accounts was particularly notable. As U.S. security priorities expanded throughout the Third World, so, too, did ESF. The program addressed a multitude of objectives. ESF aid went for budget support to El Salvador and Honduras. It rewarded African states like Djibouti, Kenya, Liberia, Morocco, Somalia, and Sudan for affording the U.S. transit and exercise arrangements and other military, navigational, and communications facilities.[36] ESF was sometimes justified on economic development grounds: that underdevelopment itself posed a present or future threat to U.S. interests.[37] And ESF was requested for international narcotics control, bolstering new democracies, and encouraging Soviet allies to move toward nonalignment.[38]

The MAP received a new lease on life. Countries like El Salvador, Turkey, and the Philippines that could not afford to purchase military equipment were given MAP grants to help them cover FMS loans. A separate MAP appropriation was maintained until FY 1989 when the program was abolished and merged into a virtually all-grant FMF program.

In addition to normal funding, the Reagan administration requested a record number of supplemental appropriations for security assistance. It received supplementals for FY 1981, FY 1983–1985, and FY 1987. El Salvador and Pakistan were principal beneficiaries of supplemental appropriations, as were some countries that had been effectively squeezed out of the foreign assistance budget by congressional earmarks.[39]

Europe. Aid to Europe went to base-rights nations: Greece, Turkey, Spain, and Portugal. Total security assistance to Europe went from $1.2 billion in FY 1982, to a high of $2.3 billion in FY 1985, to $1.1 billion in FY 1989 (see Table 3.4).[40] The United States enjoyed good relations with all these nations, except Greece—where the conservative Reagan administration and the socialist Andreas Papandreou government clashed repeatedly. In 1985, for example, Assistant Secretary of State Richard Burt castigated Athens for not participating in NATO exercises, for voicing support for provocative Soviet actions, and for providing inadequate base security for American forces.[41]

The administration sought larger aid packages for strategically located Turkey than Congress would grant. Despite repeated administration attempts to break the 7:10 ratio in military assistance between Greece and Turkey, Congress held on to this politically mandated formula. Turkey remained, nonetheless, the largest European aid recipient, and Ankara got its aid on more favorable terms than Greece. Almost $1.3 billion of Turkey's aid during the Reagan years was in the form of MAP grants, whereas all but $60 million of Greece's aid was in concessional loans. Unlike Greece, Turkey also received ESF aid. Portugal, but not

Table 3.4
Security Assistance Distribution by Region, FY 1982–FY 1989 (in millions of dollars)

REGION	FISCAL YEAR	MILITARY AID	NARCOTICS	IMET	ESF	MAP
Near East/South Asia	1982	2539.4	—	8.5	1629.1	1.0
	1983	3421.7	0.1	8.8	1597.0	40.5
	1984	3426.2	0.1	8.5	1848.2	52.0
	1985	2832.0	—	9.0	3207.0	60.0
	1986	3165.8	0.1	8.1	3137.8	73.7
	1987	3226.3	0.6	8.9	2185.3	105.4
	1988	3213.8	0.4	7.3	1982.4	94.5
	1989	3199.8	0.5	7.3	2076.8	0.5
Europe	1982	878.9	1.0	8.9	362.0	77.0
	1983	1197.9	1.0	9.8	332.0	166.6
	1984	1730.7	1.0	10.7	215.5	190.0
	1985	1736.0	0.9	11.0	282.0	285.0
	1986	1548.0	—	9.3	276.0	272.7
	1987	1028.5	0.7	10.5	220.8	392.1
	1988	925.1	0.4	9.6	113.2	266.0
	1989	959.0	0.4	9.0	133.0	99.3
East Asia/Pacific	1982	355.3	12.0	8.1	155.0	4.5
	1983	627.9	11.4	9.4	255.8	18.5
	1984	744.4	9.0	10.4	284.1	5.0
	1985	742.9	11.5	11.4	348.5	30.0

1986	693.6	13.6	11.4	590.7	93.1
1987	485.0	21.1	12.5	520.1	160.0
1988	443.6	14.0	11.1	390.3	145.0
1989	389.7	11.1	11.2	596.6	148.5

Latin America/Caribbean

Year					
1982	150.7	14.6	6.4	328.9	79.5
1983	163.9	16.1	6.2	500.4	83.9
1984	359.2	22.4	7.5	464.1	285.2
1985	269.1	28.0	8.9	970.2	235.2
1986	238.4	39.8	13.5	659.5	217.2
1987	214.9	65.0	14.5	818.5	200.4
1988	143.9	59.0	10.1	484.8	133.8
1989	164.0	55.4	10.4	461.7	153.6

Africa (Sub-Saharan)

Year					
1982	191.5	–	5.4	294.8	33.0
1983	134.2	–	7.3	286.1	89.3
1984	153.3	–	8.8	333.1	119.5
1985	163.0	–	10.5	417.8	142.6
1986	103.2	–	9.5	245.2	93.7
1987	59.0	–	9.2	164.8	46.9
1988	34.3	–	9.1	39.7	25.3
1989	33.9	–	9.2	125.5	24.7

Notes: Military assistance includes FMS credit, MAP, IMET, and other grants. Dashes (–) indicate no appropriations for that year.
Source: U.S. Agency for International Development.

Spain, received much of its military aid in grants during this period. After 1988, Spain no longer received any U.S. foreign aid.[42]

East Asia/Pacific. Total security assistance to the East Asia/Pacific area went from $534 million in FY 1982, to a high of $1.4 billion in FY 1986, to $1.1 billion in FY 1989. The budget reductions that began in 1986 cut severely into aid to this region.[43] Indonesia and Malaysia received some aid, but by the late 1980s, most security assistance went to the Philippines and, to a much lesser extent, Thailand. About one half of all military aid to the region during the first Reagan term supported the continued modernization of the Korean defense forces, but all aid to Korea, except IMET, ceased in 1986. Aid to Thailand was justified on the basis of its large Cambodian refugee population and unstable border with a Cambodia still occupied by Vietnamese troops. Considerable security and development aid flowed to the Philippines under Manila's base-rights agreement with the United States. American officials also cited an ongoing insurgency as a reason for this aid. The backing of the U.S. Congress for the democratically elected Corazon Aquino helped sustain aid to the Philippines in the late 1980s.[44]

Near East/South Asia. Of the $47.7 billion in military aid the U.S. disbursed worldwide from FY 1982 through FY 1989, $26.1 billion, or 55 percent, went to the Near East and South Asia. And 62 percent of ESF ($18 billion of $29 billion) also went to the region during this period. Beginning in FY 1982, and continuing into the early 1990s, Pakistan was a major security assistance recipient. This aid, a direct result of the 1979 Soviet invasion of Afghanistan, went to bolster Pakistan's defenses and facilitate U.S. support of various Afghan rebel groups resisting the Soviet occupation. Security aid to Pakistan during the Reagan years totaled $3.8 billion.[45]

But Israel and Egypt accounted for 52 percent of worldwide U.S. security assistance during this period. Israel received $13.3 billion in military aid and $9.9 billion in ESF; Egypt got $9.9 billion in military aid and $6.9 billion in ESF. Moreover, beginning in FY 1985, and in all subsequent years, all military aid to Israel was in grant form.[46] Congress accorded Israel numerous other special privileges. For instance, the United States paid $1.3 billion of the $1.5 billion development costs of Israel's controversial Lavi fighter, a project that was canceled in 1987 under pressure from the Pentagon. Washington then paid an additional $400 million for Lavi "cancellation costs."[47]

The early Reagan administration's relations with Israel were strained in 1981 by the sale of Airborne Warning and Control System (AWACS) aircraft to Saudi Arabia and Israel's annexation of the Golan Heights. Relations did not improve when Israel invaded Lebanon in 1982. Nonetheless, President Reagan signed unprecedented strategic cooperation agreements with Israel in November 1983 that officially acknowledged the assertion of Israel's American advocates: that the Jewish state was a U.S. "strategic asset." Ronald Reagan had little knowledge of the Middle East or foreign affairs generally, but he had a personal affection for Israel, and he saw Israel as a Cold War buffer against the Soviet

Union and its allies in the region. To the astonishment of most Middle East experts, and many others, Reagan remarked that he found it difficult "to envision Israel as being a threat to its neighbors."[48]

Despite the 1983 executive agreements with Israel, and many others that followed, most of the permanent national security bureaucracy and many senior policy officials—both before and after 1983—saw Israel as, on balance, a strategic liability. This more critical perception of Israel long predated the end of the Cold War.[49]

Latin America. The security assistance program in Latin America rose from the dead in the Reagan years. Not since the Alliance for Progress had so much attention been focused on, especially, Central America and the Caribbean. A total of $3 billion in military aid and $4.7 billion in ESF went to Latin America during this period. Human rights matters, while not wholly disregarded, were often secondary to three principal security concerns. The first was an insurgency by the Farabundo Marti National Liberation Front (FMLN) against the government of El Salvador. That government received $2.4 billion in security assistance during this period, about 33 percent of all security aid to Latin America. A second objective was to bolster the economy and security of front line states like Honduras, Guatemala, and Costa Rica against the supposed challenge from the Sandinista regime in Nicaragua. The third major issue was the flow of illicit narcotics into the United States from Latin America. Substantial resources were committed to this problem, albeit with very mixed results.[50]

Africa. More security assistance flowed to African countries during the Reagan years than at any other time: about $1.8 billion in military aid and $2.1 billion in ESF. But after reaching a peak level of $732 million in FY 1985, security aid fell off sharply. It stood at $199 million in FY 1989 and was just $174 million in the early Bush administration. Aid was dispersed throughout the continent, from Morocco to Kenya, for a variety of purposes. Compensation for the U.S. military's access to various in-country facilities was a common aid justification.[51]

Congress and Foreign Assistance

Just as the Reagan administration's security assistance program grew more complex, with its diverse goals and numerous recipients, so, too, did Congress's role become more complicated. Congress was responsive to administration security assistance requests, certainly until 1985. Indeed, Pakistan had ample aid throughout the Reagan years despite its well-known drive to acquire nuclear weapons. Likewise, while its aid levels dropped somewhat in the late 1980s, El Salvador's dismal human rights record did not prevent it from receiving substantial security aid. However, this apparent congressional support for or acquiescence in the Reagan program must be balanced against a marked increase in earmarking and conditionality (the imposition of conditions or restrictions that must be followed by implementing agencies). The multiple conditions placed on aid to El Salvador was but one example of conditionality. As for earmarking, 90-plus percent of the ESF and FMF accounts were earmarked by 1985–1986.

Changes in the authorization and appropriation processes further complicated Congress's role. Congress succeeded in passing foreign assistance authorization legislation only in 1981 (for FY 1982 and FY 1983) and 1985 (for FY 1986 and FY 1987). In those years when no separate foreign assistance authorization legislation was passed, authorizations were included within the appropriations legislation itself. This reflected the general shift in power away from the foreign affairs committees toward the appropriations committees.

Only two freestanding appropriations bills were passed during the Reagan era, in 1981 and 1988. Most foreign aid appropriations were included as just one component of a larger, sometimes omnibus, continuing resolution (CR). Lumping foreign assistance with more popular domestic programs—such as transportation, education and housing—ensured its passage. The foreign aid bill was then protected from legislators who might otherwise gut it with amendments or divert some aid funds to meet domestic priorities. This also afforded protective cover for congressmen who preferred not to go on record as voting for foreign aid.

Fundamentally, however, CRs represent a failure of the democratic process. Members of Congress and the president are left with a choice of voting yes or of closing down the government. CRs promote avoidance of accountability. They also effectively undermine the president's constitutional veto power and, in Aaron Wildavsky's words, are "strong indicators of dissensus . . . [which] testify to a breakdown . . . in ordinary modes of accommodation."[52]

Programmatic Changes. Congress made some notable changes in the security assistance program during this period. For example, the Special Defense Acquisition Fund was created by the International Security and Development Cooperation Act of 1981 (PL 97-113). This self-financing fund permitted the procurement of defense equipment in anticipation of future crises. It allowed the president to transfer defense equipment to, for example, Israel in an urgent situation without adversely affecting the readiness of U.S. forces.[53] The 1981 legislation also made aid to El Salvador conditional on presidential certification that progress was being made in human rights and political reforms. Moreover, PL 97–113 (section 669) allowed the president to waive the Symington Amendment for six years so as to provide aid to Pakistan. This permitted the administration to downplay Pakistan's nuclear ambitions in order to covertly channel military supplies through Pakistan to Afghan resistance groups.

The FY 1984 CR (PL 98–151) created an anti-terrorism assistance program to train foreign civilians to protect airports, harbors, U.S. missions, and individuals against terrorist attacks. The pervasiveness of conditionality and the clout of the appropriations committees was evident the next year concerning, for instance, El Salvador. The 1985 CR (PL 98–473) imposed elaborate reporting requirements on the executive branch and stipulated that only half of El Salvador's military aid could be obligated before March 1, 1985. The following year, PL 99–83 established a new Title IV in the Foreign Assistance Act (FAA) of 1961: international narcotics control. It authorized $115 million to assist foreign countries in eradicating illicit narcotics and conditioned U.S. aid to Peru, Bolivia, and Jamaica on their cooperation with this program.

In 1986, the National Defense Authorization Act for FY 1987 (PL 99–661), part of an omnibus CR (PL 99–591), added a new section 516 to the FAA that authorized the transfer of excess U.S. defense articles to NATO's southern flank nations, understood at the time to include only Greece, Turkey, and Portugal. Eligibility, however, was later extended to others. Three criteria must be met before such equipment may be transferred: It must be drawn from existing stocks, funds may not be spent to procure equipment for this purpose, and the president must determine that transfers will not have "an adverse impact on the military readiness of the United States."[54]

Finally, in FY 1989 the administration proposed that Congress convert security assistance to an all-grant program in order to ease the debt burden of recipient nations. Congress stopped just short of doing this, but it put most of the program on a de facto grant basis through the provision of forgiven loans for about 90 percent of the FMF program.[55]

Earmarking. By FY 1986 the Reagan administration was frustrated by a combination of earmarking and cuts in aid. The gap between the amount requested for security aid and what Congress ultimately appropriated was 10 percent in FY 1986, 24 percent in FY 1987, and 15 percent in FY 1988. In FY 1988–1989, 99 percent of all security assistance was earmarked; indeed, 49 percent of development aid was also earmarked. Secretary of State George Shultz complained repeatedly that this eliminated presidential flexibility. Moreover, because aid to Israel and Egypt was untouched as the overall foreign aid budget fell, several countries deemed important to the United States had their security assistance allocations slashed or eliminated altogether.[56]

Congress has a legitimate, constitutional prerogative to earmark federal expenditures, but presidents object when their discretion over aid allocations is stripped away entirely. However, the Reagan administration's dismay over shrinking security aid budgets was partly self-inflicted. Security assistance appropriations expanded significantly between 1981 and 1984; so did the program's goals. When budget tightening occurred during the second Reagan term, the administration seemed to approach security assistance by using the high-water mark of FY 1985 as a baseline,[57] instead of viewing the funding for that year for what is was—a uniquely high figure. In constant dollars (allowing for inflation), the FY 1989 security assistance budget was about the size of the FY 1982 budget. And the quality of aid improved notably by FY 1989, with all but a token amount in grants. Much of the supposed problem was that grandiose Reagan administration goals and ambitions simply could not be financed with anything but lavish budgets. Neither fiscal nor political reality would permit this. The administration seemed incapable of prioritizing goals; instead, everything was "high priority."[58]

BUSH ADMINISTRATION: THE END OF AN ERA

Presiding over the end of the Cold War, President George Bush led the United States at a time when the international system experienced its greatest upheaval since the end of World War II. Yet, in many ways, the Bush security assistance program remained strikingly similar to the Reagan program. Indeed, the initial Bush security assistance requests were largely in line with his predecessor's priorities.

Aid distributions remained relatively constant, and the same major security assistance recipients received their accustomed shares of aid. Even as the collapse of the Soviet Union eliminated the program's long-standing rationale of combating Soviet expansion, Bush administration justifications for security aid were virtually identical to those used in the Reagan era: promoting peace in the Middle East, maintaining base access, supporting allies against internal subversion, and sustaining cooperative relationships.[59] The most significant change during the Bush administration was the shift away from superpower confrontation and toward meeting various regional military contingencies. This shift permitted a continued reduction in both U.S. defense and security assistance expenditures.[60]

Developments in world politics and changing American domestic policy concerns did affect security assistance priorities. Encouraging the spread of democratic values and human rights and curbing illicit drugs gained salience. However, the federal budget crisis was a decisive factor, and it became clear that the post-1985 cuts in security aid would not be restored. Indeed, the end of the Cold War, criticism of military aid by powerful members of Congress, and continuing public antipathy toward foreign aid merged with the fiscal guidelines established under the Budget Enforcement Act of 1990 (PL 101–508) to reduce security assistance funding. By 1992, almost all of the smaller Reagan-era security assistance recipients had been cut off completely.

The Budget Enforcement Act set strict ceilings on FY 1991–FY 1993 budget authority and outlays for, among other things, the international affairs function of the federal budget—of which foreign assistance is a central component. This meant, in effect, that any additional funding for security aid would have to come either from supplemental appropriations (as with the Gulf War in 1990–1991) or from direct trade-offs among accounts within the international affairs function.[61] The budgetary walls separating international affairs, defense, and domestic spending that were enforced by the 1990 legislation would not come down until FY 1994, after Bush left office.

National Security Strategy

The Bush administration's national security strategy saw security assistance as supporting three of the four "fundamental elements" of U.S. defense strategy: crisis response, reconstitution, and (especially) the forward presence of

American armed forces.[62] Reducing the flow of illegal drugs into the United States also continued to be a priority objective. Toward this end, the Bush administration instituted the Andean Initiative in late 1989. Between FY 1989 and FY 1991, this provided Colombia, Bolivia, and Peru with $1.1 billion in counternarcotics aid.[63] In the administration's final year, its national security strategy statement declared: "It is time to refashion our security assistance. We need to increase funding for programs designed to facilitate . . . [the] transition of foreign militaries to democratic systems."[64]

U.S. foreign policy was now oriented toward addressing regional instabilities, with an explicit emphasis on promoting the spread of democratic institutions. Supporting the extension of democracy was a goal pursued in the belief that the United States would be more secure in a world of democratic states because democracies rarely go to war with one another.[65] The Bush administration took several significant steps in pursuit of this objective. In FY 1990, for example, $700 million in ESF was appropriated for the fragile democracies in Nicaragua and Panama. In addition, newly democratic Eastern Europe received $370 million that fiscal year under the Support for East European Democracy (SEED) Act (PL 101–513). Similarly, the so-called Freedom Support Act of 1992 (PL 102–511) authorized assistance to the nascent republics of the former Soviet Union. Virtually all of the Freedom Support aid was employed, directly or indirectly, for security reasons: to ease Russia and the other New Independent States (NIS) toward democracy, market-based economies, and less threatening military postures.

Aid Composition and Distribution

Funding levels to some security assistance recipients changed dramatically during the Bush period; however, overall program funding levels remained relatively constant before declining somewhat in FY 1992 (see Table 3.5).

Middle East. Despite the virtual absence of significant Soviet/Russian involvement in the Middle East and the sometimes strained relations between the Bush administration and the government of Israeli Prime Minister Yitzhak Shamir, Israel and Egypt together continued to receive more than 90 percent of all U.S. security assistance throughout this period. Because Jordan distanced itself from the allied effort in the 1990–1991 Gulf War, its security assistance allocation was slashed. Conversely, some who joined the allied cause, like Oman, were rewarded.

Europe/NIS. Aid to the base-rights countries of Greece, Turkey, and Portugal declined significantly; these three countries together received only $980 million by FY 1993, mostly in concessional loans. However, overall security assistance to Europe increased (see Table 3.6) largely because of new aid to the NIS, beginning in FY 1992, to almost $340 million in FMF and $124 million in ESF. Many of the former East bloc nations in Central and Eastern Europe, as well as the former Soviet Union (discussed below), now became significant recipients

Table 3.5
Security Assistance Distribution by Program, FY 1989–FY 1992 (in millions of dollars)

FISCAL YEAR	FMF	ESF	IMET	NARCOTICS
1989	4746.4	3393.6	47.1	67.4
1990	4830.9	3760.7	47.1	81.8
1991	4650.6	4058.8	46.9	99.2
1992	4630.6	2868.6	44.0	92.9
TOTALS	18858.5	14081.7	185.1	341.3

Note: FMF includes both grants and loans.
Sources: U.S. Agency for International Development; Congressional Research Service.

of foreign assistance. By the close of the Bush administration, starting with FY 1993, Russia and Ukraine had become the third and fourth largest recipients of U.S. foreign assistance.

Latin America. As aid to the former Soviet region began to flow, aid levels to Latin America plunged. Following the December 1989 invasion of Panama, and the February 1990 election in Nicaragua that ousted the Sandinista government, Congress allocated $393 million for Panama and $215 million for Nicaragua in ESF funds. By FY 1992, however, these amounts had dropped to zero and $36 million, respectively. In addition, while no Latin American nation received more aid than El Salvador during the Reagan years, by the end of the Bush era—following the January 1992 peace agreement between government and rebel forces—such assistance had all but vanished. The same was true for the other major recipient of security assistance in Central America during the Reagan administration, Honduras.[66] Overall, the Latin American region lost over one half of its security assistance during the Bush administration.

Asia/Pacific. The end of the Cold War brought a steep decline in security assistance to the Asia/Pacific region. The region received $824 million in security aid in FY 1990 but only $146 million in FY 1992. South Korea no longer received U.S. aid, security assistance to Indonesia was suspended over human rights abuses in East Timor, and nonrenewal of the basing rights agreement with the Philippines meant that security assistance to Manila went from $273 million in FY 1990 to $75 million in FY 1992.[67]

Perhaps most significant, aid to Pakistan was a casualty of the Soviet withdrawal from Afghanistan and ongoing U.S. concerns over that nation's nuclear weapons program. The president no longer certified that Pakistan did not have a nuclear device, a prerequisite for security assistance since the passage of the 1985 Pressler amendment. Pakistan had been the fifth largest security assistance recipient during the 1980s, but it received virtually none after FY 1990.

Africa. Security assistance to sub-Saharan Africa remained at constant, low

Table 3.6
Security Assistance Distribution by Region, FY 1989–FY 1992 (in millions of dollars)

REGION	FISCAL YEAR	FMF	NARCOTICS	IMET	ESF
Near East/South Asia	1989	3199.8	0.5	7.3	2076.8
	1990	3235.2	0.3	7.5	2157.4
	1991	3182.6	0.8	6.6	2720.4
	1992	3158.7	–	5.2	2167.6
Europe	1989	959.0	0.4	9.0	133.0
	1990	939.7	0.4	8.7	102.8
	1991	1007.9	0.4	7.9	320.4
	1992	1298.9	0.4	9.7	115.9
East Asia/Pacific	1989	389.7	11.1	11.2	596.6
	1990	383.2	9.1	10.8	420.9
	1991	208.1	10.0	8.1	286.9
	1992	32.3	8.8	7.3	98.1
Latin America/Caribbean	1989	164.0	55.4	10.4	461.7
	1990	234.1	72.0	11.3	1052.4
	1991	214.2	88.0	15.8	674.9
	1992	123.8	83.7	13.4	442.3
Africa (Sub-Saharan)	1989	33.9	–	9.2	125.5
	1990	38.7	–	8.8	27.2
	1991	37.8	–	8.5	56.2
	1992	16.9	–	8.4	44.7

Notes: FMF includes both grants and loans. Europe includes $339.2 in FMF, $123.9 in ESF, and $0.2 in IMET funds for the NIS in FY 1992.

Sources: U.S. Agency for International Development; Congressional Research Service.

levels during the Bush years, although Angola, Mozambique, and Namibia experienced modest increases.

Congress and Security Assistance

Continuing a trend set during the Reagan administration, the Democrat-controlled Congress continued to reduce the security assistance program over the opposition of a Republican president. Simultaneously, Congress was instrumental in beginning the process of rethinking and refocusing this program, and foreign aid in general. Aid to Egypt-Israel was untouchable politically, but while aid to the base-rights states (and many others) fell, Congress appropriated substantial security assistance and other aid for the emerging democracies of central and Eastern Europe. It also authorized the so-called Nunn-Lugar, or Cooperative Threat Reduction program (sometimes called the Safe and Secure Dismantlement program) for the four NIS that were nuclear weapons inheritors of the former Soviet Union (discussed below).

Reform. Led by Congressmen Lee Hamilton (D-Ind.) and Benjamin Gilman (R-N.Y.) (the Hamilton Task Force), the House Foreign Affairs Committee issued an important report in early 1989 (see Chapter 4) that declared that

[c]hanges in the international environment and the position of the United States, ... domestic budgetary pressures, ... and the loss of public and Congressional support for the aid program all demand major changes in foreign aid legislation. U.S. foreign assistance needs a new premise, a new framework, and a new purpose to meet the challenges of today.[68]

The Hamilton Task Force maintained that foreign aid remained important to promoting the interests of the United States but asserted that the program was "hamstrung by too many conflicting objectives, legislative conditions, earmarks, and bureaucratic red tape." The study uncovered 33 declared objectives of foreign assistance in 500-plus pages of statutory language. Many of the objectives were found to be obsolete, contradictory, or simply unnecessary.[69]

Among other things, the Hamilton Task Force recommended a relative shift in emphasis away from security assistance and toward development assistance; a reduction in earmarks not "politically inevitable"; phasing out base-rights aid over a five-year period; more effective accountability for the expenditure of program funds; the consolidation of military assistance into one funding source; and the substitution of sweeping new legislation for the 1961 Foreign Assistance Act and the 1976 Arms Export Control Act.[70] While some task force recommendations were ultimately adopted, the overall foreign aid program was affected only marginally.

Nunn-Lugar. Among the most significant developments related to U.S. security assistance during the Bush years was the 1991 congressionally mandated establishment of the Nunn-Lugar, or CTR program. The CTR program addressed nonproliferation problems spawned by the demise of the Soviet Union in late 1991.

Two particularly pressing nonproliferation concerns were the so-called loose nukes and brain drain issues. The former referred to concerns about the safety, security, and command and control of the Soviet nuclear arsenal in the midst of deunionization. Of primary importance to the Bush administration was the ultimate fate of the approximately 27,000 former Soviet nuclear weapons concentrated in Russia, Ukraine, Belarus, and Kazakhstan. The success of just-negotiated strategic arms control treaties also hinged on the effective management of this worrisome problem.[71] The brain drain problem dealt with the potential outflow of weapons-related scientific expertise from the former Soviet Union. To meet these problems, CTR focused on several primary areas: destruction and dismantlement of nuclear and chemical weapons; "chain of custody," that is, weapons security and nuclear fissile material protection, control, and accounting; nonproliferation through funding of science centers and improving export controls; and defense conversion and demilitarization.

CTR is not part of the *formal* security assistance program.[72] Nonetheless, it is a bilateral aid effort funded largely through the DOD budget that directly advances the security interests of the United States. Moreover, it shares the essential characteristics of statutorily defined security assistance programs.[73] Because Congress is more receptive to defense than it is to foreign aid, the Nunn-Lugar bill's chief sponsor, Senator Sam Nunn (D-Ga.), denied that it constituted "foreign aid."[74] Rather, it was presented as "defense by other means."[75]

Surprisingly, despite the acknowledged importance of Senator Nunn's measure, it was not welcomed by the Bush administration. Although the White House did acquiesce in the diversion of a total of $800 million from DOD's budget to fund CTR between FY 1992 and FY 1993, the Nunn-Lugar legislation was considered an improper intrusion by Congress into the foreign policy realm. The program was, indeed, a creature of Congress and, as such, was treated as another instance of attempted congressional micromanagement of foreign policy. The administration, therefore, effectively dragged its feet in implementing CTR.[76]

There were also other reasons the program took so long to get off the ground, including the necessity of establishing the requisite degree of mutual trust between the United States and its former adversaries, the reluctance of both sides to reveal what had long been among their most guarded secrets, and the bureaucratic maneuvering in both Washington and Moscow over which departments or ministries would be involved.[77] As a consequence, Nunn-Lugar's full implementation awaited the next administration. Only then would the program, and security assistance generally, begin to move substantially "beyond containment."

CLINTON ADMINISTRATION: A NEW ERA

The central objectives of the administration of William Clinton included the promotion of democracy, stability, free market economies, and denuclearization in Russia, the other former Soviet republics, and elsewhere. In 1993, the Congress granted the administration's request for a $2.5 billion aid package for the former Soviet republics. However, this was politically doable only because Congress insisted on a trade-off under which it simultaneously and severely cut aid to most other regions and countries (except, of course, Israel and Egypt).[78] For example, Congress approved only 43 percent of the administration's foreign aid request for Latin America. For Russia and the other NIS, however, total U.S. foreign aid—*excluding* the DOD-budgeted Nunn-Lugar aid, which, by FY 1995, reached a total of $1.6 billion—amounted to $2 billion in FY 1993, $904 million in FY 1994, and $842 million in FY 1995. The administration reduced its FY 1996 aid request for the former Soviet region in the face of congressional concerns about ineffective use of some of the aid and allegations of arms control treaty noncompliance and human rights violations.[79]

Relative to development aid and most other forms of assistance, security assistance actually increased as a percentage of the budget. Security aid went from 38 percent of a $16.3 billion foreign assistance budget in FY 1993 to 48 percent of a $12.1 billion budget in FY 1996 under the Republican-controlled 104th Congress. There were several reasons for this. First, as the foreign aid budget fell, the bulk of security assistance—aid to Egypt-Israel—remained frozen at customarily high levels. Second, the budgetary walls separating international affairs, defense, and domestic spending that were enforced by the 1990 Budget Enforcement Act came down in 1993. While this allowed the international affairs budget (of which foreign aid is a component) to "raid" DOD's budget for aid to Russia—as in a 1994 supplemental to the FY 1993 budget—it also exposed foreign aid to even greater reductions than during the Bush years. A third factor was the 104th Congress: Conservatives tend to be less critical of security aid than liberals. Finally, President Clinton, like his Cold War predecessors, discovered that foreign aid, and security assistance in particular, was an important implement of foreign policy in an international system where the United States still played a pivotal role. In 1995, Clinton's national security adviser, Anthony Lake, denounced "back-door isolationists" in Congress who slashed foreign aid, thereby damaging "tools America has used for fifty years to maintain our leadership in the world: aid to emerging markets, economic support for peace, international peacekeeping, [and] programs to fight terrorism."[80]

National Security Strategy: Post–Cold War Security Aid

It was in the Clinton administration that the United States truly began to pursue a postcontainment foreign policy and, with it, a post–Cold War security assistance program. However, the program retained a decided continuity with the past in many respects. This was nowhere more evident than in President Clinton's conventional arms transfer policy, which was announced in February 1995 in Presidential Decision Directive (PDD) 34 (PD 34). The Clinton policy was squarely in line with the largely open-ended Reagan-Bush approach. That is, arms transfers were justified and encouraged on a wide variety of often vague or even contradictory grounds.[81]

Clinton's national security statements linked security assistance to four of the five principal elements of his foreign policy: enlarging the community of free market democracies, maintaining strong military forces with peacetime forward presence commitments, responding to such global threats as those posed by terrorists and narcotics traffickers, and meeting other security needs such as supporting multilateral peace operations.[82] This same declaratory policy statement gave security aid a prominent role "through training programs, . . . military contacts, and security assistance programs that include judicious foreign military sales," by which the United States "can strengthen . . . our friends and allies."[83] This was as vigorous a rationale for security assistance as was set forth by the Bush administration.

Attempted Reform. Under prodding from a Congress still controlled by Democrats, the Clinton administration attempted to overhaul the entire foreign assistance program and, in so doing, offer its vision of the future of security assistance.[84] The proposed Peace, Prosperity, and Democracy Act (H.R. 3765), which was transmitted to Congress in early 1994, would have abandoned the practice of budgeting foreign aid resources around functional accounts such as FMF, ESF, development aid, and so forth. Rather, it sought to reorganize foreign assistance policy and budget allocations around five thematic foreign policy objectives: sustainable development, building democracy, promoting peace, promoting humanitarian and crisis aid, and promoting economic growth through trade and investment.[85]

The administration asserted that this new framework would strengthen public and congressional support for foreign aid by restoring coherence and direction to the program through a focus on the goal of "enlarging" the sphere of democracy. All foreign aid was intended to support one or more thematic objectives and was not to be country oriented; instead, it was designed to advance broad U.S. goals (democracy, free market economies, etc.) and to meet shared global concerns, such as weapons proliferation, refugees, and so forth. Most security assistance in the draft bill fell under Title II (Building Democracy) and, especially, Title III (Promoting Peace). Title II would direct economic and military aid to countries making the transition to democracy, although authorization of aid to the NIS and Eastern Europe would remain, respectively, under the Freedom Support and SEED Acts. Title III stated that regional conflicts posed continuing threats to the United States; it noted the U.S. interest in Middle East peace; and most sweepingly, it allowed the use of aid for any of three purposes: to resolve conflict, to counter security threats, or to promote collective security.

H.R. 3765 was somewhat elusive about how funds would be programmed, but the president was granted broad authority to offer aid for political, economic, and security reasons. There was a provision, however, for Congress to separately authorize and appropriate military aid programs administered by DOD, thereby allowing Congress to set the respective levels of military and economic aid. Sensitive to congressional concerns about global arms transfers, the bill urged— but did not require—the president to tilt toward development assistance once regional threats subside. Much to the chagrin of many members of Congress, the bill also attempted to pursue one of the principal recommendations of the 1989 Hamilton Task Force: the virtual elimination of earmarks. However, *none* of the traditional functions performed by security assistance programs would have disappeared under the proposed Peace, Prosperity, and Democracy Act; only their packaging, organization, and (perhaps) funding levels would have changed.

But Congress failed to act in 1994, and H.R. 3765 was a short-lived attempt to reform the cumbersome foreign aid program. Many members of Congress objected that the proposed Peace, Prosperity, and Democracy Act would shift excessive power to the president. Moreover, there was no political constituency for reform. In fact, the powerful pro-Israel lobby opposed changing a system under which it was the primary beneficiary.[86] With the onset of a Republican Congress in January 1995, other priorities took precedence. Indeed, Senator Jesse Helms (R-N.C.), the new chairman of the Senate Foreign Relations Committee, denounced foreign aid as this "stupid business of giving away taxpayers' money."[87] Senator Helms then launched a campaign to abolish the Agency for International Development as part of a restructuring of Washington's Cold War apparatus.

Aid Composition and Distribution

Only $13.4 billion was appropriated for foreign aid in FY 1994 (slightly more in FY 1995), and several accounts were reduced as budget levels fell to only $12.1 billion in FY 1996. Greece and Turkey received just $770 million in Treasury rate (not concessional) loans in FY 1994 and $620 million in FY 1995. Despite the Clinton administration's assessment that more military aid was required to help dismantle drug trafficking operations in South America, the State Department's international narcotics control budget was reduced by Congress until the 104th Congress increased it in FY 1996 (see Table 3.7). The process of decapitalizing the Special Defense Acquisition Fund also began at this time. The SDAF was established in 1982 to ensure that U.S. defense stocks would not be seriously depleted if an ally needed rapid delivery of military equipment.

Responding to congressional directives, the International Military Education and Training program—which retained most of its funding—expanded its mission in 1991 and 1992 to include instruction in civilian control over the military, improving military justice systems, and training national legislators for overseeing their national militaries (PL 101–513; PL 102–391). IMET and a parallel

Table 3.7
Security Assistance Distribution by Program, FY 1993–FY 1996 (in millions of dollars)

FISCAL YEAR	FMF	ESF	IMET	NARCOTICS	TERRORISM	NDE	PKOs
1993	3449.2	2670.0	42.5	147.8	15.6	–	27.2
1994	3352.6	2582.0	42.5	147.8	15.6	10.0	77.2
1995	3151.3	2349.0	25.5	105.0	15.2	10.0	72.0
1996	3715.5	2346.4	19.0	150.0	15.0	20.0	72.0
TOTALS	13668.6	9947.4	129.5	550.6	61.4	40.0	248.4

Note: FMF includes both grants and loans.
Sources: Congressional Research Service; House Committee on Appropriations, Subcommittee on Foreign Operations (H.R. 104–143).

Pentagon-funded effort established in 1989—the military-to-military contact program—focused heavily on Eastern Europe and the former Soviet region.

Some other accounts actually increased. Voluntary U.S. funding of United Nations' peacekeeping operations rose from $27 million in FY 1993 to $72 million in FY 1996. Moreover, three new accounts were actually created. First, due to the sweeping changes in Central and Eastern Europe since the fall of the Berlin Wall, $60 million in foreign operations funds (joined by $40 million in Department of Defense money) were requested in FY 1996 for increased defense cooperation among "Partnership for Peace" members to facilitate and expedite the probable future expansion of the NATO alliance. Second, the Nonproliferation and Disarmament Fund was established with $10 million in FY 1994 to help create viable export control systems in the former Soviet republics. The NDF was under the rubric of Nunn-Lugar but funded out of the International Affairs budget rather than the DOD budget. The allocation for the NDF rose to $20 million in FY 1996 in part to help bolster export controls throughout the former Soviet region. Lastly, to help counter North Korea's fledgling nuclear weapons program, the U.S. government spent $48 million between FY 1994 and FY 1996 for the provision of heavy fuel oil and partial financing of two light-water reactors in support of the 1994 "Agreed Framework" agreement with that "rogue" state.

Middle East. There were few notable changes in levels of security aid to Egypt and Israel under Clinton, but assistance to Jordan rebounded in FY 1993. Much more important to Jordan, however, was the $275 million in debt forgiveness that year, Washington's reward for signing on to the Israeli-Palestinian peace process. Another "peace process recipient," the West Bank/Gaza Strip, received $75.5 million in FY 1995 ESF funds and an equal amount in FY 1996.

Europe/NIS. Aid to base-rights nations continued to decline during the Clinton presidency (see Table 3.8). Greece maintained a relatively constant level of $315 million in loans throughout this period, but aid to Turkey fell and Portugal "graduated" as an aid recipient. Otherwise, the most noticeable feature of security assistance operations in Europe (excluding Nunn-Lugar) was the widespread participation of most NIS in the IMET program by FY 1996.

Latin America. The most striking component of the security assistance program in Latin America during the Clinton era was the continued post–Cold War reduction in both ESF and FMF aid. Much of the small counternarcotics and IMET program aid continued to go to Latin America, but only Haiti received a notable level of security assistance. Parallel with the U.S. invasion (peace operation) and subsequent military occupation of the island to restore democracy, Haiti went from zero program support in FY 1993 to $36 million in ESF in FY 1994, and more than $90 million in each of the next two years, plus a small amount of FMF.

Asia/Pacific. Despite the growing importance of Asia for U.S. security and foreign economic policy, security aid to the region plunged to a record-low level. A particularly telling indicator of the role of security assistance in the region

Table 3.8
Security Assistance Distribution by Region, FY 1993–FY 1996 (in millions of dollars)

REGION	FISCAL YEAR	FMF	NARCOTICS	IMET	ESE
Near East	1993	3158.1	–	5.6	2075.4
	1994	3109.0	–	3.1	1863.0
	1995	3107.3	–	4.3	2413.6
	1996	3130.0	–	4.6	2101.2
Europe/NIS	1993	864.4	0.4	9.1	316.6
	1994	846.0	0.4	6.8	74.4
	1995	620.7	0.4	7.8	200.3
	1996	850.0	4.4	12.9	144.6
Asia	1993	21.9	10.2	6.9	70.1
	1994	–	8.4	2.9	40.0
	1995	–	7.4	4.0	35.6
	1996	3.0	7.5	6.3	84.3
Latin America/Caribbean	1993	73.9	75.4	11.3	334.4
	1994	12.2	53.2	5.1	172.9
	1995	15.8	53.4	4.8	190.3
	1996	10.0	150.6	9.1	117.8
Africa (Sub-Saharan)	1993	24.0	–	9.0	9.3
	1994	485.0	–	4.0	16.1
	1995	–	–	5.1	7.8
	1996	–	–	6.6	24.4

Notes: FMF includes both grants and loans. FY 1995 levels are estimates, as of February 1995. FY 1996 figures are based on administration requests, not finalized disbursements. Dashes (–) indicate zero disbursements.
Sources: U.S. Agency for International Development; Congressional Research Service.

was that a country of tertiary significance to the United States, Cambodia, was the major aid recipient (for UN peacekeeping).

Africa. Only Africa received less security assistance than Asia during the Clinton years. The African subcontinent continued to receive development and humanitarian assistance, but no country in sub-Saharan Africa received substantial levels of security aid. Many African states still participated in the IMET program; otherwise, the region was effectively severed from the security assistance program.

Congress and Security Assistance

The 103d Congress continued to reduce overall security assistance levels while protecting the two largest aid recipients. Congress pressured Clinton to submit comprehensive reform legislation in 1993, but (as discussed above) Congress did not act on H.R. 3765 when it was submitted by the president the next year.

The demise of Clinton's proposed Peace, Prosperity, and Democracy Act was assured with the election of a more conservative 104th Congress in November 1994. Dedicated to fiscal soundness, the new Congress reduced FY 1996 spending on foreign operations to the lowest level in decades. However, as overall foreign aid expenditures declined, security assistance levels stabilized and even increased. Still, the Nunn-Lugar program, despite being a creature of Congress, initially became a target of the new Congress. Hence, its future seemed to be in some question.

Nunn-Lugar. By April 1993, the Clinton administration began to broaden and deepen its relations with the non-Russian former Soviet republics. Whereas President Bush had used Nunn-Lugar aid as an incentive to persuade the former Soviet republics to denuclearize as a precondition for a more broad-based relationship with the United States, Clinton's approach was one of more across-the-board constructive engagement.[88]

The Clinton administration became an ardent advocate of a CTR program that it viewed as opening valuable channels of communication, affording the United States a "seat at the table" for regional security affairs, and ultimately, achieving the denuclearization of Ukraine, Kazakhstan, and Belarus.[89] There was enthusiastic, virtually unanimous support for CTR within the national security bureaucracy, largely because, as Undersecretary of Defense for Policy Walter Slocombe said: "Dollar for dollar, there is no better way to spend national security resources than to help eliminate a former enemy's nuclear weapons and convert its defense industry to peaceful purposes."[90] The 103d Congress agreed; it was fully supportive of Nunn-Lugar.

This situation changed in 1995, especially in the House of Representatives. Some House members, particularly conservative Republicans, charged that Russia had not complied with its arms control obligations concerning chemical and biological weapons,[91] that CTR funds were being employed by Russia to modernize its weapons of mass destruction,[92] and that the General Accounting Office was highly critical of the program.[93] The House then slashed the administration's $371 million CTR budget request for FY 1996 to a mere $200 million. However, the Senate was more supportive, and $298 million was ultimately appropriated.

Nunn-Lugar, while certainly not problem free, was considered vital by most U.S. security specialists, whether inside or outside government. Moreover, the cumulative cost of the CTR program through FY 1996 was relatively modest—one-third less than the *annual* U.S. security assistance subsidy to Israel. While this centerpiece of U.S.-Russian relations faced significant congressional scrutiny particularly in 1995–1996, with questions over the scope of the assistance, overall funding levels, and the pace of its disbursal, it appeared probable that the program would run, in some form, through its anticipated end date of FY 2001.[94]

NOTES

1. Zbigniew Brzezinski, *Power and Principle: Memoirs of the National Security Adviser, 1977–1981* (New York: Farrar, Straus & Giroux, 1983), pp. 52–55.

2. Ibid., p. 56.

3. Jimmy Carter, *Keeping Faith: Memoirs of a President* (New York: Bantam Books, 1982), p. 143.

4. Paul Hammond, David J. Louscher, Michael D. Salomone, and Norman A. Graham, *The Reluctant Supplier: U.S. Decisionmaking for Arms Sales* (Cambridge, Mass.: Oelgeschlager, Gunn & Hain, 1983), p. 170.

5. "President Carter Announces Policy on the Transfer of Conventional Arms," *Department of State Bulletin* [hereafter, *DOS Bulletin*] 76 (June 13, 1977), pp. 625–26.

6. Ibid.

7. "Administration Officials Testify on Arms Transfer Policy," *DOS Bulletin* 78 (March 1978), pp. 45–46; Lucy Wilson Benson, "Security Assistance: Conventional Arms Transfer Policy," *DOS Bulletin* 78 (March 1978), p. 44.

8. See "Administration Officials Testify," p. 46.

9. Andrew J. Pierre, *The Global Politics of Arms Sales* (Princeton, N.J.: Princeton University Press, 1982), p. 58.

10. One of the better assessments is Richard Betts, "The Tragicomedy of Arms Trade Control," *International Security* 5 (Summer 1980), pp. 80–110.

11. Seymour Weiss, *President Carter's Arms Transfer Policy: A Critical Assessment* (Miami, Fla.: Advanced International Studies Institute, University of Miami, 1978).

12. See Nicole Ball and Milton Leitenberg, "The Arms Sales Policy of the Carter Administration," *Alternatives* 4 (1979), pp. 527–56; Jo L. Husbands, "The Arms Connection: Jimmy Carter and the Politics of Military Exports," in Cindy Cannizzo, ed., *The Gun Merchants* (New York: Pergamon Press, 1980), pp. 18–49; Pierre, *The Global Politics of Arms Sales*, p. 57.

13. Brzezinski, *Power and Principle*, p. 145.

14. Duncan L. Clarke, *Politics of Arms Control: The Role and Effectiveness of the U.S. Arms Control and Disarmament Agency* (New York: Free Press, 1979), pp. 227–28.

15. U.S. Congress, House, Committee on Foreign Affairs, *Staff Report: U.S. Security Assistance and Arms Transfer Policies for the 1980s*, 97th Cong., 1st sess., 1981, pp. 8–9; Pierre, *The Global Politics of Arms Sales*, p. 55.

16. Brzezinski, *Power and Principle*, pp. 128–29.

17. Cyrus Vance, "Foreign Assistance and U.S. Policy," *DOS Bulletin* 79 (March 1979), p. 37.

18. U.S. Agency for International Development [hereafter, AID], *U.S. Overseas Loans and Grants, Volume V: Europe, Oceania, Canada and Interregional—Obligations and Loan Authorizations, FY 1946–1990* [hereafter, *Europe*], Washington, D.C., 1991 (not paginated).

19. Cyrus Vance, "Europe: Assistance Programs to Greece, Turkey, and Cyprus," *DOS Bulletin* 78 (May 1978), p. 33.

20. AID, *U.S. Overseas Loans and Grants, Volume III: East Asia—Obligations and Loan Authorizations, FY 1946–1990* [hereafter, *East Asia*], Washington, D.C., 1991 (not paginated).

21. AID, *U.S. Overseas Loans and Grants, Volume I: Near East and South Asia— Obligations and Loan Authorizations, FY 1946–1990* [hereafter, *Near East and South Asia*], Washington, D.C., 1991 (not paginated); Clyde Mark, "U.S. Laws that Benefit Israel," Congressional Research Service, Washington, D.C., 1988, pp. 1–2.

22. Gerald Felix Warburg, *Conflict and Consensus: The Struggle between Congress and the President over Foreign Policymaking* (New York: Harper & Row, 1989), pp. 199–202; Brzezinski, *Power and Principle*, pp. 247–49; Mitchell Geoffrey Bard, *The Water's Edge: Defining the Limits to Domestic Influence on United States Middle East Policy* (New Brunswick, N.J.: Transaction, 1991), pp. 39–50.

23. AID, *U.S. Overseas Loans and Grants, Volume II: Latin America and Caribbean—Obligations and Loan Authorizations, FY 1946–1990* [hereafter, *Latin America and Caribbean*], Washington, D.C., 1991 (not paginated); U.S. Congress, House, Committee on Foreign Affairs, *Congress and Foreign Policy, 1981*, Comm. Prt., 97th Cong., 2d sess., 1982, p. 116.

24. Cyrus Vance, "Secretary Vance Emphasized Importance of Foreign Assistance Programs," *DOS Bulletin* 76 (April 11, 1977), p. 338; Richard Moose, "Africa: Security Assistance to the Sub-Sahara," *DOS Bulletin* 78 (April 1978), p. 30; idem, "Africa: FY 1980 Assistance Proposals," *DOS Bulletin* 79 (April 1979), p. 11.

25. AID, *U.S. Overseas Loans and Grants, Volume IV: Africa—Obligations and Loan Authorizations, FY 1949–1990* [hereafter, *Africa*], Washington, D.C., 1991 (not paginated).

26. See, for example, Nigel Bowles, *The White House and Capitol Hill: The Politics of Presidential Persuasion* (New York: Oxford University Press, 1987), pp. 194–97.

27. See John Felton, "Carter Is Pressing Congress to Soften Vietnam-Era Restrictions on Presidency," *Congressional Quarterly Weekly Report* (April 26, 1980), pp. 1136–37; Matthew Nimetz, "Security Assistance Programs: Promoting U.S. Interests," *DOS Bulletin* 80 (June 1980), pp. 60–62. One result of the 1980 exemptions was to facilitate the transfer of military equipment to Turkey by NATO members other than the United States.

28. U.S. Congress, Senate, Committee on Foreign Relations, *Senate Report No. 95-841* [to accompany S. 3075], 95th Cong., 2d sess., 1979, p. 1848.

29. Quoted in Lou Cannon, *President Reagan: The Role of a Lifetime* (New York: Simon & Schuster, 1991), pp. 316–17.

30. For a presentation of this point of view, see Robert W. Tucker, *The Purposes of*

American Power: An Essay on National Security (New York: Praeger Publishers, 1981), pp. 1–37. Tucker contended (pp. 36–37) that Kissinger, Nixon, Carter, and others who pointed to the limits of American power suffered from "a political pathology."

31. "Conventional Arms Transfer Policy," *DOS Bulletin* 81 (September 1981), p. 61.

32. The meaning of "the Reagan Doctrine" was always a mystery to the administration. President Reagan did not use the term, nor did it appear in any of the 200-plus National Security Decision Directives signed by him. The term was invented by neoconservative columnist Charles Krauthammer in April 1985. See Cannon, *President Reagan*, pp. 365–70.

33. *International Security and Development Cooperation Act of 1985*, PL 99–83, sec. 722, 811, 904–5.

34. Stanley J. Heginbotham and Larry Q. Nowels, *An Overview of U.S. Foreign Aid Programs*, Congressional Research Service [hereafter, CRS] Report for Congress, Washington, D.C., March 30, 1988, pp. 18–19.

35. U.S. Congress, House, Committee on Foreign Affairs, *Report of the Task Force on Foreign Assistance*, Comm. Prt., 101st Cong., 1st sess., 1989, pp. 10–11.

36. Larry Nowels, "Economic Security Assistance as a Tool of American Foreign Policy," Research Report, National War College, Washington, D.C., February 1987, p. 13; William Schneider, "FY 1987 Security Assistance Requests," *DOS Bulletin* 86 (August 1986), p. 78.

37. See Nowels, "Economic Security Assistance," p. 15.

38. See "International Affairs: The FY 1987 Budget," *DOS Bulletin* 86 (April 1986), p. 4; Schneider, "FY 1987," pp. 77–79.

39. See, for example, U.S. Department of State, *Congressional Presentation Document for FY 1988: Security Assistance Programs* (Washington, D.C.: Government Printing Office [hereafter, GPO]), 1987).

40. AID, *Europe*.

41. Richard Burt, "FY 1986 Assistance Requests to Europe," *DOS Bulletin* 85 (May 1985), pp. 71–74.

42. AID, *Europe*; "U.S.-Spain Framework for Defense Cooperation," *DOS Bulletin* 88 (March 1988), p. 69.

43. AID, *East Asia*.

44. Ibid.; see Gaston Sigur, "U.S. Security Interests in the Philippines," *DOS Bulletin* 86 (June 1986), pp. 41–42.

45. AID, *Near East and South Asia*.

46. Ibid.; AID, *U.S. Overseas Loans and Grants: Obligations and Loan Authorizations, July 1, 1945–September 30, 1990*, Washington, D.C., 1991.

47. Clyde Mark, *Israel: U.S. Foreign Assistance*, CRS Issue Brief, Congressional Research Service, Washington, D.C., August 30, 1995, p. 7; Duncan L. Clarke and Alan S. Cohen, "The United States, Israel and the Lavi Fighter," *Middle East Journal* 40 (Winter 1986), pp. 16–32.

48. Quoted in Cannon, *President Reagan*, p. 157.

49. See Chapter 7; Helena Cobban, *The Superpowers and the Syrian-Israeli Conflict: Beyond Crisis Management?* (New York: Praeger Publishers, 1991), pp. 78–111.

50. AID, *Latin America and Caribbean*. See Cynthia Arnson, *Crossroads: Congress, the Reagan Administration, and Central America* (New York: Pantheon Books, 1989); Robert A. Pastor, *Whirlpool: U.S. Foreign Policy toward Latin America and the Caribbean* (Princeton, N.J.: Princeton University Press, 1992), pp. 65–82.

51. AID, *Africa*; Roy Stacy, "FY 1988 Assistance Requests for Sub-Sahara Africa," *DOS Bulletin* 87 (May 1987), p. 12; Nowels, "Economic Security Assistance," p. 13.

52. Aaron Wildavsky, *The New Politics of the Budgetary Process*, 2d ed. (New York: HarperCollins, 1992), pp. 234–36.

53. For the rationale for the SDAF, see U.S. Congress, Senate, Committee on Foreign Relations, *Senate Report No. 97–88*, 97th Cong., 1st sess., 1981, pp. 2417–19.

54. Louis J. Samelson, "Congress and the Fiscal Year 1987 Security Assistance Budget: A Study in Austerity," *DISAM Journal* 9 (Winter 1986–1987), pp. 23–24.

55. See Louis J. Samelson, "Fiscal Year Military Assistance Legislation: An Analysis," *DISAM Journal* 11 (Winter 1988–1989), p. 13.

56. William Schneider, Jr., "FY 1984 Security Assistance Requests," *DOS Bulletin* 83 (May 1983), p. 73; idem, "FY 1986 Security Assistance Requests," *DOS Bulletin* 85 (June 1985), p. 69; Louis J. Samelson, "Supplemental FY 1987 and Pending FY 1988 Security Assistance Appropriations," *DISAM Journal* 10 (Fall 1987), pp. 8–10; George Shultz, "The Foreign Affairs Budget Crisis: A Threat to Our Vital Interests," *DOS Bulletin* 87 (March 1987), pp. 7–13; Louis J. Samelson, "Another Year of Austerity: The Fiscal Year 1988 Security Assistance Budget," *DISAM Journal* 10 (Spring 1988), pp. 1–37; House, *Report of the Task Force on Foreign Assistance*, p. 27.

57. For example, see the testimony of Secretary of State George Shultz, "Matching Foreign Policy Resources with Goals," *DOS Bulletin* 87 (October 1987), p. 7.

58. See the insightful analysis in Nowels, "Economic Security Assistance," pp. 17–26.

59. U.S. Department of State, *Congressional Presentation Document for Security Assistance Programs: Fiscal Year 1991*, Washington, D.C., 1990, p. 2.

60. See Patrick J. Garrity and Sharon K. Weiner, "U.S. Defense Strategy after the Cold War," *Washington Quarterly* 15 (Spring 1992), pp. 57, 61.

61. Larry Nowels and Ellen Collier, *Foreign Policy Budget: Issues and Priorities for the 1990s*, CRS Report for Congress, Washington, D.C., 1991, p. 3.

62. White House, *National Security Strategy of the United States*, Washington, D.C., December 1991, pp. 9, 27.

63. U.S. Department of State, "Fact Sheet on U.S. Economic, Military, and Counter-Narcotics Program Assistance," *U.S. Department of State Dispatch*, Washington, D.C., March 2, 1992, p. 167.

64. White House, *National Security Strategy of the United States*, Washington, D.C., January 1993, pp. 14–15, 20.

65. See Francis Fukuyama, *The End of History and the Last Man* (New York: Free Press, 1992).

66. See U.S. Department of State, *Congressional Presentation Document for Security Assistance: Fiscal Year 1994*, Washington, D.C., 1993.

67. AID, *U.S. Overseas Loans and Grants, Obligations and Loan Authorizations: July 1, 1945–September 30, 1993*, Washington, D.C., 1994.

68. House, *Report of the Task Force on Foreign Assistance*, p. 29.

69. Ibid., pp. v, 27.

70. Ibid., pp. v–vi, 29–42.

71. See generally Michael R. Beschloss and Strobe Talbott, *At the Highest Levels: The Inside Story of the End of the Cold War* (Boston, Mass.: Little, Brown, 1993), pp. 165–68.

72. However, some professional associations do label Nunn-Lugar a security assis-

tance program. See "U.S. Security Assistance to the Former Soviet Union," *Arms Control Today* 25 (April 1995), pp. 24–25.

73. U.S. Department of Defense [hereafter, DOD], Joint Chiefs of Staff, *Dictionary of Military and Associated Terms* (Washington, D.C.: GPO, 1979), p. 306. Nunn-Lugar is much like the DOD-funded, Vietnam-era Military Assistance Service Fund. The MASF was universally viewed as security assistance. Both programs provided defense-related goods and services in furtherance of national policy.

74. Quoted in Pamela Fessler, "Congress Clears Soviet Aid Bill in Late Reversal of Sentiment," *Congressional Quarterly Weekly Report*, November 30, 1991, p. 3536.

75. DOD, "Cooperative Threat Reduction," Washington, D.C., April 1995, p. 1 (mimeographed).

76. Jason Ellis, "Nunn-Lugar's Mid-Life Crisis," *Survival* 39 (Spring 1997), p. 96; Theodor Galdi, *The Nunn-Lugar Program for Soviet Weapons Dismantlement: Background and Implementation*, Congressional Research Service, Rpt. 94–985F, Washington, D.C., June 8, 1995, p. 2.

77. Heather Wilson, "Missed Opportunities: Washington Politics and Nuclear Proliferation," *National Interest* 34 (Winter 1993–1994), p. 29; Mitchell Reiss, *Bridled Ambition: Why Countries Constrain Their Nuclear Capabilities* (Baltimore, Md.: Johns Hopkins University Press, 1995), pp. 89–182; interview of former White House official by Jason Ellis, July 1995. See also William C. Potter, *The Politics of Nuclear Renunciation*, Occasional Paper No. 22 (Washington, D.C.: Henry L. Stimson Center, April 1995).

78. See Jeremy D. Rosner, *The New Tug-of-War: Congress, the Executive Branch, and National Security* (Washington, D.C.: Carnegie Endowment for International Peace, 1995), pp. 45–64.

79. See Curt Tarnoff, *U.S. and International Assistance to the Former Soviet Union, CRS Issue Brief*, Congressional Research Service, Washington, D.C., 1995; idem, *Conditions on U.S. Foreign Assistance to Russia*, CRS Report for Congress, Congressional Research Service, Washington, D.C., June 26, 1995; Larry Nowels, *Appropriations for FY 1996: Foreign Operations*, CRS Report for Congress, Congressional Research Service, Washington, D.C., July 13, 1995.

80. Anthony Lake, address before the National Press Club, White House, Washington, D.C., April 27, 1995.

81. Richard F. Grimmet, *Conventional Arms Transfers: President Clinton's Policy Directive*, CRS Report for Congress, Congressional Research Service, Washington, D.C., May 17, 1995; Lora Lumpe, "Clinton's Conventional Arms Export Policy: So Little Change," *Arms Control Today* 25 (April–May 1995), pp. 9–14.

82. White House, *National Security Strategy of Engagement and Enlargement*, Washington, D.C., February 1995, pp. 1–17.

83. Ibid., p. 10.

84. For an account of this episode, see Duncan L. Clarke and Daniel O'Connor, "Security Assistance Policy after the Cold War," in Randall Ripley and James Lindsay, eds., *U.S. Foreign Policy After the Cold War* (Pittsburgh, Pa.: University of Pittsburgh Press, 1997).

85. See Larry Q. Nowels, *Foreign Aid: Clinton Administration Policy and Budget Reform Proposals*, CRS Issue Brief, Congressional Research Service, Washington, D.C., January 28, 1994.

86. Caren Benjamin, "Clinton Wants to Revamp Aid," *Washington Jewish Week*, December 16, 1993, p. 4.

87. John M. Goshko, "Foreign Aid May Be Early Test of New Hill Order," *Washington Post*, November 21, 1994, p. A14.

88. Jason D. Ellis, "The 'Ukranian Dilemma' and U.S. Foreign Policy," *European Security* 3 (Summer 1994), pp. 251–80.

89. By June 1996, Kazakhstan and Ukraine were nuclear weapons free, and Belarus was rid of nuclear weapons by December 1996.

90. Testimony of Undersecretary of Defense for Policy Walter Slocomb, Senate Armed Services Committee, hearings on START II, May 17, 1995 (mimeographed).

91. The administration was concerned about this but professed confidence that problems could be resolved. U.S. Department of State, *U.S. Assistance and Related Programs for the New Independent States of the Former Soviet Union: 1994 Annual Report* (Washington, D.C.: GPO, 1995), p. 200. The Pentagon asserted: "Linking all CTR assistance to Russia, including nuclear systems dismantlement assistance, to Russian chemical and biological arms control compliance threatens programs which directly improve U.S. security, and amounts to cutting off our nose to spite our face." DOD, "Point Paper: Cooperative Threat Reduction 'Nunn-Lugar' Program, House, National Security Committee, FY 1996 Defense Authorization Bill Markup," July 1995, p. 2 (mimeographed).

92. News accounts that Russia was using CTR money for weapons modernization were denied by the administration. Letter from Secretary of Defense William Perry to Representative Floyd Spence (R-S.C.), May 23, 1995 (mimeographed).

93. The General Accounting Office [hereafter, GAO] did issue a report that raised some questions about the CTR program, especially concerning the U.S. agreement to help Russia construct a chemical weapons destruction facility. U.S. GAO, *Weapons of Mass Destruction: Reducing the Threat from the Former Soviet Union: An Update*, NSIAD-95-165, Washington, D.C., June 1995. However, the GAO cautiously concluded that the CTR's "long-term prognosis for achieving its objectives may be promising" (p. 2).

94. Interviews of Defense, State, and Energy Department officials by Jason Ellis, July–August 1995, February–March 1996. Significantly, the DOD transferred programmatic and budgetary responsibility for nine separate Nunn-Lugar program elements to the Departments of Energy and State in FY 1996 in order to ensure continued funding. Clearly, one measure of this successful approach is that while DOD's CTR funding diminished, aggregate program funding actually *increased* to $401 million in FY 1996.

4

Congress and Security Assistance

Foreign aid is influenced profoundly by Congress. Indeed, the annual foreign assistance bill is perhaps the most visible and significant of the many mechanisms through which Congress helps determine U.S. foreign policy. Even those, such as Barbara Hinckley, who challenge the widely held view that Congress has been increasingly assertive in foreign policy since the early 1970s acknowledge that presidents routinely "bargain for whatever [foreign] assistance they can get" and that, at least in this area of foreign policymaking, "Congress has not acquiesced to the executive branch."[1]

Congress takes a special interest in foreign aid because the foreign assistance bill is the one regularly scheduled opportunity to debate and influence foreign policy.[2] Indeed, foreign assistance generally affords the most direct avenue for various members to affect policy.[3] Legislators realize that foreign aid, while commonly supported by elite leadership opinion, does not normally enjoy substantial broad-based support from the general American public. There are few political costs for voting to cut foreign aid (or rhetorically lambasting it while voting to approve it anyway) with the exception of very specific constituencies, such as influential ethnic or defense-export lobbies (see Chapter 5).

Debates over security assistance reflect the larger executive-legislative struggle for influence over foreign policymaking. Security assistance spans the institutional interests and prerogatives of both branches. For the executive branch, security assistance is a useful, relatively low-cost tool for implementing policy. For Congress, it not only represents a vehicle for influencing the substance of policy but also is a tangible expression of the legislative branch's coequal stature with the executive in the realm of foreign policy, as well as a mechanism to satisfy powerful special interests.

Congress ultimately controls the purse strings for security assistance, and through the budget process and such legislative vehicles as earmarking and conditionality, it can determine the purposes for which funds are to be employed. This often constrains the president's freedom of action and, as such, is a source of interbranch tension. This chapter examines, respectively, the congressional interest in security assistance, the tools Congress uses to influence security assistance policy, and congressional committees and processes for decisionmaking in this area.

CONGRESSIONAL INTEREST IN SECURITY ASSISTANCE

The interplay between Congress and the president over security assistance is a subset of the perennial question of the appropriate role of Congress in foreign policy. The issue here—unlike long-standing constitutional debates over executive agreements, executive privilege, and the shared war powers of the two branches—is less one of constitutionality than it is of mutually legitimate, clashing institutional prerogatives and policy preferences. While the federal courts have generally granted the president considerable constitutional leeway in foreign relations, concerning foreign assistance, presidents do not usually contest the several specific constitutional grants of power that enable Congress to, for instance, appropriate funds, regulate foreign commerce (such as the transfer of military goods), or (Article IV, Section 3) dispose and make rules for property belonging to the United States. Rather, the focus of executive-legislative differences over foreign aid in general and security assistance specifically concerns both substantive policy differences and the degree of latitude to be accorded the president in utilizing what he considers to be a valuable policy tool. Moreover, it is widely recognized that Congress lacks the institutional competence to effectively manage ("micromanage") the program; instead, it is for Congress to set policy guidelines, review executive branch actions, and disapprove executive actions that contravene those policy guidelines.[4]

Members of Congress have voiced various policy concerns over the years about security assistance. Indeed, economic development assistance is generally more popular than military aid, especially among more liberal legislators. Despite persistent concerns, however, the security assistance portion of the foreign aid budget has consistently hovered between roughly 40 and 60 percent since the inception of the program, thus revealing a substantial degree of congressional support or at least acquiescence.[5] Legislators have been variously concerned that security assistance does not really "work"; that it diverts resources from pressing domestic problems; and that it worsens the U.S. balance of payments. Moreover, some have feared that security aid programs may entangle the United States in questionable overseas commitments. Many liberal and moderate members of Congress have faulted security assistance programs for sometimes supporting repressive authoritarian regimes; legislators have also been concerned that military assistance may destabilize governments and foster regional instability by contributing to conventional arms races. Still others oppose assisting countries that are actively engaged in the proliferation of weapons of mass destruction or in systematic abuses of internationally recognized human rights. Legislators also occasionally look into program mismanagement or maladministration by the Defense Security Assistance Agency or the Agency for International Development.[6]

Yet Congress continues to provide security aid long after the end of the Cold War, despite a critical public and the reservations of individual members. Congressman David Obey (D-Wis.) once remarked that foreign aid is the program that members' constituents "most want to see cut."[7] However, many members of Congress who support foreign aid simply ignore public opinion, believing the general public does not follow their voting records closely and will not punish them electorally for their votes. In other cases, members may "balance" their vote for the foreign aid budget by also voting to cut or restrict aid. Members also use select provisions of the foreign aid legislation to curry favor with influential interest groups. Finally, of course, there are legislators who simply want to contribute to the formulation of sound public policy.[8]

Legislators are often partial to certain countries or programs. For example, some members have favored tight restrictions on security assistance to certain Central American countries because of human rights concerns, while they simultaneously support aid to such violators of human rights as Turkey. Congressmen in key positions use their influence to protect preferred-country programs. For example, Congressman Charles Wilson (D-Tex.) used his leverage as a swing vote on the Subcommittee on Foreign Operations of the House Appropriations Committee to preserve aid to Pakistan in the 1980s. Similarly, pro-Greece legislators have worked effectively to maintain the 7:10 Greece-Turkey aid ratio.[9]

Members of Congress are regularly responsive to aid requests from their ethnic compatriots, or they may otherwise work to help countries with which they identify. Senator Robert Dole (R-Kans.), for instance, repeatedly championed aid to post-Soviet Armenia because an Armenian doctor saved his life in World War II.[10] Other legislators may favor one security assistance program over another because the military equipment to be provided comes from their districts. For example, in 1991 Senator Christopher Dodd (D-Conn.) pushed for allowing U.S. allies to use Export-Import Bank credits to purchase military equipment, a move that would have aided the Connecticut-based Sikorsky Aircraft company in its bid for a contract to sell military helicopters to Turkey.[11]

There are other ways to categorize members' approaches to foreign aid. Most broadly, perhaps, there are those who favor more foreign aid and those who favor less. Some legislators simply do not favor any foreign aid. Congressman Sonny Callahan (R-Ala.), for instance, never voted for a foreign aid bill until he became chairman of the influential foreign operations subcommittee in 1995; similarly, Senator Jesse Helms (R-N.C.)—who supports aid to Israel but little else—regularly criticizes foreign aid.[12] Many other members of Congress approach foreign aid largely on how it is apportioned between security assistance and development aid. This effectively constitutes a liberal-conservative fault line. Liberals usually tilt toward humanitarian and development aid, in the belief that American interests are best served by helping in the development of the poorer members of the international community. On the other hand, those conservatives who do support foreign aid often favor security assistance. Conservatives often see the primary threats to American interests as instability stemming from external military threats to governments friendly to the United States and/or from such transnational challenges as international narcotics trafficking or terrorism. In any case, it should be noted that there has usually been a significant level of support for foreign aid from congressional moderates. Concerning the continuing downward spiral of security assistance funds since 1985, for example, Senator Mitch McConnell (R-Ky.) declared that a foreign assistance budget as low as the FY 1996 budget could "leave this president [and] our nation . . . with no global options other than sending in troops."[13]

CONGRESSIONAL APPROACHES TO SECURITY ASSISTANCE

In general, and with infrequent exceptions, successive Congresses have supported presidential requests for security assistance funds to regions deemed by the president to be of vital national interest: Europe in the 1940s, Asia in the 1950s and 1960s, the Middle East since the 1970s, (to a lesser degree) Central America in the 1980s, and Eastern Europe and the former Soviet Union in the 1990s. Presidents, then, have been able to assert their traditional leadership roles in foreign affairs through the use of security assistance. During the Cold War, there was a broad band of opinion within Congress that security assistance programs were necessary; these programs often followed U.S. troop commitments and supported supposed American regional interests, or they were implemented as an alternative to and substitute for direct U.S. military intervention.

However, congressional support for the program has never been unqualified. During the first decade of the program, foreign assistance (and NATO, too) was viewed by Congress as a temporary, if necessary, measure for a dangerous world.[14] Legislators were regularly critical of program management, planning, and accountability. They also complained that aid priorities were obscure and, by the mid-1950s, that aid was going to prosperous nations that could pay for their own defense.[15] However, these criticisms diminished somewhat when, with the Foreign Assistance Act of 1961, Congress took the major legislative step of codifying a freestanding foreign assistance program.

Congress, of course, is a divided institution with a fluid membership. Positions taken by legislators in the House and Senate on security assistance have changed over the years as membership and attitudes have changed. In the late 1970s, for instance, while the Senate Foreign Relations Committee was questioning the general rationale and effectiveness of the program, arguing that it wanted to "end grant military assistance as a 'habit' and bureaucratic 'addiction,' " the

House International Relations Committee was declaring aid an "important tool" of foreign policy.[16] In the early and mid-1980s, these positions were reversed: A Republican-controlled Senate backed the Reagan administration's push for increased security assistance, while many in a Democrat-controlled House resisted. Even after the Democrats regained control of the Senate in 1986, that body continued to be more supportive of military aid than the House. In the Republican 104th Congress (1995–1996), security assistance rose as a percentage of a falling foreign aid budget.

While Congress traditionally appropriates funds for security assistance to complement foreign policies that it finds acceptable, it nonetheless usually makes cuts in administration requests. For example, Congress cut the president's request every year between 1963 and 1982, often by more than 20 percent. Indeed, as Table 4.1 indicates, Congress routinely cuts roughly 10 percent of the administration request. However, this provides the executive with an incentive to "pad" each year's request by at least 10 percent ("cut insurance"), thereby permitting legislators to present themselves to their constituents as "cost cutters" on foreign aid.[17] While Congress makes policy statements in authorization/appropriations bills and, less formally, in reports, it generally will not force important policy measures on a resistant president. However, if the president pursues a foreign policy that polarizes the Congress, or if the president attempts to curtail or circumvent the customary prerogatives of Congress, there may be a vigorous congressional policy response, one that takes statutory form.

For instance, during the later phases of the war in Vietnam, Congress inserted mandatory reporting requirements in foreign assistance authorizations in an attempt to get more and better information from the Nixon administration. Congress also stipulated in the 1970s that significant proposed military sales agreements had to be submitted by the executive for prior approval. The 1974 Turkish arms embargo was especially demonstrative of the deterioration of executive-legislative relations in the 1970s. Despite the Ford administration's continuous exhortations about the importance of Turkey to American security interests in the eastern Mediterranean, Congress voted to cut off aid, partly because of a pervasive distrust of the presidency in the wake of the Nixon administration and partly because of its determination to reclaim an important role in foreign policy decisions.[18] This action led to a sweeping revision of the Foreign Assistance Act in 1976 through the passage of the International Security and Arms Export Control Act (PL 94–329), which embodied a widely held belief in Congress that arms sales contributed to international conflict.

When the Reagan administration's interventions in Central America during the 1980s encountered an increasingly hostile response from the authorizing committees, the administration simply moved to bypass them by seeking support from the appropriations committees.[19] Concerning the Central Intelligence Agency (CIA)–sponsored "Contras" who operated against the Sandinista government in Nicaragua, the executive and legislative branches came to pursue rival foreign policies.[20] While Congress enacted an evermore restrictive series

Table 4.1
Executive Requests and Congressional Appropriations, FY 1981–FY 1995 (in millions of dollars)

FISCAL YEAR	Executive Branch Requests				Congressional Appropriations			
	EMF	MAP	IMET	ESF	EMF	MAP	IMET	ESF
1981	734	104	33	2,031	500	110	28	2,105
1982	1,482	131	42	2,932	800	171	42	2,926
1983	950	557	54	2,886	1,175	383	46	2,962
1984	1,000	747	57	2,949	1,315	712	52	3,254
1985	5,100	925	61	3,438	4,940	805	56	6,084
1986	5,655	949	66	4,024	5,190	798	54	3,800
1987	5,861	1,257	69	4,391	4,053	950	56	3,600
1988	4,421	1,330	56	3,600	4,017	701	47	3,201
1989	4,460	467	53	3,281	4,272	467	47	3,259
1990	5,027	40	55	3,849	4,828	—	47	3,917
1991	5,017	—	51	3,358	4,663	—	47	3,175
1992	4,610	—	53	3,240	3,929	—	47	3,217
1993	4,099	—	48	3,123	3,245	—	43	2,670
1994	3,232	—	43	2,582	3,052	—	22	2,365
1995	3,131	—	26	82	3,151	—	26	2,369

Notes: Figures represent total budgetary authority requested and appropriated for FMF. Numbers rounded to nearest million. Dashes (–) indicate zero request or appropriation.

Source: U.S. Department of State.

of reporting procedures, presidential certifications, and congressional review requirements, the Reagan administration interpreted these restrictions very loosely and even found alternative means for funding the Contras. In one glaring instance of "loose" interpretation, the administration interpreted the congressional stipulation that aid could be used only for humanitarian purposes to include "equipment and supplies necessary for defense against air attack" and "training in radio communications, collection and utilization of intelligence, logistics, and small-unit skills and tactics."[21]

In the post–Cold War era, both the White House and Congress lack a clearly defined policy imperative, such as containment, into which the security assistance program can fit conceptually. Many members of Congress and much of the public seem unsure of America's new role and weary of the internationalist burden. Greater attention has been given to domestic problems and to those international economic issues that bear directly on the U.S. economy. More than one half of the members of the 104th Congress were elected after the fall of the Berlin Wall, and the new members, particularly in the House, were considerably less deferential to presidential or even congressional leadership than in previous years. The Senate, however, given its traditionally higher profile in foreign affairs and the continued presence of much of its old guard, remained more attuned to international developments.

CONGRESSIONAL TOOLS OF INFLUENCE

Congress has a variety of tools with which to influence policy, the most important of which is its constitutional authority to allocate or deny funds to certain activities and to earmark, condition, or otherwise direct the use of appropriated funds. These congressionally imposed restrictions may be contained in the language of the final bill or in committee reports. Congress can also attach policy statements to a bill and impose various reporting requirements. While statutory policy statements are binding, the president is virtually always given considerable discretion in policy implementation. Congress also frequently inserts "sense of the Congress" statements into resolutions or legislation that, while not binding, send a clear message to the executive branch about congressional intentions and aid concerns and preferences.

Budgetary Authority

While there are important exceptions, Congress is generally cautious about using the foreign assistance bill to directly challenge major presidential foreign policy actions. However, Congress sharply rebuffs presidents who intrude on constitutionally established congressional prerogatives. A priority congressional objective is to ensure that all funds expended by the president are lawfully authorized and appropriated. Presidents who attempt to "create" funds outside the normal process, or redirect appropriated funds for purposes not approved by

Congress, risk being severely sanctioned. For instance, Congress passed the Foreign Military Sales Act in 1968 in part because it believed the executive branch had created a de facto revolving fund that could bypass congressional processes. Likewise, the Reagan administration ran headlong into congressional sensitivities when it asserted a right to move funds without clear congressional approval.[22]

Congress, of course, determines the level of foreign assistance appropriations and, often, how they should be spent. While some in Congress—more so in the House than in the Senate—have resisted earmarking funds in order to allow the executive branch at least *some* flexibility to meet unforeseen developments, no member disputes Congress's right to earmark. "Some people would accuse us of micromanagement," said Congressman Howard Berman (D-Calif.), "but that stems from our frustration. This is the only vehicle on which we can do anything. Otherwise it's all talk."[23]

From a procedural standpoint, annual foreign aid appropriations are supposed to be authorized by the House Foreign Affairs and Senate Foreign Relations Committees, with differences in their respective bills resolved in conference. When Congress fails to enact authorizing legislation, however, the authorization is incorporated within the appropriations legislation itself and is drafted by the Foreign Operations Subcommittees of the House and Senate Appropriations Committees. Indeed, since the early 1980s, Congress has usually been unable to pass foreign assistance authorization legislation. Even supporters of congressional activism in foreign affairs such as James Lindsay note that the House Foreign Affairs and Senate Foreign Relations Committees became "remarkably ineffective" in shaping U.S. foreign policy by the 1980s; the Senate Foreign Relations Committee, in particular, from 1985 to 1996, "failed in its main legislative task: drafting a foreign aid authorization bill acceptable to the Senate."[24]

In contrast to the 1960s and 1970s, the 1980s saw a dramatic increase in the use of continuing resolutions to keep the foreign aid programs running (see Table 4.2). Between 1983 and 1989, annual foreign assistance funding and policy were provided for in CRs. Between 1989 and 1995, by contrast, regular bills were passed each year except for FY 1992. Foreign assistance was funded under CR authority in FY 1996 as part of the general budget standoff between President Clinton and a Republican Congress. Whereas traditional foreign aid authorization bills are freestanding, during much of the Reagan-Bush era foreign aid appropriations constituted just one component of huge, omnibus resolutions that lumped foreign aid spending with other federal programs.

Such CRs had a certain appeal to both the administration and congressional leaders. For proponents of foreign aid they offered protection from legislators who might otherwise burden the bill with amendments that could effectively constrain the smooth operation of the program. For the administration, the CRs offered hopes of fewer earmarks and conditions on aid, a partial lessening of congressional oversight, and by extension, increased flexibility in discretionary

Table 4.2
Comparison of Foreign Aid Authorizations, 1960s/1980s (in fiscal years)

Year	Authorization	Year	Authorization
1961	PL 87-195	1981	PL 97-113 (2 years)
1962	PL 88-205 (2 years)	1982	Continued from 1981
1963	Continued from 1962	1983	None
1964	PL 88-633	1984	None
1965	PL 89-171	1985	PL 99-83 (2 years)
1966	PL 89-583	1986	Continued from 1985
1967	PL 90-137	1987	None
1968	PL 90-554	1988	None
1969	PL 91-175 (2 years)	1989	None
1970	Continued from 1969	1990	None

Source: Data compiled by the authors.

aid allocations. The executive branch also negotiated with fewer members since only the two foreign operations subcommittees and the congressional leadership were involved in the process.[25] This translated into fewer political deals to be struck. For Congress, CRs provided protective political cover for those members who did not want to go on record as voting for a separate, highly visible foreign aid bill, yet could not afford to vote against it because of the financial and political clout of powerful ethnic lobbies. Yet CRs ultimately reflect a basic weakness in the democratic process because they sanction the avoidance of accountability, effectively require approval lest the government cease to function, and are "strong indicators of dissensus [which] testify to a breakdown . . . in ordinary modes of accommodation."[26]

Two pieces of legislation had a significant impact on the foreign assistance budget. The Gramm-Rudman-Hollings Deficit Reduction Act of 1985 ended the Reagan-era growth in the foreign aid budget and marked the beginning of a process of retrenchment that lasted through the Clinton years. A second statute was the Budget Enforcement Act of 1990 (PL 101–508), which set strict caps on FY 1991–FY 1993 budgetary outlays and authority for, among others, the international affairs function of the federal budget. This meant, in effect, that any additional funding for security assistance would have to come from supplemental appropriations (as with various Gulf War outlays) or from direct trade-offs from other accounts within the international affairs budget.[27] The budgetary walls separating the international affairs, national defense, and domestic spending components of the federal budget that were enforced under this legislation came down in FY 1994. This allowed the international affairs budget to raid the budget of the Department of Defense for additional funds but also exposed the foreign assistance budget to even greater reductions than it experienced during the Bush years.

Earmarks

"Earmarks" are congressionally mandated set-asides for specified countries, regions, or programs. They are tangible indicators of congressional foreign policy preferences and constrain the president's discretion to allocate foreign assistance to recipients of his choosing. They are, not surprisingly, politically popular among members of Congress. In the late 1980s, for instance, Congress routinely earmarked about 92 percent of military aid, between 80 to 98 percent of ESF, and 50 percent of development aid.[28] Said Senator Robert Kasten: Reducing earmarks just "doesn't make any sense" to senators, who generally earmark more than their colleagues in the House.[29]

Former chairman of the House Foreign Operations Subcommittee David Obey campaigned in FY 1995 with some apparent success for an appropriations bill that, except for the virtual entitlements to Israel and Egypt, was earmark free. The Senate took a more traditional approach that year and included earmarks for Egypt, Israel, and a host of other countries and programs. In the end, the only earmarks that survived the conference report (H.R. 103–267) were the assistance levels for Egypt and Israel, an additional $80 million in refugee aid for Israel, and a requirement that the administration provide $15 million in economic aid to Cyprus—a program long supported by the Greek lobby. Nonetheless, a full 96 percent of the FY 1995 *security assistance* funds were thereby earmarked, a percentage that rose to more than 98 percent in FY 1996. Moreover, although officially nonbinding, restrictive language in the committee's report constituted additional earmarks.

Earmarking has never been popular with the executive branch because it reduces the president's freedom of action to meet his priorities and to address unforeseen contingencies. It also inhibits efficient, comprehensive management of the entire aid program. Earmarking likewise limits U.S. leverage over the policies and practices of politically favored recipient nations, such as Israel and Egypt, because they know in advance that they will receive assistance; indeed, they usually know the exact amount of that aid.[30] Earmarks are such irritants for the executive branch that administrations continuously press for earmark-free legislation. The Clinton administration, for instance, proposed an end to both earmarks and country-specific foreign aid allocations in 1994. The proposal fell on deaf ears, however, as Congress has few champions of earmark-free legislation and little political incentive to alter customary practices.

Conditionality/Certifications

Conditionality refers to conditions or restrictions in legislation or committee reports on recipient countries and/or the executive branch. In contrast to earmarking, which tells the president for what or for whom aid is to be used, conditionality indicates what foreign assistance funds can *not* be used for. Over the years, for instance, Congress has disallowed the use of foreign aid for countries engaged in a "consistent pattern of gross violations of internationally recognized human rights" (PL 94–161). The effectiveness of congressional restrictions varies considerably, and many recipient countries view conditionally allocated aid as an "invasion of sovereignty."[31] Regardless of its effectiveness, however, and despite frequent executive branch resistance, conditionality is here to stay.[32]

Whereas earmarking has no support in the executive branch, conditionality is less unwelcome. Although the president prefers maximum flexibility, congressional restrictions may occasionally provide a diplomatically useful shield for the administration when it imposes unwanted policies on recipient countries as a condition of aid delivery. For instance, Reagan administration Assistant Secretary of State Elliott Abrahms observed that restrictive human rights legislation was "occasionally useful" as a negotiating tool with other—especially repressive—governments: "We could say, 'You'd better be good or Congress will take action.' "[33]

Another prominent example of conditionality is the congressional prohibition on aid to countries seeking to develop or otherwise acquire nuclear weapons (PL 99–83). A 1985 amendment sponsored by Senator Larry Pressler (R-S. Dak.) prohibited economic or military aid to Pakistan unless the president annually certified to Congress that Pakistan "does not possess a nuclear device." The conditioning of aid through restrictions is almost always accompanied by an "escape hatch" clause that allows the president to permit the aid to go forward, even if congressional conditions are not met, by submitting an official finding that such aid is in the "national interest" of the United States. Often, such an escape clause is insisted on by an administration as a precondition to the president signing the legislation. Even if a president never uses, or even intends to use, this authority, the quest for maximum flexibility has reigned supreme.

Conditionality gives Congress a policy role in foreign affairs. Members are able to translate their views into law, while avoiding ultimate responsibility if a policy goes astray. At the same time, however, Congress cedes primary control of U.S. foreign policy to the president when it allows sweeping exceptions to congressional preferences. Says Pat Holt, former staff director of the Senate Foreign Relations Committee: "[A]nything a president wants to do, he will think is 'vital' to national security. [With such loopholes] Congress doesn't have to pass the law in the first place."[34]

Other Vehicles of Influence

Reporting Requirements. Since the early 1970s, reporting requirements have skyrocketed.[35] DOD, for one, complained of congressional micromanagement as requests for reports and studies more than tripled between 1980 and 1991, from 223 requests to 733.[36] Such reporting requirements increase the pressure on scarce resources and distract bureaucrats away from managing their programs. In financial terms alone for DOD, this translates into roughly $50 million per year (and rising) in expenditures to address these requests. This is roughly equivalent to the entire FY 1995 combined allocation for the IMET, anti-terrorism, and nonproliferation and disarmament programs in the international affairs budget.

Reprogramming. A favored tool of the executive has been to reprogram funds within and between accounts, something Congress has moved to curb. Since 1977, written appropriations committee approval has been required to reprogram funds, and Congress has often denied the president the ability to do so. For example, the Bush administration's FY 1990 request to transfer money between foreign aid accounts, once appropriated by Congress, was denied.

Policy Statements. Congress can, of course, make policy through the foreign aid legislation it passes. With the collapse of the authorization process (discussed below), it is common for policy language to be added to foreign aid appropriations bills. Congress (as discussed above) also makes policy statements through nonbinding "sense of the Congress" provisions or resolutions. While not legally binding on the executive branch, presidents are well advised to heed them.

Legislation and Security Assistance Reform

Over the years, Congress has variously sought to reform the security assistance program. In the first twelve years of the program, Congress passed four major laws: the Mutual Defense Assistance Act of 1949, the Mutual Security Act of 1951, the Mutual Security Act of 1954, and the Foreign Assistance Act of 1961 (see Chapter 1). These early acts created the Military Assistance Program, the Foreign Military Sales Program, and the forerunner to the Economic Support Fund.

From 1961 to the end of the Cold War (circa 1989), Congress used the Foreign Assistance Act of 1961, as amended, as its legislative vehicle to make desired changes in the security assistance program. Major program revisions occurred in 1968 and 1976, and smaller changes were made in 1978, 1981, and 1985. Reforms between 1961 and 1976 led to greater congressional oversight of the program and moved the program toward cash and credit sales and away from grants of military equipment. Congressional reforms in 1978, 1981, and 1985 moved the program back toward grant funding and low-interest concessional loans.

With the end of the Cold War, many in Congress believed that the time had come to overhaul, rather than simply amend, the foreign assistance law written almost 30 years before. In February 1989, a task force led by Congressman Lee Hamilton (D-Ind.) released a report containing recommendations on reforming foreign assistance legislation. The Hamilton Task Force decried the state of the foreign assistance program. It proposed new legislation to eliminate obsolete and redundant provisions and to streamline the legal guidelines for U.S. foreign aid. Hamilton found that the current system lacked effective accountability and impeded effective implementation of the program.[37]

The Hamilton Task Force called for a much-needed overhaul of the unwieldy foreign assistance legislation and urged a substantial reduction in the 288 annual individual reporting requirements mandated by Congress that took AID alone some 140 man-years to fulfill annually. It also recommended that security assistance be better integrated with overall U.S. foreign policy and with U.S. policy toward individual recipient nations. The task force recommended greater in-country monitoring of military aid, a genuinely centralized accounting system in DOD for military sales, and more congressional oversight of the process.[38]

With respect to military assistance, the report recommended that the administration do the following: consolidate military assistance into a single funding account; establish a separate aid account for countries that provide the United States with access to their military bases and gradually terminate such assistance; and examine alternative funding mechanisms for military sales.[39] The report further recommended that a small "regional contingency fund" equal to 2 percent of the total bill be established to give the executive branch some flexibility in light of increasing earmarking of the foreign aid bill. With respect to ESF, the task force recommended that project aid under ESF be moved to the development assistance account. The administration opposed this provision because it could become more difficult to grant economic aid to countries like Egypt if development criteria became primary.[40]

The Hamilton Task Force report had some effect, and some of its prescriptions were even adopted in subsequent years. But while the House passed a bill in June 1989 (H.R. 2655), which incorporated most of the report's recommendations, the House leadership needed, but never received, the active support of the Bush administration and the Senate. The administration failed to grasp the opportunity to realign foreign aid with post–Cold War developments. The administration seemed distrustful of the congressional initiative and refused to endorse the House effort in a timely or effective manner. The executive branch remained entrenched in the mind-set established in previous years: that it gained flexibility by circumventing the authorization process and striking a deal with the appropriators (discussed below). The Senate also did not cooperate with the House, thereby effectively rendering the bill dead on arrival.[41]

Even when Congress does not itself recommend specific reforms, it has encouraged the administration to do so—especially in the post–Cold War era. A tactic employed in 1995–1996 by the 104th Congress, for instance, was to sharply curtail program funds in order to force the executive to make difficult trade-offs between, on the one hand, funding for favored programs and, on the other, agencies such as AID.[42] All things considered, efforts at reform since 1989 demonstrate both the difficulty of enacting a sweeping change in the foreign assistance program and the need for both chambers and the president to work together to effect such change. As in many issues, both the president and key members of Congress agree that reform is needed. The shape of the reform is what is in dispute.

SECURITY ASSISTANCE DECISIONMAKING ON CAPITOL HILL

Four congressional committees hold primary jurisdiction over foreign aid: the House Foreign Affairs and Senate Foreign Relations Committees, which set—or are supposed to set—the policy parameters for assistance, and the House and Senate Foreign Operations Subcommittees of the Appropriations Committees, which effectively decide how much funding to appropriate, within the authorized amount, to various foreign aid accounts.[43] The role a committee performs is determined by several sets of factors, including constitutional stipulations regarding the expenditure of funds, rules of the respective chambers regarding authorizations and appropriations and the rights of members to amend bills, the personalities of subcommittee or committee chairmen and the role they believe the committees should play, the composition of the committee, and the general political climate.

Authorizing Committees

The House Foreign Affairs (sometimes titled International Relations) Committee and the Senate Foreign Relations Committee have a long and distinguished history in the Congress dating from 1822 and 1816, respectively. Within Congress, the authorization committees are charged with examining the policy questions related to the provision of foreign assistance. Authorizing committees can stipulate conditions for the provision of aid and establish aid ceilings and earmarks for countries. The authorization of aid does not mean it will be provided, but more aid cannot be appropriated than is authorized. Thus, the authorization committee's role is distinct from that of the appropriations committee. As one authorization chairman argued, his committee "ought to make the decisions about what programs [exist]. . . . That doesn't mean you can afford those programs. . . . The authorizers should say what we need to fit changing social circumstances. Appropriators should say what we can afford at the time, what programs are working."[44]

Formally, the Senate Foreign Relations and House Foreign Affairs Committees occupy a central role in congressional decisionmaking on foreign policy. Their jurisdiction enables them to play a role in almost every major foreign policy issue. In practice, however, the two committees are often ineffective.[45] Foreign aid authorizations were common before 1981. In fact, authorizations were an annual occurrence (except in 1972) after the passage of the FAA of 1961. During the 1980s and 1990s, however, the authorizing committees lost much of the power they once had; only two authorizing bills for foreign assistance, each for two years, were passed (Table 4.2). Bills were regularly stalled, either in committee or on the floor of one of the chambers. The failure to pass authorization bills was both a cause and a consequence of the decline in power of the authorizing committees, and those committees lost the respect of many members of Congress.[46]

The inability to pass an authorization bill stemmed from several sources. Leadership was a central problem. Both authorization committees were fractionalized, and their chairmen seemed unable to control the debates and conflicts within their committees. In the early 1980s, the House Foreign Affairs Committee suffered from the reforms of the 1970s that transferred substantial power to various subcommittees. At that time, House Foreign Affairs Committee Chairman Clement Zablocki (D-Wis.) could not control the conflicts among committee and subcommittee members and consequently was unable to produce an authorizing bill. His successors, Dante Fascell, Lee Hamilton, and Benjamin Gilman, proved more effective—mainly because they employed a subcommittee system for channeling some of these political divisions, thereby enabling some disputes to be waged outside of the full committee.[47]

The House committee's work suffered, however, because its companion committee in the Senate, where polarization was even worse, proved unable to function. The Senate Foreign Relations Committee experienced significant leadership problems under Chairman Percy (R-Ill.), 1981–1984, and especially under Claiborne Pell (D-R.I.), 1987–1994. Senator Percy got a bill passed in 1981 with considerable administration support. However, as time went on and administration support declined, Percy proved unable to pull together an increasingly fractious committee. Richard Lugar (R-Ind.), in his two-year chairmanship (1985–1986), managed to produce a bill and get it passed on the Senate floor with much less administration support. Senator Pell's difficulties stemmed from his leadership deficiencies and his inability to lead the committee on policy questions. The accession of Senator Jesse Helms (R-N.C.) to the chairmanship of the Senate Foreign Relations Committee in 1995 added another divisive element to the mix. During his first year as chairman, for instance, Helms delayed two major arms control treaties and confirmation hearings for more than a dozen ambassadors in order to pressure the Clinton administration to fold AID, the U.S. Information Agency, and the Arms Control and Disarmament Agency into the State Department.[48]

An ideological rift among members of the two authorization committees contributed to many of these problems. In the 1960s, even with the Vietnam War, this was a manageable problem, but by the 1980s, differences had widened so considerably that a close observer of ideological tensions on the Senate Foreign Relations Committee lamented that "they just can't get anything done."[49]

When the committees did pass a bill, they often proved unable to get the House Speaker and Senate Majority Leader to schedule time for it to come to the floor. This was a particular problem in the Senate because of its crowded legislative calendar and deficit reduction matters that consumed considerable time after 1985. Furthermore, there were simply more authorization bills to bring to the floor than in, say, the 1950s. Members of Congress also did not like to go on record as having supported foreign aid; legislators feared that a public debate on foreign aid and a recorded vote registering their support for aid could work against them at election time.[50] This gave them even less incentive to schedule floor debate for the foreign assistance bill.

The executive branch, particularly in the Reagan and Bush administrations, made the legislator's job more difficult by sometimes withdrawing its traditional support for the bills and by issuing veto threats against authorizing bills containing objectionable language. These actions had the effect of undercutting the bill in the other chamber. For example, a veto threat against the House bill left the Senate with a dilemma: If the Senate supported the objectionable House provision, it risked a presidential veto; but if it removed the provision, it might lose House support on the conference bill. In essence, then, members might vote on the bill only to see it rejected in the other chamber or vetoed; hence, their vote would hurt them politically and be essentially meaningless.

For its part, the executive branch also discovered that it could get along quite nicely without an authorization bill because the absence of authorizing legislation meant fewer restrictions on foreign aid. Especially during the Reagan years, "killer amendments" in the authorization bills threatened to so hinder presidential authority that the president was unlikely to sign them.[51] The executive branch arguably benefits from only one vote per year on foreign aid, and the only vote *necessary* is on the appropriations bill (and in the appropriations committees). Moreover, Congress has passed authorization bills for key areas as needed, such as the Support for East European Democracy Act in the early post–Cold War era.[52]

Another problem facing the authorizing committees is that authorizing legislation is not required by the Constitution or by law but only by the rules of each chamber. These rules, which state that no funds can be appropriated that are not authorized, can be waived by a vote in each chamber.[53] Once it becomes clear that the authorization bill will not be passed, it is only a matter of time before the authorization requirement is waived despite the best efforts of the committee chairmen (particularly of the House Foreign Affairs Committee) to get congressional action on the bill. Some individual authorization committee members, especially in the House, have approached the foreign operations subcommittee about putting authorizing language in the appropriations bill. But the authorization committee chairmen have resisted because this undermines their authority. Nevertheless, when these chairmen conclude that their bill will not pass, they do often agree to this arrangement. In a variant of this approach, the House Foreign Affairs and Appropriations Committees have developed an "informal arrangement" to bring authorization personnel into appropriations deliberations.[54]

While the authorization committees were battered and disparaged during the 1980s and 1990s, they should not be completely discounted. The Reagan administration did have a freestanding authorization bill for four of its eight years;

in contrast, Bush and Clinton had none. The authorization bills, when enacted, contributed to substantive policy, such as the authorization of the Special Defense Acquisition Fund. In the 1990s, although authorization bills were not passed, the foreign aid authorization debate did allow for a vigorous policy dialogue both within Congress and between the administration and Capitol Hill on the direction, size, and management of foreign assistance.

The authorization committees foster dialogue, but the policy and housekeeping tasks done by these committees through the annual authorizing legislation can be done biannually, or even less frequently, if special legislation is passed that authorizes foreign assistance–type programs outside of the general foreign aid budget (such as the SEED Act or the Cooperative Threat Reduction program). The real problem in failing to pass authorization legislation is that it eliminates from the policy process the very committees with the most expertise on foreign policy. Accordingly, the House Foreign Affairs Committee, with 43 members and 62 committee and subcommittee staff, and the Senate Foreign Relations Committee, with 18 members and 6 staff, are replaced functionally by the House and Senate foreign operations subcommittees, each with 13 members and 4 full-time staff members.

Thus, foreign assistance policy has been directed since the 1980s by the appropriations subcommittees. One senator remarked, with some exaggeration, that "it's the little old foreign operations [subcommittee], which is never on TV, that sets the foreign policy of the United States."[55]

Appropriations Committees

The appropriations committees, of course, control the power of the purse. In principle, they are concerned with the merits of a program that has been authorized by Congress. The practice, however, has been quite different. The effective demise of the authorization process has blurred the jurisdictional lines between authorization and appropriations committees, and concerning foreign aid, de facto responsibility for the passage of annual foreign assistance legislation has devolved to the appropriations committees.[56]

Given the relatively large size of the House of Representatives, most individual legislators have difficulty influencing legislation outside of committee. The appropriations committees, of course, draw their formidable power from Article 1, section 9 of the Constitution: "No money shall be drawn from the Treasury, but in consequence of Appropriations made by law." And the Constitution further stipulates (Article 1, section 7) that "all bills for raising revenue shall originate in the House of Representatives." Joseph White, in his study of the House Appropriations Committee, states that the committee's two primary functions are to "fit the House's preference about budget details into the majority's sense of an acceptable total [and to] . . . manage the details in a manner that preserves and projects Congress' power over federal activities vis-à-vis the president, while satisfying member demands for a rough fairness in the distribution of district benefits.''[57] A second, and even more basic, task of the appropriations committee and its thirteen subcommittees is to jealously guard its designated constitutional role.[58] While budgeting should not be policymaking by default, and while committee members are usually respectful of the jurisdiction of the authorization committees, the job must still be done in whatever reasonable manner.

The rules of the Senate give individual senators much greater power than their House counterparts. Senators can much more easily affect legislation from the Senate floor than can members of the House; for instance, a bill that originated in a Senate subcommittee can be amended from the floor. Moreover, the recourse, or threatened recourse, to a filibuster gives minority party senators leverage and creates a strong incentive for the majority to cooperate with the minority.[59] The considerable power of individual senators also gives them less incentive to work with their colleagues on subcommittees and full committees to influence legislation.[60]

The foreign operations subcommittee reviews foreign assistance bills before they go to the full appropriations committee. The subcommittee's role is critical because, in both houses, the bill that is reported out of the subcommittee usually passes the full chamber without many substantive modifications. The heavy workload and sheer size of the appropriations committee necessitates a dependence by the full committee on subcommittee recommendations.[61] Frequently, the full committee chair will allow the subcommittee chairs to take the lead on their portions of the bill in full markup. In both chambers, subcommittees are the best place to impact legislation.

Ultimately, the power of the foreign operations subcommittees depends on several factors, including the fate of the authorization bill, the role of subcommittees in each chamber, the personalities and styles of the chairmen and members, the political adeptness of the subcommittee chairman, the political balance in the chamber and its relation to the party in control of the White House, the substance of the issues being addressed, the administration request, and the budgetary situation faced by the Congress that year.[62] The policy role of the foreign operations subcommittee hinges importantly on the effectiveness of the authorizing committee. If the authorization committee is strong and passes its bills, the appropriators' leeway for setting foreign aid policy in the appropriations bill is constricted. If the authorization committees fail to pass a bill, key policy functions devolve to the appropriations committee. A weak authorization committee will also incline the State Department and the White House to look to the appropriations subcommittees for legislative provisos.[63]

The rules of each chamber also influence the subcommittees' roles. Subcommittees are less important in the Senate because that chamber's rules allow a legislator to amend legislation on the floor. However, because House rules make it very difficult to amend legislation from the floor, subcommittee membership becomes more important for influencing the contents of a bill. Indeed, particularly in the House, a traditional subcommittee function is to give members a venue from which to aid their districts. Thus, relative to the traditional interests of members of Congress, the foreign operations subcommittee is somewhat unusual in that it has few strictly domestic political concerns. Indeed, members of the subcommittee often have a genuine interest in foreign affairs. Still, foreign operations is often quite partisan for an appropriations subcommittee because it makes decisions "about which countries we like and how much" and because many members have a political stake in being responsive to ethnic groups and other special interests for whom the foreign assistance bill is of utmost importance.[64] Yet few members have interests in the entire bill. As one former committee member asserted, "[Foreign operations] is a hefty document. Rather than attempt to understand all the parts, such as Foreign Military Sales Credits, I pay attention to what I'm concerned about most, military versus economic aid, bilateral versus multilateral."[65]

In both chambers the personality of the chairman and his conception of his role are critical to the functioning and effectiveness of the committees. If the chairman is politically savvy and is a respected leader, the committee can function effectively. If the chairman is not an effective broker among feuding members, or if he does not see the shaping of the final product as his role, then the committee will be less effective. Often the chairman sets the tone for the annual budget process, and he can signal likely congressional support for administration policy, or lack thereof, at the outset of the hearings.[66]

Through the drafting of the chairman's "mark," the subcommittee chair has the power to allocate preferences. He sees the full range of committee interests and pressures. He has, says Joseph White, an "especially great advantage on member-interest matters. If the requester challenges the chair in markup, the other members have to decide whom to support. Since the chair can do them more good or harm later, members will support him unless he violates a norm of fairness or the challenger has a strong case on the merits."[67] Historically, the chairman's role has been to see that divergent member interests are accommodated in exchange for their support for the rest of the bill. To succeed, the chairman must be a good negotiator and take a broad view of the bill. Moreover, he must accurately count votes in subcommittee, in full committee, and on the chamber floor; the chairman should be sure that he has the votes to sustain positions in all three arenas. Part of the chairman's power to broker deals lies in the implicit bargain that the subcommittee bill will be supported and secured in a floor vote.

The political balance in Congress also has a strong impact on foreign aid policymaking. In a divided Congress, with Democrats and Republicans each controlling a chamber, the president will probably work with the chamber his party controls. Ideological splits within parties create additional opportunities for coalition building between the White House and Congress. In a situation where the president is of one party and Congress the other, Congress has the opportunity to take bolder initiatives. However, this is usually done in the context of the president's proposals. That is, the subcommittees generally accept or reject the president's requests instead of originating new initiatives. While the threat that the president will veto major appropriations bills is usually not a pressing concern, the president's considerable authority in foreign affairs is an important source of leverage in dealing with the subcommittees.

Presidents Reagan and Bush often clashed with a Democratic Congress over foreign aid. President Clinton was able to work with Congress in his first two years in office when, for the first time since 1978, the presidency and both houses of Congress were controlled by the same party.[68] The 1994 Republican election victory brought about a clash of priorities on a number of fronts, with the Republican leadership using the foreign aid bill to make statements about alternative policy preferences.

The substance of the issues is also a key concern of lawmakers, both on the subcommittees and in the full Congress. The subcommittees must operate within the context of anticipating probable congressional support for the issues at hand. For example, aid to Israel, Egypt, Greece, and (usually) Turkey has received consistent support. When there is no clear congressional position on an issue, the subcommittees and committees have some leeway to take the initiative. Still, the dominant pattern of operation is to assess the president's request and work from this request as a basis for action, rather than to start from scratch and propose an ambitious congressionally initiated foreign policy agenda.

The budgetary situation, particularly the federal deficit, has been an overriding consideration for foreign assistance funding. The 1985 Gramm-Rudman-Hollings Act, among other things, introduced the budget committees as new actors in the process by giving them the initial authority to determine the ceilings that each committee would have for their overall appropriations. In the early 1990s, the budget agreement between the Bush administration and the Congress set levels of foreign assistance spending for FY 1991–FY 1993. In FY 1996, congressional Republicans made deficit reduction a top priority and cut foreign aid spending further. In reality, of course, the foreign aid budget will have a minuscule effect on the budget deficit. Subcommittee chairs have employed the budget deficit issue variously, arguing either that foreign aid impacts minimally on the deficit or, alternatively, that foreign aid should bear its fair share of deficit reduction.

CONCLUSION

Foreign assistance lies at a distinct crossroad in executive-legislative relations. The president sees aid as a major foreign policy tool, while Congress sees it as a vital mechanism for influencing the direction of that policy. Over the years, Congress gradually enhanced its control over the program. The president, on the other hand, generally resisted this trend and maneuvered for freedom of action to manage the program.

In varying degrees, Congress has always been somewhat skeptical that security assistance and other forms of aid constituted a wise use of scarce resources. Within Congress, authority over the program has shifted decisively to the appropriations committees; resources are likely to remain under pressure; and the outdated, universally criticized Foreign Assistance Act of 1961, as amended, continues to carry the program. Continued struggle over the size and composition of the U.S. foreign assistance program is certain.

Foreign aid is utterly fused with domestic political and economic considerations. It resides at the intersection of executive-legislative relations where institutional, partisan, interest group, public opinion, and individual preferences regularly meet and collide. Foreign assistance legislation gives Congress a voice in foreign policy. Unless Congress decides to turn inward and sharply reduce its role in foreign policy—an unlikely prospect—foreign assistance, in *some* form, is here to stay. Of course, foreign aid and security assistance will continue to be adjusted, albeit haltingly and imperfectly, to emerging international realities.

NOTES

1. Barbara Hinckley, *Less Than Meets the Eye: Foreign Policy Making and the Myth of the Assertive Congress* (Chicago, Ill.: University of Chicago Press, 1994), p. 106.

2. Gerald Warburg, *Conflict and Consensus: The Struggle between Congress and the President over Foreign Policymaking* (New York: Harper & Row, 1989), p. 234.

3. Hinckley, *Less Than Meets the Eye*, pp. 101–24; Warburg, *Conflict and Consensus*, pp. 231–73.

4. Jeffrey A. Meyer, "Congressional Control of Foreign Assistance," *Yale Journal of International Law* 13 (Winter 1988), pp. 93–96.

5. See Chester J. Pach, Jr., "Military Assistance and American Foreign Policy: The Role of Congress," in Michael Barnhart, ed., *Congress and United States Foreign Policy* (Albany, N.Y.: SUNY Press, 1987), p. 138.

6. See Steven A. Hildreth, "Perceptions of U.S. Security Assistance, 1959–1983: The Public Record," in Ernest Graves and Steven A. Hildreth, eds., *U.S. Security Assistance: The Political Process* (Lexington, Ky.: Lexington Books, 1985), p. 50.

7. David Obey and Carol Lancaster, "Funding Foreign Aid," *Foreign Policy* 71 (Summer 1988), p. 146.

8. See James M. Lindsay, *Congress and the Politics of U.S. Foreign Policy* (Baltimore, Md.: Johns Hopkins University Press, 1994), p. 42.

9. The 7:10 ratio is an informal formula that gives Greece $7 in military assistance for every $10 that Turkey receives. The formula does not apply to economic assistance (discussed in Chapter 6).

10. For example, Senator Robert Dole attempted to earmark $18 million in humanitarian aid for Armenia in the FY 1995 foreign assistance legislation (H.R. 2295).

11. David S. Cloud, "Members Question Proposal to Boost Weapons Sales," *Congressional Quarterly Weekly Report* (March 23, 1991), p. 735.

12. John M. Goshko, "Foreign Aid May Be Early Test of New Hill Order," *Washington Post*, November 21, 1994, p. A14.

13. Thomas W. Lippman, "Hill Battle Lines Pit Foreign Aid against National Economic Interests," *Washington Post*, May 16, 1994, p. A7.

14. John Holcombe and Alan Berg, *MAP for Security* (Columbia: University of South Carolina Press, 1957), p. 10.

15. See U.S. Congress, House, Committee on Government Operations, *U.S. Military Aid and Supply Programs in Western Europe*, 85th Cong., 2d sess., 1958, H. Rpt. 1371, p. 3.

16. Quoted in William H. Lewis, "Political Influence: The Diminished Capacity," in Stephanie G. Neuman and Robert E. Harkavy, eds., *Arms Transfers in the Modern World* (New York: Praeger, 1979), p. 195.

17. Cut insurance is also common in the president's defense budget requests. See Richard A. Stubbing, *The Defense Game* (New York: Harper & Row, 1986), pp. 96–98.

18. Thomas Franck and Edward Weisband, *Foreign Policy by Congress* (New York: Oxford University Press, 1979), p. 35.

19. Warburg, *Conflict and Consensus*, p. 234.

20. What is striking was how little money was at stake. Between 1982 and 1990, Congress appropriated a total of just $321.4 million in both military and nonlethal aid to the Contras, or less than 10 percent of the *annual* appropriation for Israel alone. Nonetheless, the issue of the Contras was extremely important and occupied approximately one half of Congress's working foreign policy agenda between 1982 and 1987. See Hinckley, *Less Than Meets the Eye*, p. 154; William M. LeoGrande and Philip Brenner, "The House Divided: Ideological Polarization over Aid to the Nicaraguan 'Contras,' " *Legislative Studies Quarterly* 18 (February 1993), pp. 105–136; Cynthia Arnson, *Crossroads: Congress, the Reagan Administration, and Central America* (New York: Pantheon Books, 1989).

21. See *Weekly Compilation of Presidential Documents* 21 (August 8, 1985), p. 973; and 22 (March 19, 1986), p. 391. See also U.S. Congress, House, Select Committee to Investigate Covert Arms Transactions with Iran, *Iran-Contra Affair*, 100th Cong., 1st sess., 1987, H. Rpt. 100–433. This violated the express terms of the *International Security and Development Cooperation Act of 1985* (PL 99-83), sec. 722(g)(5).

22. See John Felton, "Jousting Over Congressional Prerogatives," *Congressional Quarterly Weekly Report* (October 1, 1988), p. 2734.

23. Steven V. Roberts, "Congress Has Its Ways of Influencing Foreign Aid," *New York Times*, April 7, 1985, sec. IV, p. 3.

24. Lindsay, *Congress and the Politics of U.S. Foreign Policy*, p. 55.

25. Obey and Lancaster, "Funding Foreign Aid," p. 148.

26. Aaron Wildavsky, *The New Politics of the Budgetary Process*, 2d ed. (New York: HarperCollins, 1992), pp. 234–36.

27. Larry Q. Nowels and Ellen C. Collier, *Foreign Affairs Budget: Issues and Priorities for the 1990s*, Congressional Research Service, Washington, D.C., 1991, p. 3.

28. U.S. Congress, House, Committee on Foreign Affairs, *Report of the Task Force on Foreign Assistance*, 101st Cong., 1st sess., 1989, p. 28.

29. John Felton, "Hill, Administration at Odds over Foreign Aid Measure," *Congressional Quarterly Weekly Report* (November 4, 1989), p. 2965.

30. Stanton H. Burnett, *Investing in Security: Economic Aid for Noneconomic Purposes* (Washington, D.C.: Center for Strategic and International Studies, 1992), pp. 2–14.

31. Joan M. Nelson with Stephanie J. Eglinton, *Encouraging Democracy: What Role for Conditioned Aid?* (Washington, D.C.: Overseas Development Council, 1992), p. 3.

32. Warburg, *Conflict and Consensus*, pp. 232–33.

33. Carroll J. Doherty, "Foreign Policy Rules Riddled with Presidential Loopholes," *Congressional Quarterly Weekly Report* (December 5, 1992), p. 3755.

34. Quoted in ibid., pp. 3754, 3757.

35. See Ellen C. Collier, "Foreign Policy by Reporting Requirement," *Washington Quarterly* 11 (Winter 1988), pp. 75–88; U.S. Congress, House, Committee on Foreign Affairs, *Required Reports to Congress on Foreign Policy*, 100th Cong., 2d sess., 1988; idem, *Foreign Assistance Reporting Requirements*, 103d Cong., 1st sess., 1989.

36. See Pamela Fester, "Complaints Are Stacking Up as Hill Piles on Reports," *Congressional Quarterly Weekly Report* (September 7, 1991), pp. 2565–66. For a defense of the reporting requirements, see Lindsay, *Congress and the Politics of U.S. Foreign Policy*, pp. 165–66.

37. For an analysis of the work of the Hamilton-Gilman task force, see Duncan L. Clarke and Steven Woehrel, "Reforming United States Security Assistance," *American University Journal of International Law and Policy* 6 (Winter 1991), pp. 233–41.

38. House Committee on Foreign Affairs, *Report of the Task Force on Foreign Assistance*, pp. 28, 34–35, 42.

39. Larry Q. Nowels, *Foreign Assistance: Congressional Initiatives to Reform U.S. Foreign Aid in 1989*, Congressional Research Service, Washington, D.C., May 10, 1990.

40. John Felton, "Intention to Change System Encounters Hill Reality," *Congressional Quarterly Weekly Report* (May 22, 1989), p. 1265.

41. U.S. Congress, House, Committee on Foreign Affairs, *Congress and Foreign Policy, 1989*, 101st Cong., 2d sess., 1990, pp. 103, 105.

42. Susan B. Epstein, Larry Q. Nowels, and Steven A. Hildreth, *Foreign Policy Agency Reorganization*, Congressional Research Service, Washington, D.C., July 27, 1995, pp. 1–4.

43. Other committees are also important. The House and Senate Budget Committees decide the broad figure under which appropriations must operate, and the Armed Services Committees can pass legislation that may amend the Foreign Assistance Act with regard to military assistance.

44. Joseph White, "The Functions and Power of the House Appropriations Committee" (Ph.D. diss., University of California at Berkeley, 1989), p. 196.

45. Lindsay, *Congress and the Politics of U.S. Foreign Policy*, p. 55.

46. See Lawrence J. Haas, "Unauthorized Action," *National Journal* (January 2, 1988), pp. 17–21.

47. James M. McCormick, "Decision Making in the Foreign Affairs and Foreign Relations Committees," in Randall B. Ripley and James M. Lindsay, eds., *Congress Resurgent: Foreign and Defense Policy on Capitol Hill* (Ann Arbor: University of Michigan Press, 1993), p. 137; Rochelle Stanfield, "Floating Power Centers," *National Journal* (December 1, 1990), p. 2916.

48. Epstein, Nowels, and Hildreth, *Foreign Policy Agency Reorganization*, pp. 2–8.

49. Interview by Dan O'Connor, Senate staff member, Washington, D.C., August 23, 1994; Lindsay, *Congress and the Politics of U.S. Foreign Policy*, p. 56.

50. Larry Q. Nowels, "Foreign Aid: The Changing Legislative Process," in U.S. Congress, House, Committee on Foreign Affairs, *Congress and Foreign Policy, 1984*, 95th Cong., 1st sess., 1985, p. 80.

51. Ibid., p. 82.

52. Interview by Dan O'Connor of a former House Foreign Affairs Committee staff member, Washington, D.C., August 1994.

53. See Louis Fisher, "The Authorization-Appropriations Process in Congress: Formal Rules and Informal Practices," *Catholic University Law Review* 29 (1979), pp. 51–105; White, "The Functions and Power," p. 452. The Senate's Rule XVI against unauthorized appropriations dates back to 1850.

54. McCormick, "Decision Making in the Foreign Affairs and Foreign Relations Committees," p. 147.

55. Joseph White, "Decision Making in the Appropriations Subcommittees on Defense and Foreign Operations," in Ripley and Lindsay, *Congress Resurgent*, p. 197.

56. Cecil V. Crabb, Jr., and Pat M. Holt, *Invitation to Struggle: Congress, the President, and Foreign Policy*, 3d ed. (Washington, D.C.: Congressional Quarterly Press, 1989), p. 49.

57. White, "The Functions and Power," pp. 16–17. See also Richard F. Fenno, Jr., *The Power of the Purse: Appropriations Politics in Congress* (Boston: Little, Brown, 1966).

58. White, "The Functions and Power," p. 29.

59. For example, a sweeping plan by Senator Jesse Helms to reorganize the foreign affairs agencies was derailed by the minority Democrats in August 1995 as the Republicans lacked the 60 votes to invoke cloture. See Carroll J. Doherty, "Helms Reorganization Plan Stymied by Democrats," *Congressional Quarterly Weekly Report* (August 5, 1995), p. 2388.

60. See Christopher J. Deering and Steven S. Smith, "Subcommittees in Congress," in Lawrence C. Dodd and Bruce I. Oppenheimer, eds., *Congress Reconsidered*, 3d ed. (Washington, D.C.: Congressional Quarterly Press, 1985), pp. 195, 205.

61. Steven S. Smith and Christopher J. Deering, *Committees in Congress* (Washington, D.C.: Congressional Quarterly, 1984), p. 145.

62. See Daniel B. O'Connor, "United States Security Assistance in the Reagan Administration: Political Processes and Policy Outputs" (Ph.D. diss., American University, 1997), pp. 187–97.

63. Nowels, "Foreign Aid," p. 83.

64. White, "Decision Making in the Appropriations Subcommittees on Defense and Foreign Operations," pp. 192–93.

65. White, "The Functions and Power," p. 321.

66. Interview by Dan O'Connor of a House staff member, Washington, D.C., August 12, 1994.

67. White, "Decision Making in the Appropriations Subcommittees on Defense and Foreign Operations," pp. 191.

68. One clear example relating to foreign aid was the administration's success in securing $2.5 billion for the former Soviet region in FY 1994. See Jeremy Rosner, *The New Tug-of-War: Congress, the Executive, and National Security* (Washington, D.C.: Carnegie, 1995), pp. 10–15.

5

Perceptions of the Security Assistance Program

This chapter examines elite (professional or influential) and general public perceptions of the security assistance program and discusses the role of interest groups in the security assistance allocation process. It is conventional wisdom that the American public is generally uninformed about foreign aid and skeptical of its utility. There is more than a grain of truth to this, but polling data consistently reveal that the public supports *some* level of foreign assistance and often favors the provision of development and, especially, humanitarian aid over security assistance.[1] Moreover, some sectors of the voting public consistently and vigorously support security assistance, particularly influential ethnic groups and the defense-industrial lobby. While the available public opinion data do not allow for meaningful differentiation among "schools of thought," as can cautiously be attempted with elite opinion, the general public has commonly had a rather negative view of military assistance and a mixed (but still somewhat unfavorable) opinion about economic aid. However, elite opinion has clearly had a greater effect on the course of the security assistance program and is the focus of most of this chapter.

The elite sector of society almost always reacts more favorably to the provision of foreign aid than does the general public. While the public is usually uninformed about the particulars of the foreign aid program, much of the foreign policy elite regularly attempts to influence the composition and direction of the program. Within the elite category there appear to be three roughly identifiable schools of thought concerning security assistance: the traditionalists, the reformers, and the abolitionists. The *traditionalists* generally accepted the officially declared premises of security assistance during the Cold War and, today, broadly agree that the United States must remain vigilant in an unstable, rapidly evolving, threat-filled international environment. *Reformers* compose the broadest, most diverse school. Some reformers would merely economize on security aid by eliminating waste and streamlining management; others would reduce security assistance in favor of, especially, economic development programs; some view security assistance as a necessary, if exceptional, instrument of foreign policy; and still others would reorganize or restructure the various security assistance program elements to better align them with changing international conditions. Finally, the *abolitionist* group ranges from those who oppose all forms of foreign aid to those who argue that security assistance, and perhaps other forms of aid, should be drastically curtailed in today's less threatening world. These schools of thought, of course, are constructed as ideal types and are not definitive. Indeed, the three groups inevitably overlap one another.

ELITE OPINION

Traditionalists

Since World War II, American presidents have viewed security assistance as an important, flexible, and even "indispensable"[2] tool of foreign policy. Indeed, security assistance became a key vehicle for U.S. worldwide engagement in conjunction with the global goal of containing the Soviet Union. It was used to, among other things, demonstrate U.S. political commitments to friendly and allied states and assist them to defend themselves; to supplement U.S. economic aid to these states; to help secure a U.S. forward presence through basing agreements; and to improve the interoperability of U.S. and allied armed forces. Moreover, supporters of security assistance argued that it offered a financially and politically less costly alternative to direct U.S. military involvement abroad.[3] Thus, the traditionalist school viewed security assistance as both a legitimate and necessary tool of American foreign policy.

While this anti-Soviet rationale was rendered obsolete with the dissolution of the Soviet Union, contemporary traditionalists—always prominent in the executive branch—hold that security assistance remains a viable policy tool for U.S. relations abroad. Although the specific composition of U.S. aid, and the recipients themselves, have changed over time, the security assistance program clearly retains its strategic value as a foreign policy instrument intended to advance the national security interests of the United States. Post–Cold War traditionalists assert that security assistance enhances deterrence, encourages the sharing of defense responsibilities, supports U.S. military readiness, encourages interoperability of forces among U.S. allies, improves bilateral and multilateral cooperation, promotes regional stability through U.S. engagement, serves as a "cost-effective alternative" to maintaining larger U.S. forces in the region, and remains "an integral part of peacetime engagement" by promoting American overseas military presence and demonstrating U.S. commitment to defending common interests.[4] Ultimately, timely and collaborative military action—as in the 1990–1991 Persian Gulf War—is only possible as a result of years of security assistance and commercial arms sales that facilitate military coordination between the United States and its allies.[5]

As early as 1987, administration officials began to redefine the basic utility of security assistance, rearticulating new rationales for the program in light of waning Cold War tensions. Admiral William Crowe, chairman of the Joint Chiefs of Staff, testified that security assistance was a "vital pillar of our national strategy," indicating that the "extremely disappointing" allocation for FY 1987 was "simply not enough for smaller, poorer countries to protect their sovereignty, deal effectively with state-sponsored terrorism and subversion, and curtail local trafficking in drugs."[6] This view had little to do with the Soviet Union or Cold War politics; rather, it represented a concrete attempt to build a cohesive alternative program rationale. While the FY 1989 *Congressional Presentation Document for Security Assistance* [*CPD*] still focused on containing the spread of Soviet influence in the developing world, it indicated that U.S. security assistance programs were important for other reasons as well.[7] Just three years later, the FY 1992 *CPD* noted that as the international system had evolved away from a bipolar Cold War framework, now regional instability in the form of ethnic conflict and insurgency might erupt as states seek to assert themselves in an emerging multipolar system. Hence, security aid "remain[s] one of the most important tools available for us to manage this process of change"[8] in an "uncertain" environment.[9]

Traditionalists generally argue that security assistance yields both military and political benefits for the United States and its allies. Proponents of this school of thought operate from the basic premise that arms sales and security assistance can promote regional stability. Given the continuous search for flexible policy instruments short of the actual use of force, every post–World War II administration has embraced this view to a greater or lesser extent. Under Presidents Richard Nixon and Gerald Ford, commercial sales of U.S. weaponry jumped from $1 to $2 billion per year in 1970–1971 to a startling $15 to $20 billion by 1975.[10] Under Ronald Reagan, this trend continued, and overall levels of military assistance allocations (in constant dollars) rose to heights not seen since before the Eisenhower administration. While both arms sales and security assistance allocations dropped substantially after the Cold War, arms sales averaged $11 to $13 billion annually from 1990 through 1996 and seemed likely to rise further.[11]

The Reagan administration wholeheartedly embraced this traditional approach, as did the Bush administration and, to the surprise of some, the Clinton administration as well. Reagan's conventional arms transfer policy statement, for instance, asserted that the United States viewed the transfer of conventional arms and other defense articles and services as an "essential element of its global defense posture" and an "indispensable component of its foreign policy," since the United States could not "defend the free world's interests alone."[12] President Clinton's pronouncement on arms transfers had the following objectives: (1) to ensure that U.S. military forces would continue to enjoy technological advantages over potential adversaries; (2) to help allies and friends defend themselves while promoting interoperability with U.S. forces when combined operations were required; (3) to promote regional stability in areas critical to U.S. interests while preventing proliferation of weapons of mass destruction and their missile delivery systems; (4) to promote peaceful conflict resolution and arms control, human rights, democratization, and other U.S. foreign policy objectives; and (5) to enhance the U.S. defense industrial base.[13] Interestingly, human rights did not figure prominently in Clinton's declared security objectives, as it did in Carter's or even Bush's. But the promotion of democracy was pursued with much more vigor; it constituted one of the administration's three primary foreign policy goals as articulated in the February 1995 national security strategy document.[14]

Traditionalists go beyond geopolitical generalizations to detail what they consider to be specific benefits that accrue to the United States from security assistance. For instance, purchases of advanced weapons systems can lead to a desirable dependency on the United States for technical support and spare parts, a condition that is difficult for the recipient nation to alter.[15] The experiences of Iran and Egypt are instructive. Iran's post-1979 armed forces were severely hampered by the absence of American parts and technical support. Similarly, it took Egypt many years and billions of dollars to rebuild its armed forces once it turned away from its main arms supplier, the Soviet Union. In addition, the English-language training and close military-to-military working relationships fostered through the International Military Education and Training program serve to enhance American influence. Such programs provide low-cost tools of influence for the United States. Moreover, U.S. economic assistance from the Economic Support Fund can help stabilize nations experiencing economic difficulties.

In addition to these strategic benefits, traditionalists argue that security assistance also benefits the U.S. defense industry by giving it additional contracts for equipment and services. This, in turn, keeps production lines open, thereby lowering the cost of military equipment purchased by the U.S. armed services and maintaining the U.S. defense industry's competitive advantage.[16] It also translates directly into jobs for American workers and, since most foreign assistance funds are spent in the United States, into a more robust domestic economy through export promotion. As one study asserts: ''A strong commitment to foreign aid is now necessary if America is to advance its economic, political and humanitarian interests abroad. [Otherwise] we are simply going to fall further behind in the race for jobs, markets, and increased exports.''[17]

The 1988 Commission on Integrated Long-Term Strategy (Gorman Commission) endorsed the traditionalist view that a ''marginal dollar invested'' in security assistance ''buys more security for the United States than if allocated instead to U.S. forces.''[18] The authors of the Gorman Report emphasized the role of perception, specifically recipients' perceptions of U.S. commitment to their well-being. Accordingly, security assistance can play an important part in maintaining alliances and key security relationships. For instance, arms *will* be sold or otherwise transferred on the international market. Lt. Gen. Howard Fish made this point in 1980: ''[U]ltimately, the United States simply cannot decide whether there will be arms sales. We can only determine, in a negative sense [by not transferring weapons], where the arms will come from.''[19]

The traditionalists do not necessarily dismiss the issue of human rights and its relationship to the provision of American security aid. However, they usually speak of the need to ''balance'' human rights (and other considerations) with U.S. security interests. Indeed, traditionalists even argue that some forms of security assistance, such as IMET aid, may improve human rights in recipient nations. During the Bush era, for instance, the promotion of human rights was listed as one of the five main objectives of the security assistance program, but it was the fifth element listed—well behind such goals as securing base rights and promoting regional stability through arms transfers.[20]

The end of the Cold War certainly did not spell the demise of the traditionalist perspective. A case continues to be made for a robust security assistance program, especially by many who advocate an activist global leadership role for the United States. If the United States devoted the same percentage of its national resources to the defense and international affairs budgets (the latter includes foreign aid) as it did in 1949, it would have spent in 1995 an estimated $302 billion and $162 billion, respectively, instead of the approximately $260 billion and $18.7 billion it actually did spend. For one such traditionalist, lower foreign aid expenditures mean that ''except for a handful of [recipient] nations,'' the United States now finds itself ''in the second row. . . . The European Community representative or the Japanese ambassador can bring more to the table than we can, so our influence continues to erode.''[21] Traditionalists tend to see the reduction in security aid as a neo-isolationist development that would ''turn the American eagle into an ostrich.''[22]

Reformers

Under the banner of reformers lies a broad spectrum of opinion regarding military assistance and arms sales. (Indeed, it is perhaps the case that nearly everyone has an idea of what the foreign assistance program should do— whether military, economic development, or humanitarian assistance should be emphasized or deemphasized.) Ultimately, what separates reformers from traditionalists and abolitionists are their core assumptions about the utility of the program and the nature of the international environment in which the program operates. Their policy prescriptions tend to flow from these assumptions.

Reformers run the gamut from those who value security assistance as a useful policy instrument in need of retooling to those who may dislike the program but bow to one or both of two political realities: that the president insists on a security assistance program and that elements of the program have powerful friends in Congress among key electoral constituencies. In general, most reformers would agree with Ernest Graves that the end of the Cold War has "left the U.S. foreign assistance program without a coherent organizing principle and with declining resources and a host of structural problems . . . [but it] can continue to be a powerful force in support of U.S. interests abroad."[23] While reformers would be divided over Graves's additional assertion that the post–Cold War era requires a shift in program emphasis toward economic, environmental, and social objectives, there is a widespread belief that a "vigorous housecleaning needs to be undertaken at both ends of Pennsylvania Avenue."[24]

Specifically, three broad reformist approaches to security assistance are discernible: (1) the *economizers*, who want to economize and/or redress a perceived imbalance between security assistance and development aid within the foreign aid budget; (2) the *exceptionalists*, who view security assistance and arms transfers as sometimes necessary, but usually exceptional, instruments of state; and (3) the structural *tinkerers*, who argue, variously, that a radical overhaul of the Foreign Assistance Act is necessary, that only minor reforms are necessary, or that major surgery should be performed on one or more specific elements of the program.

Economizers. Those who support a less security-oriented foreign aid program often argue that many of the threats that the United States and its allies face today are more economic than military in nature.[25] Indeed, some believe that the domestic political battle lines in the emerging international order appear to have shifted from the "Cold Warriors versus Do-Gooders" to the "Economic Warriors versus Do-Gooders."[26] At the same time, there are many in Congress and elsewhere who doubt the efficacy of various components of the foreign aid program. Conservatives, for instance, frequently criticize development assistance. Senator Mitch McConnell (R-Ky.), who assumed the chairmanship of the Foreign Operations Subcommittee of the Senate Appropriations Committee in 1995, lamented that "most poor countries are still poor" despite decades of U.S. assistance. He is not supportive of an economic development program that "subsidizes failure."[27]

The quest for streamlining foreign aid is not new, but there have been some innovative suggestions to help reduce overhead costs while maintaining a significant assistance program, such as the push toward privatization of bureaucratic responsibility for administering aid.[28] The Agency for International Development, at congressional insistence, has engaged in nearly continuous downsizing since the end of the Cold War. By mid-1995, this had resulted in the reduction of 1,200 personnel and the elimination of 21 overseas missions. The total number of AID missions was projected to fall from 108 in the early 1990s to approximately 50 by the year 2000.[29] Moreover, the congressional urge to cut foreign assistance for the ostensible purpose of reducing the national deficit— whatever the merits of this rationale—is deemed politically prudent, especially by those members who find it unacceptable to increase aid while reducing domestic expenditures.[30]

Nonetheless, while advocating reduction and redirection of the foreign aid program, Senator McConnell sharply criticized those who would eliminate the program entirely.[31] And liberal members like Congressman David Obey (D-Wis.) have long argued that making U.S. aid more effective requires reversing the aid priorities away from military assistance toward humanitarian and development programs and curtailing expensive de facto entitlement programs to favored recipients. In reality, says Obey, more military aid translates directly into less economic assistance, and the latter is a greater source of international leverage.[32]

Exceptionalists. Further along the spectrum of reformers are those who feel that security assistance and arms transfers, while occasionally necessary, should be tightly controlled. While Obey and others would redress the balance between development and security assistance, this subgroup would go much further toward nonuse of arms transfers and military aid as policy tools. Indeed, this group, somewhat like the early Carter administration, generally views arms transfers as inherently destabilizing.[33] Such transfers are part of the problem, not the solution, to regional instability. Moreover, the economic cost for the recipient nations of paying for arms transfers could itself upset domestic political stability within those nations. All things considered, there are various high-cost, potentially negative consequences of such sales. Specifically, they may arm potential adversaries and, thereby, increase the possible threats faced by U.S. forces in critical regions; fuel local and regional conflicts; weaken the long-term economic health of recipient nations and encourage an unhealthy dependent relationship with the supplier; and foster instability by promoting skewed priorities in developing nations and supporting undemocratic regimes that are likely to wage war against their own citizens or neighbors.[34]

In addition to these assertions, many exceptionalists (and abolitionists, too) would point out that respected, rigorous analysts conclude that the "long-term impact [of arms transfers] to the U.S. economy is often far less clear" than their proponents allege,[35] and that there is no necessary or clear correlation between maintaining a sound defense industrial base and aggressively pursuing foreign military sales.[36] Finally, the contention that military aid is positive for American workers and the U.S. economy is, quite simply, erroneous. This is so partly because that aid comes from American taxpayers, and even if it is never misspent, used contrary to U.S. laws or policies, or spent outside the United States (none of which are true), there obviously could be no *net* economic benefit for Americans. Moreover, by the 1990s, well over 50 percent of all U.S. military grant aid went to Israel, and since FY 1988, the Jewish state has been permitted to spend much of its annual $1.8 billion in military assistance—$475 million yearly since FY 1991—in Israel rather than in the United States.[37] And a Congressional Research Service (CRS) study based on DOD and Department of Commerce data and analytical models found that when U.S. military aid funds are spent overseas on this scale, thousands of American jobs are lost.[38]

Exceptionalists may concede reluctantly that military aid is a *potential* source of short- or medium-term political leverage and influence, but they hold, espe-

cially over the long term, that arms sales and military assistance are often unreliable or even counterproductive elements of national policy. Hence, careful
executive and legislative branch review and oversight, as well as strict export
controls and other restrictions, are essential.

Over the years, reformist legislators (and others) have attempted to condition
the provision of military assistance or arms sales to the recipient's meeting
various criteria. So, for example, foreign aid is to be denied to countries engaged
in a "consistent pattern of gross violations of internationally recognized human
rights" (PL 94–161). Yet such restrictions usually include an "escape hatch"
where the president is permitted to submit a finding to Congress indicating that
"extraordinary circumstances exist warranting provision of such assistance"
(section 502 [b]). An example of attempted conditionality was the unsuccessful
effort by Congress in 1995 to legislate a "code of conduct" for prospective
buyers of U.S. arms and recipients of U.S. military assistance. This provision
would have prohibited countries from making such purchases or receiving such
aid unless the president certified to Congress that the recipient government promoted democracy, respected human rights, did not engage in armed aggression
in violation of international law, and participated fully in the UN Register of
Conventional Arms.[39]

Tinkerers. Another branch of the reformer school concedes that presidents
will insist on at least some form of security aid, but these reformers focus
primarily on revising various program elements or overhauling the program's
legislative charter in order to make it more reflective of a changing international
security environment. Robert Zimmerman, who raises serious questions about
the wisdom of ESF aid, finds that the end of the Cold War "created unparalleled
new opportunities . . . to use . . . foreign assistance *for* social-political change
rather than *against* a foreign ideology."[40] Others have noted that despite the
opportunities for positive change presented by the end of the Cold War, they
have thus far gone largely unrealized. While foreign assistance should promote
American political interests, said the Senate Appropriations Committee in 1995,
this cannot be done by sustaining "a business as usual approach."[41]

Despite cyclical calls in the past to reform foreign assistance, there is today
a widespread understanding of the need for a sweeping overhaul of the post–
Cold War aid program. Thirty-five years after the Foreign Assistance Act of
1961 was passed, that overburdened legislation contained 33 often contradictory
goals and a maze of 75 different priorities, the sum total of which symbolized
the utter lack of coherence of the entire aid program. As the Hamilton Task
Force (see Chapter 4) concluded in 1989, "U.S. foreign assistance needs a new
premise, a new framework, and a new purpose to meet the challenges of today.
It is time to start anew."[42] Yet despite the powerful and persuasive report of
the Hamilton Task Force, President Clinton's early post–Cold War attempt to
offer a sweeping overhaul of the foreign aid program—his proposed Peace,
Prosperity, and Democracy Act of 1994—was little more than dead on arrival
when it was sent to Congress.

Because of their diversity, evaluating the assumptions of the reformers is difficult. Their prescriptions, too, whether in program design, levels of funding, or objectives, vary widely. The absence of a single, clear-cut, overarching threat to the United States means that the foreign policy elite will remain divided over the foreign aid program and the purpose it is to serve. For instance, although the Clinton administration made the promotion of democracy a central objective, 1994 polling data of the foreign affairs elite indicated that while 62 percent agreed that this should be a "priority," only 28 percent felt that it should be the "top priority."[43]

Abolitionists

Those who want to abolish or radically curtail security assistance represent the smallest of the three schools of thought, but their numbers appeared to be growing by the mid-1990s. Abolitionists, although politically diverse, see security assistance as an anachronistic relic of the Cold War. Conservative isolationists and libertarians generally oppose all or most forms of foreign aid, including security assistance. They urge a reduction in America's global role. Liberal abolitionists, on the other hand, generally view military assistance and most arms transfers as counterproductive and, perhaps, immoral. They want to slash security assistance and, sometimes, sharply curtail or redirect economic development aid.

The late Congressman Otto Passman (D-La.), chairman of the House Foreign Operations Subcommittee of the Appropriations Committee in the 1950s and 1960s, epitomized the isolationist approach. He consistently opposed foreign aid as a waste of taxpayer money. Passman cited gross program mismanagement and the relative lack of tangible "proof" of aid's effectiveness as reason enough to curtail the program.[44] Senator Jesse Helms (R-N.C.), who assumed the chairmanship of the Senate Foreign Relations Committee in 1995, repeatedly denounced foreign assistance as a "stupid business of giving away taxpayers' money."[45] Senator Helms, who supported aid to Israel, but little else, introduced legislation that year to abolish AID. Similarly, Ted Galen Carpenter of the libertarian Cato Institute has little, if anything, positive to say about foreign aid.[46]

Liberal abolitionists, however, generally believe that the United States must remain engaged abroad, albeit in a less security-centered manner. For many, military aid and arms sales are simply ineffective and unreliable tools of policy. Roger Labrie, John Hutchins, and Edwin Peura, for instance, argue even more pointedly than reformist-exceptionalists that arms sales often provide the United States with little diplomatic leverage over recipients, their economic benefits are overstated, they can exacerbate regional tensions and increase the risk of war, and they can undermine the internal stability of countries friendly to the United States.[47] Moreover, the so-called boomerang effect of arms sales, or the prospect of U.S.-supplied weapons later being used against U.S. troops, is especially worrisome to this group—and many supporters of security assistance as well.[48]

Other liberal abolitionists see U.S. military aid and arms sales as enabling dictators in Third World states to suppress internal dissent. Michael Klare and Cynthia Arnson argue that rather than advancing democracy or fostering respect for human rights, U.S. security assistance has commonly supported authoritarian, repressive regimes.[49] David Isenberg of the liberal Center for Defense Information holds that the United States "should have no desire to be known as the arsenal of autocracy."[50]

Moreover, some abolitionists assert that the central U.S. foreign policy concern should not be security related, as during the Cold War; instead, economic concerns must be central.[51] While a number of reformers also are in agreement, they would not generally go as far as some abolitionists and effectively deny the continued relevance of a military-oriented security assistance program in the present era.[52]

Some liberal abolitionists argue that the Cold War was a time when "people were given machine guns to replace machetes as weapons of choice . . . [, and consequently,] many people who should have been sowing seeds are now digging holes to bury their neighbors."[53] Accordingly, they would utilize the post–Cold War moment to develop a new, noninterventionist policy through which the United States would remain engaged culturally, economically, and politically but "bring its military home and curtail expensive foreign aid programs."[54] For others, however, the end of the Cold War requires the "transfer [of] resources from the military sector to development," especially from security assistance, which has enabled some countries to maintain military establishments "significantly larger than they could have supported with domestic resources."[55]

Similarly, analysts at the Washington-based Overseas Development Council (ODC) proposed in 1991 that the United States make several important post–Cold War changes in the security assistance program. Above all, programs designed to prevent Soviet expansion should be phased out. They further proposed that security assistance for Israel and Egypt be moved to a separate account, something vigorously opposed by the American Israel Public Affairs Committee (AIPAC). They also wanted to eliminate payments to base-rights countries and recommended shifting the FMF program to DOD's budget. The ODC's prescriptions would have reduced security aid to a mere 22 percent of the foreign aid budget, created a large "Sustainable Development Fund," and emphasized economic aid that supported multilateral development banks and the Development Fund for Africa.[56]

The abolitionist school's key assumptions clearly diverge from those of the traditionalist and reformist schools. Even in a post–Cold War era, most of the abolitionists' policy preferences have thus far gone largely unrealized. The frequent liberal abolitionist proposal, often supported by some reformers, to channel resources away from security into development assistance has sometimes resonated with Washington policymakers, but the strength of this sentiment in Congress has varied substantially. Recommendations to scrap security assistance entirely have found almost no support in the executive branch.

GENERAL PUBLIC OPINION

There is considerable evidence to confirm the conventional wisdom that foreign aid rarely enjoys sustained, broad-based public support.[57] Indeed, weak public support for security assistance inclines some analysts to characterize it as the "political equivalent of an orphan."[58] However, a significant percentage of the American people usually supports *some* level of foreign assistance. Polling data over time reveal that the public is far more supportive of economic development and humanitarian aid than it is of military assistance. Moreover, the public has definite opinions on certain issue-specific subjects. In various polls conducted in 1993 and 1994, for instance, respondents opposed increasing U.S. economic aid to Russia.[59] Similarly, a B'nai B'rith Anti-Defamation League–sponsored poll on aid to Israel found in 1992 that 53 percent of the American public believed that such assistance should be decreased or stopped altogether, while 44 percent felt that it should be increased or remain the same.[60]

Public skepticism about foreign aid stems from several sources, not the least of which is a widespread misunderstanding of the program, including how much is actually appropriated. Some surveys reveal that much of the general public believes that the United States routinely spends as much as 40 percent of the federal budget on foreign assistance and that large amounts of assistance are largely cash giveaways that could be better spent in the United States. Similarly, a 1993 Harris Poll found that only 12 percent of the public thought the United States spent less than 9 percent of its GNP on foreign aid, with 23 percent indicating the amount as over 50 percent annually.[61]

Of course, what the general public thinks appears to vary greatly, with one poll reporting that a full 41 percent believed that less than $.10 out of every $1 was spent on foreign aid,[62] and another indicating that 25 percent of those polled estimated that the federal government spent more on foreign aid than on defense, welfare, or interest on the national debt.[63] One survey conducted in 1995 uncovered substantial popular support for a foreign aid program that was as large as roughly 5 percent of the GNP.[64] In reality, of course, the annual appropriation for foreign assistance is less than 1 percent of the federal budget (and falling), and more than 70 percent of annual bilateral foreign aid allocations are eventually spent in the United States.

Moreover, the general public has doubts as to what foreign aid can actually accomplish abroad, as well as what it can do for America at home. Especially where military assistance is concerned, the American public has consistently expressed concern that security aid could lead to U.S. military involvement in overseas conflicts. As Table 5.1 and other polls suggest, the American public has seldom rallied behind the security assistance program. Even during the Cold War, when the threat was clearer and the public tended to be more supportive of active internationalism, support was generally withheld for the program's key elements: military aid, ESF assistance (mostly cash transfers, not development

Table 5.1
Perceptions of Economic and Military Aid and Arms Sales, 1974–1994

	1974		1978		1982		1986		1990		1994	
	P	E	P	E	P	E	P	E	P	E	P	E
Economic Aid	52	–	46	90	50	94	53	91	45	90	45	86
Military Aid	22	–	29	60	28	59	33	73	28	39	–	–
Arms Sales	35	–	33	67	39	68	37	–	32	50	15	45

QUESTIONS ASKED: First, "On the whole, do you favor or oppose giving economic aid to other nations for purposes of economic development and technical assistance?" Second, "On the whole, do you favor or oppose giving military aid to other nations? By *military aid* I mean arms and equipment but not troops." Finally, "On the whole, do you favor or oppose our government selling military equipment to other nations?"

Notes: Percentage *in favor* of aid. P = general public responses; E = elite responses. Figures marked by dashes (–) indicate responses unavailable.
Source: John E. Reilly, ed., *American Public Opinion and U.S. Foreign Policy* (Chicago, Ill.: 1974–1994).

aid), and arms sales. The wide divide between elite and general public attitudes toward security assistance is also evident.

The repeatedly and strongly emphasized Cold War rationale for American security assistance—to aid states threatened by Soviet expansion—now works against the program, as the world and the United States have moved into an era where the old rationale is irrelevant. A disjuncture between elite and general public opinion remains, but there also seems to be a significant gap emerging between both of these groups and the actual nature of the program as implemented. For instance, contemporary elite opinion seems generally supportive of select aid programs to Latin America, Eastern Europe, and (concerning the CTR program) Russia and other former Soviet republics. It appears to be considerably less supportive of aid to Israel, Egypt, and the developing nations of Africa.[65] By the mid-1990s, however, Congress had slashed all of these programs except aid to Israel and Egypt. Also, there has been substantial elite and mass-based support for counternarcotics programs since the late 1980s,[66] but this element of the assistance program came under congressional attack in the Clinton years.

While public and elite opinion is generally supportive of the *idea* of promoting democracy and human rights, this support wavers when it is thought to require a commensurate commitment of *resources*. Indeed, there is an inherent limit to popular support for programs that (rightly or wrongly) are perceived as trade-offs with the domestic well-being of American citizens. This is especially true in an era of "donor fatigue," "peace dividend" sentiments, and "America first" rhetoric.[67]

LOBBIES AND SECURITY ASSISTANCE

Lobbies and interest groups play an active role in the congressional process regarding security assistance, forming a primary vehicle through which some elements of the foreign policy elite influence security assistance policy.[68] Just as lobbies work through Congress to realize their goals, so does Congress utilize lobbies. For instance, lobbies and interest groups can provide information and viewpoints at variance with the executive branch and offer constructive policy alternatives. And the success of lobbies depends to a great extent on the level of congressional interest in issues important to the lobbies themselves.

Lobbies use various means to influence the allocation of security assistance. For example, they contact legislators directly—whether privately or through open congressional testimony. They usually work closely with a core group of legislators predisposed toward their agendas or even with individual members of Congress such as former Senator Robert Dole (R-Kans.) for aid to Armenia or Senator Robert Byrd (D-W.Va.) on aid to Turkey. Of course, lobbies can also mobilize constituents to contact members of Congress and, at times, the White House, and to cast their votes for supportive candidates. And political action committees (PACs) and individuals can channel donations to favored candidates. While the amount each PAC can contribute directly to a candidate is relatively small, the cumulative effect of a number of PACs donating to a single candidate on the basis of a single issue can be substantial. Moreover, the amount of an individual's contribution is unlimited by law. For instance, the Center for Responsive Politics reported that people who donated to pro-Israel PACs in the 1990 elections also contributed $3.6 million as individuals to the same candidates supported by those PACs. This resulted in donations "much larger than those given to other ideological groups such as gun control or abortion rights."[69]

A spectrum of organizations join the debate over the allocation of security assistance funds, but the most prominent are the ethnic groups, defense industry organizations and firms, and regionally oriented organizations or groups supportive of development/humanitarian aid.

The ethnic lobbies represent a variety of diasporas with a demographic presence in the United States. Some of these interest groups have been uniquely influential. These groups tend to embrace their geographical or cultural/ideological homeland in a manner they hope or expect will not jeopardize their identities as patriotic American citizens. Yet they must always be prepared to "defend themselves against the charge of divided loyalties."[70] That is, while closely relating to the interests of their ethnic homelands, such groups must be careful to simultaneously identify these interests with the larger foreign policy priorities of the United States. In addition to promulgating and maintaining perceived legitimacy, ethnic groups usually need to make a reasonable case for their positions and provide useful services to policymakers—such as information, draft legislation, paid trips overseas, votes, campaign contributions, and so on.[71] Those ethnic groups (and other special interests) that rest their cases largely on moral or humanitarian grounds, but are unable to deliver tangible benefits to legislators, are usually not serious players. This partly explains why funding for Israel (and Egypt) remained strong after the end of the Cold War and why development assistance to Africa was slashed by the mid-1990s.

No lobby, ethnic or otherwise, rivals AIPAC's influence on security assistance allocations and foreign assistance generally. Since 1954, AIPAC has been a tireless proponent of American aid to Israel. While AIPAC's primary target is Congress, it is probably the only ethnic lobby to focus, with some considerable effect, on the executive branch as well. At the 1995 annual meeting of the American Israel Public Affairs Committee in Washington, D.C., for instance, approximately 100 representatives and 54 senators attended, and President Clinton delivered the keynote address. With the rare exception of FY 1996,[72] AIPAC has almost always lobbied for the entire foreign assistance budget instead of focusing narrowly on Israel's slice of the foreign aid pie. A principal reason for this is that Israel's huge annual aid allocation *appears* less striking if the overall foreign assistance budget is sizable. This is also why AIPAC opposes shifting Israel-Egypt aid to a separate line item in the Defense budget, as some development-oriented groups have urged (as it would highlight the size and distinctiveness of what many supporters of Israel came to consider a de facto "entitlement").

AIPAC cites professionalism, grassroots organization, and "key contacts . . . in all 50 states" as factors contributing to its effectiveness.[73] AIPAC sometimes adopts a low profile; at other times it appears to wish to reinforce its image as a "heavyweight" or "King of the Hill."[74] It has been instrumental in thwarting the reelection bids of some of its perceived political opponents,[75] and among many other things, AIPAC helped to devise and promote the notion that Israel was a strategic asset for the United States in the Middle East. By such reasoning, security assistance to Israel was in the national security interest of the United States (see Chapter 7).

In contrast to AIPAC, the National Association of Arab Americans (NAAA) is effectively a non-player in the aid game.[76] Disunity within the Arab-American community, insufficient levels of financial contributions to political candidates, and the hostility of much of the Arab or Islamic world toward the United States are a few of the many reasons for the NAAA's ineffectiveness.

The American Hellenic Institute (AHI) Public Affairs Committee lobbies routinely for Greek interests in Congress.[77] AHI was formally established in 1975 in the wake of the Turkish invasion of Cyprus. In the 1980s, AHI's main achievements were the preservation of the Greek-Turkish 7:10 aid ratio at a time when the Reagan administration wanted to alter the ratio in favor of Turkey. AHI also helped to win a variety of other security assistance benefits for Greece such as low-interest loans and some outright aid grants. Eugene Telemachus Rossides, a former Nixon administration official, founded the organization and directed it for many years. AHI drew on a well-organized grassroots activation network provided by AHEPA (American Hellenic Educational Progressive Association).[78] Utilizing AHEPA's connections with the American Greek community at large, AHI was able to remain organizationally small, cohesive, and centralized.

Other countries, such as Turkey and, in the past, El Salvador and the Philippines, have also lobbied for security aid, as have subnational actors like the Contras during the Reagan era. Lacking the powerful lobbies of Greece and Israel, however, these countries have often employed professional lobbying firms, embassy staff, and sympathetic nongovernmental organizations to plead their case to Congress. Turkey, for example, has contracted with firms such as Hill and Knowlton to lobby on its behalf,[79] although by the 1990s Turkey, and even Jordan, benefited from AIPAC's efforts on their behalf. In the case of Nicaragua, by contrast, more than 200 domestic private voluntary and nongovernmental organizations were involved in a "lobby war" in which some supported the democratically elected Nicaraguan government and others the Contra rebels.[80] Similarly, in Bosnia, strong grassroots political pressure was certainly one factor in the "equip-and-train" provision of the 1995 Dayton Accord.[81] Moreover, Washington-based ambassadors and other senior officials from those countries receiving U.S. *military* assistance regularly implore Congress for increased levels of aid.[82]

In the early post–Cold War era, lobbies representing sixteen East European states formed the Central and East European Coalition (CEEC), an umbrella organization with a significant ethnic political base in the midwestern and northeastern sections of the United States.[83] This group took some credit in 1995 for persuading the House to clarify the U.S. position on NATO expansion, and it has consistently advocated closer military ties between the United States and East European states. One of the major thrusts of this group is also to ensure that aid money is distributed to non-Russian republics of the former Soviet Union.[84]

In addition to the ethnic lobbies, the defense-export lobby sometimes attempts to influence the allocation of foreign aid resources. Arguing that the provision of military aid and arms transfers accounts for up to 1 million jobs domestically and advances U.S. interests,[85] proponents of arms exports work mainly with congressional conservatives. Minor coalitions such as the Aerospace Industries Association (AIA) and large umbrella organizations like the American League for Exports and Security Assistance (ALESA) routinely lobby for military aid. While AIA represents only a few firms with foreign aid interests,[86] ALESA represents firms and unions that depend to some degree on security assistance funds for part of their income, and as a consequence, it lobbies for increases in security assistance. However, ALESA's ''corporate member interests are sometimes divergent,''[87] and neither it nor AIA has been viewed as a particularly effective lobby in Washington.

Other nongovernmental groups have been ardent opponents of security assistance. They generally urge giving priority to development assistance. Organizations such as Bread for the World, InterAction, TransAfrica, and others—mainly human rights and development-oriented groups—routinely issue reports promoting development aid and condemning military assistance and arms transfers. Says Caleb Rossiter, director of the Project on Demilitarization and Democracy: ''[W]hat we really have on the [arms] selling side is welfare for the corporations at home and, on the buying side, welfare for the dictators abroad.''[88] Among the best known of the development lobbies is the Overseas Development Council, which issues reports on development issues and annually testifies before Congress.

CONCLUSION

Despite weak public support for security assistance, special interest groups, especially Greek and Jewish groups, play an active, assertive, and often decisive role. These groups have frequently exerted an inordinate degree of influence on policy partly because, in close elections, ''the 1 percent of the electorate that is seriously concerned with providing security assistance to a given country may be 50 percent of a candidate's margin.''[89] Moreover, Jewish groups and individuals may provide up to 50 percent of the funding for major Democratic political campaigns, and 15 to 20 percent of the funding for major Republican campaigns.[90] Of course, Congress is well aware that foreign aid is not liked by the general public, and most members would agree with Congressman Obey that foreign aid is the program their constituents "most want to see cut."[91] But on this issue, Congress listens to the special interests, not the general public, largely because, as former Congressman Matthew McHugh (D-N.Y.) observed, foreign aid is "not a cutting-edge political issue" with most people.[92] It *is* a cutting-edge issue with key ethnic lobbies.

While the general public's influence on security assistance appears to be limited, and while the size and composition of the program are always in flux, the program will not soon disappear. It has too many champions in the elite sector, among interest groups, and in the executive and legislative branches of government. And wholly apart from domestic political considerations, many are convinced of its utility.

NOTES

1. See, generally, Christine Contee, *What Americans Think: Views on Development and U.S.–Third World Relations* (Washington, D.C.: Overseas Development Council, 1987); John R. Reilly, ed., *American Public Opinion and U.S. Foreign Policy* (Chicago, Ill.: Chicago Council on Foreign Relations [hereafter, CCFR], 1972, 1974, 1978, 1982, 1986, 1990, 1994); The Times Mirror Center, *America's Place in the Post–Cold War World* (Washington, D.C., November 1993); Steven Kull, Program on International Policy Attitudes, *Americans and Foreign Aid: A Study of American Public Attitudes* (College Park: University of Maryland, 1995); U.S. Agency for International Development, "Polls and Public Opinion: The Myth of Opposition to Foreign Assistance," January 23, 1995 (mimeographed).

2. U.S. Department of State, *Congressional Presentation for Foreign Operations, Fiscal Year 1996* [hereafter, *CPD . . . 1996*], Washington, D.C., 1995, p. 480.

3. See Richard Nixon, "Asia after Vietnam," *Foreign Affairs* 46 (October 1967), pp. 113–14; see also *CPD . . . 1996*, pp. 7–8, 480.

4. Department of Defense [hereafter, DOD], Joint Chiefs of Staff, *National Military Strategy of the United States of America: A Strategy of Flexible and Selective Engagement*, Washington, D.C., February 1995, pp. 8–9; White House, *National Security Strategy of Engagement and Enlargement*, Washington, D.C., February 1995, p. 10; DOD, *Annual Report to the President and the Congress*, Washington, D.C., February 1995, p. J-1; Association of the United States Army, *Security Assistance: An Instrument of U.S. Foreign Policy* (Washington, D.C., June 1990), p. 6; Commission on Integrated Long-Term Strategy, Regional Conflict Working Group [hereafter, Gorman Report], *Commitment to Freedom: Security Assistance as a Policy Instrument in the Third World* (Washington, D.C.: DOD, 1988), p. 1.

5. Ernest Graves, "The Future of U.S. Security Assistance and Arms Sales," *The Washington Quarterly* 14 (Summer 1991), pp. 55–56. See also Lt. Gen. Teddy G. Allen, "Security Assistance in Changing Times," *DISAM Journal* 14 (Summer 1992), p. 20.

6. Testimony, Admiral William J. Crowe, U.S. Navy, U.S. Congress, House, Com-

mittee on Foreign Affairs, hearing, *Concurrent Resolution on the Budget for FY88*, 99th Cong., 1st. sess., February 18, 1987, p. 53.

7. U.S. Department of State, *Congressional Presentation Document for Security Assistance, Fiscal Year 1989*, Washington, D.C., 1988, p. 5.

8. U.S. Department of State, *Congressional Presentation for Security Assistance Programs, Fiscal Year 1992*, Washington, D.C., 1991, p. 5.

9. *CPD . . . 1996*, pp. 7–8.

10. Defense Security Assistance Agency, *Fiscal Year Series as of September 1981* (Washington, D.C.: Government Printing Office [hereafter, GPO], 1982), pp. 2–3. See also Lewis Sorely, *Arms Transfers under Nixon: A Policy Analysis* (Lexington: University of Kentucky Press, 1983).

11. DOD, Office of the Under Secretary for Research and Technology, *Worldwide Conventional Arms Trade (1994–2000): A Forecast and Analysis*, Washington, D.C., December 1994; Richard F. Grimmett, *Conventional Arms Transfers to the Third World: 1986–1994*, Congressional Research Service [hereafter, CRS] Report for Congress, Washington, D.C., 1995.

12. Conventional Arms Transfer Policy statement, reprinted in *Department of State Bulletin* 81 (September 1981), p. 61.

13. One review found that the guidelines for arms transfers ''are sufficiently broad so as to permit most U.S. sales on the grounds of advancing the national interest.'' Richard F. Grimmett, *Conventional Arms Transfers: President Clinton's Policy Directive*, CRS Report for Congress 95–639F, Washington, D.C., May 17, 1995, p. 1. See also Lora Lumpe, ''Clinton's Conventional Arms Export Policy: So Little Change,'' *Arms Control Today* (May 1995), pp. 9–13.

14. Cf. note 4, *National Security Strategy of the United States*, pp. 1–3.

15. Roger P. Labrie, John Hutchins, and Edwin W.A. Peura, *U.S. Arms Sales Policy: Background and Issues* (Washington, D.C.: American Enterprise Institute, 1982), p. 79.

16. Joel Johnson, ''What the U.S. Gains by Arms Transfers,'' in Center for Defense Information [hereafter, CDI], *Conventional Arms Transfer Restraint in the 1990's* (Washington, D.C.: CDI, 1995), pp. 10–16.

17. Mayer Alan Brenner, Martin J. Ingall, Steven F. Liebes, and Steven L. Spiegel, *The Value of Foreign Aid to the American Taxpayer*, Occasional Paper No. 5 (Los Angeles, Calif.: Center for Foreign Policy Options, July 1992), pp. 1, 4. This review estimates that between 1980 and 1991 approximately $54 billion, or 94.5 percent of U.S. military aid, was spent domestically (p. 13). Foreign aid in general (based on $12.5 billion in spending) accounts for about 238,750 jobs in the United States, according to the authors.

18. Gorman Report, p. 13.

19. U.S. Congress, Senate, *Conventional Arms Transfer Policy*, 96th Cong., 2d sess., 1980, Rpt. No. 381–26, pp. 137–40.

20. U.S. Department of State, *Congressional Presentation for Security Assistance, Fiscal Year 1993*, Washington, D.C., 1992, pp. 4–5.

21. Charles A. Stevenson, ''Global Leadership on the Cheap'' (paper presented at the conference on New Frontiers in International Security, Washington, D.C., October 13, 1995), p. 4 (mimeographed).

22. Deputy Secretary of State Strobe Talbott, ''American Eagle or Ostrich? The Case for U.S. Leadership,'' *U.S. Department of State Dispatch* 6 (March 27, 1995), p. 245.

23. Ernest Graves, "Restructuring Foreign Assistance," *The Washington Quarterly* 16 (Summer 1993), p. 189.

24. Richard Bissell, "After Foreign Aid—What?" *The Washington Quarterly* 14 (Summer 1991), p. 30.

25. See C. Fred Bergsten, "The Primacy of Economics," *Foreign Policy* 87 (Summer 1992), pp. 15, 24.

26. Mark Lowenthal, *U.S. Foreign Aid in a Changing World: Options for New Priorities*, CRS Report prepared for the House Committee on Foreign Affairs, Subcommittee on Europe and the Middle East, 102d Cong., 1st sess., February 1991, pp. 2, 7.

27. Thomas W. Lippman, "Key GOP Senator Proposes Revamping Foreign Aid Program," *Washington Post*, December 13, 1994, p. A34. See also Joshua Muravchik, *The Imperative of American Leadership* (Washington, D.C.: American Enterprise Institute Press, 1996), pp. 182–84.

28. See Henrietta Holsman Fore, "Lean Development and the Privatization of U.S. Foreign Assistance," *The Washington Quarterly* 17 (Winter 1994), pp. 183–96; Brian Robertson, "Can the World Find Aid in the Private Sector?" *Washington Times*, Insight, December 5, 1994, pp. 6–9.

29. U.S. Agency for International Development, "Ten Questions Commonly Asked About U.S. Foreign Assistance Programs," Washington, D.C., p. 2 (mimeographed); Ben Barber, "US AID Director Aims to Target Assistance, Boost Human Rights," *Christian Science Monitor*, June 17, 1993, p. 3.

30. David Obey and Carol Lancaster, "Funding Foreign Aid," *Foreign Policy* 71 (Summer 1988), p. 144. See also Thomas W. Lippman, "Hill Battle Lines Pit Foreign Aid against National Economic Interests," *Washington Post*, May 16, 1994, p. A7.

31. See Lippman, "Hill Battle Lines," p. A7.

32. Obey and Lancaster, "Funding Foreign Aid," p. 145; John Felton, "House Panel Acts to Shift Foreign Aid Priorities," *Congressional Quarterly Weekly Report* (June 16, 1990), pp. 1896–98.

33. See Conventional Arms Transfer Policy Statement, *Department of State Bulletin*, 76 (June 13, 1977).

34. William D. Hartung, "Negative Consequences of the Weapons Trade: What the United States Loses by Arms Transfers," in CDI, *Conventional Arms*, p. 27; Harry Shaw, "Debts and Dependency," *Foreign Policy* 50 (Spring 1983), pp. 105–23; Eric Nordlinger, *Isolationism Reconfigured: American Foreign Policy for a New Century* (Princeton, N.J.: Princeton University Press, 1995), p. 210. See also Vernon W. Ruttan, *United States Development Assistance Policy: The Domestic Politics of Foreign Economic Aid* (Baltimore, Md.: Johns Hopkins University Press, 1996).

35. Jacques S. Gansler, *Defense Conversion: Transforming the Arsenal of Democracy* (Cambridge, Mass.: MIT Press, 1995), p. 61.

36. Craig M. Brandt, "American Weapons Sales and the Defense Industrial Base: Can Arms Transfers Save Defense Production?" (paper presented at the International Studies Association Convention, San Diego, Calif., April 1996).

37. Clyde Mark, *Israel: U.S. Foreign Assistance*, CRS Issue Brief, Congressional Research Service, Washington, D.C., August 30, 1995, pp. 7, 14.

38. Linda Legrand and Robert Shuey, *A CRS Analysis of the Employment Effect of Spending Foreign Military Sales Credits Outside of the United States*, Congressional Research Service, Washington, D.C., September 17, 1984, pp. 6–10.

39. R. Jeffrey Smith, "Arms Sales 'Conduct Code' Opposed," *Washington Post*, May

24, 1995, p. A6; Cynthia McKinney and Caleb Rossiter, "It's Time the US Stopped 'Boomerang' Arms Sales," *Christian Science Monitor*, May 23, 1995, p. 19.

40. Robert F. Zimmerman, *Dollars, Diplomacy, and Dependency: Dilemmas of U.S. Economic Aid* (Boulder, Colo.: Lynne Reinner Publishers, 1993), p. 179.

41. U.S. Congress, Senate, Committee on Appropriations, Subcommittee on Foreign Operations, *Foreign Operations, Export Financing, and Related Programs Appropriation Bill, 1996*, 104th Cong., 1st sess., 1995, Rpt. 104–143, pp. 20–21. See also James C. Clad and Roger D. Stone, "New Mission for Foreign Aid," *Foreign Affairs* 72 (Winter 1992–1993), pp. 196–98.

42. U.S. Congress, House, Committee on Foreign Affairs, *Report of the Task Force on Foreign Assistance*, 101st Cong., 1st sess., 1989, p. 29; Bissell, "After Foreign Aid," p. 23.

43. The Times Mirror Center, *America's Place*, pp. 90, 92.

44. See, for instance, Otto Passman's "Foreign Aid: Success or Failure?" *National Review* 14 (May 21, 1963), pp. 401–3.

45. John M. Goshko, "Foreign Aid May Be Early Test of New Hill Order," *Washington Post*, November 21, 1994, p. A14.

46. Ted Galen Carpenter, *A Search for Enemies: America's Alliances after the Cold War* (Washington, D.C.: The Cato Institute, 1992).

47. Labrie, Hutchins, and Peura, *U.S. Arms Sales Policy*, pp. 58–60.

48. William Hartung observes that in many instances where the United States has been involved in overseas conflicts (for instance, Panama, 1989; Iraq, 1990–1991; Somalia, 1992–1994; and Haiti, 1994–1995), it has faced forces that had received arms, training, or military technology from the United States during the period leading up to the conflict. Moreover, while some traditionalists may argue that countries with U.S. weapons do not start wars due to a fear of being cut off from the United States, abolitionists would note that some 48 of the 50 ethnic and territorial conflicts under way in early 1993 involved countries that had received U.S. arms prior to the start of hostilities. For Lawrence Korb, the result of a policy that permits the export of increasing levels of conventional weapons technology is a "vicious cycle" in which Washington allows the export of technology, and the U.S. military then argues that it could be used against the United States, then further uses that assertion to justify DOD's purchase of even more sophisticated technology. This is a phenomenon that Natalie Goldring asserts is the equivalent of a leading supplier becoming involved in an arms race with itself. See Hartung, "Negative Consequences," pp. 22–23; idem, *U.S. Weapons at War: United States Arms Deliveries to Regions of Conflict* (New York: World Policy Institute, 1995), p. 2; Lawrence Korb, "Overview of the Conventional Arms Trade," in CDI, *Conventional Arms*, p. 61; Natalie J. Goldring, "Finding Effective Arms Transfer Restraint Measures," in CDI, *Conventional Arms*, p. 65.

49. Michael T. Klare and Cynthia Arnson, *Supplying Repression: U.S. Support for Authoritarian Regimes Abroad* (Washington, D.C.: Institute for Policy Studies, 1981), p. 4. See also Leslie Gelb, "Arms Sales," *Foreign Policy* 24 (Winter 1976–1977), pp. 3–24; Martin Edwin Anderson, "The Military Obstacle to Latin Democracy," *Foreign Policy* 73 (Winter 1988–1989), pp. 95–97; Nicole Ball and Milton Leitenberg, "The Foreign Arms Sales Policy of the Carter Administration," *Alternatives* 4 (March 1979), pp. 527–56.

50. David Isenberg, "The Sins of the Security Assistance Program," *Foreign Policy Briefing*, vol. 18 (Washington, D.C.: The CATO Institute, February 27, 1992), p. 10.

51. Susan Strange, "The Name of the Game," in Nicholas X. Rizopolous, ed., *Sea-Changes: American Foreign Policy in a World Transformed* (New York: Council on Foreign Relations, 1990), pp. 238, 271. See also John Stremlau, "Clinton's Dollar Diplomacy," *Foreign Policy* 97 (Winter 1994–1995), pp. 18–35.

52. See Peter G. Peterson with James K. Sebenius, "The Primacy of the Domestic Agenda," in Graham Allison and Gregory F. Treverton, eds., *Rethinking America's Security: Beyond Cold War to New World Order* (New York: W. W. Norton, 1992), pp. 61, 92; John Sewell and Christine Contee, "Foreign Aid and Gramm-Rudman," *Foreign Affairs* 65 (Summer 1987), p. 1016.

53. Bread for the World Institute, *Countries in Crisis: Hunger 1996* (Silver Spring, Md., 1995), p. 1.

54. Doug Bandow, "Keeping the Troops and the Money at Home," *Current History* 93 (January 1994), pp. 12–13.

55. Nicole Ball, *Pressing for Peace: Can Aid Induce Reform?* Overseas Development Council, Policy Essay No. 6 (Washington, D.C.: ODC, 1992), pp. 1–4, 36–37; Bread for the World, *Countries in Crisis*, pp. 21–38; ACTIONAID, *The Reality of Aid 95* (London: Earthscan Publications Ltd., 1995), pp. 95–98; John W. Sewell, "Foreign Aid for a New World Order," *The Washington Quarterly* 14 (Summer 1991), pp. 34–45; Ernest H. Preeg, "The Aid for Trade Debate," *The Washington Quarterly* 16 (Winter 1993), pp. 99–114; Kim R. Holmes, *Focus on Free Markets: How to Cut Foreign Aid* (Washington, D.C.: The Heritage Foundation, 1995).

56. John W. Sewell and Peter M. Storm, *United States Budget for a New World Order* (Washington, D.C.: Overseas Development Council, 1991), p. 23. Neither the Bush nor Clinton administration reacted favorably to most of these proposals.

57. Eugene Wittkopf, *Faces of Internationalism: Public Opinion and American Foreign Policy* (Durham, N.C.: Duke University Press, 1990), p. 71.

58. Robert B. Mahoney, Jr., and David L. Wallace, "The Domestic Constituencies of the Security Assistance Program," in Ernest Graves and Steven A. Hildreth, eds., *U.S. Security Assistance: The Political Process* (Lexington, Mass.: Lexington Books, 1985), p. 126.

59. See Gallup/*Newsweek* poll, March 25, 1993, 75 percent indicating that the United States was already providing enough; the March 8–11, 1994, CBS News/*New York Times* poll, with 71 percent agreeing that the United States should not give an increased level of economic assistance to Russia; and the Gallup/CNN/*USA Today* poll, September 20, 1994, in which 67 percent opposed an increase in economic aid to Russia (polling data available through Lexis-Nexis from the Roper Center, Connecticut).

60. B'nai B'rith Anti-Defamation League poll, April 28–May 1, 1992 (polling data available through Lexis-Nexis from the Roper Center, Connecticut). Cf. Jon Krosnik and Shibley Telhami, "Public Attitudes toward Israel: A Study of the Attentive and Issue Publics," *International Studies Quarterly* 39 (December 1995), pp. 535–54.

61. Harris Poll, October 1–6, 1993 (polling data available through Lexis-Nexis from the Roper Center, Connecticut).

62. I.C.R. Survey Research Group poll, March 3, 1993 (polling data available through Lexis-Nexis from the Roper Center, Connecticut).

63. ABC News/*Washington Post* poll, February 25–28, 1993 (polling data available through Lexis-Nexis from the Roper Center, Connecticut).

64. Program on International Policy Attitudes, *Americans and Foreign Aid*, p. 3.

65. The Times Mirror Center, *America's Place*, p. 81.

66. Reilly, CCFR, p. 25.

67. The Times Mirror Center issued polling results indicating that a full 79 percent of the American public agreed in April 1993 (up from 60 percent in 1985) that "we should not think so much in international terms but concentrate more on our own national problems and building up our strength and prosperity here at home." At the same time, however, only 37 percent (compared with 34 percent in 1985) agreed that "the U.S. should mind its own business internationally and let other countries get along the best they can on their own." A September 1993 poll conducted by the same firm reported that a full 81 percent allowed that the United States should have a *shared* world leadership role with other nations. See The Times Mirror Center, *America's Place*, October 21–23, 1993, supplemental questionnaire, p. 8.

68. See Chapter 4 for an overview of Congress. See also Joseph White, "Decision Making in the Appropriations Committees on Defense and Foreign Operations," in Randall B. Ripley and James M. Lindsay, ed., *Congress Resurgent: Defense and Foreign Policy on Capitol Hill* (Ann Arbor: University of Michigan Press, 1993), pp. 183–207; Thomas M. Franck and Edward Weisband, *Foreign Policy by Congress* (New York: Oxford University Press, 1979), pp. 251–53; James M. Lindsay, *Congress and the Politics of U.S. Foreign Policy* (Baltimore, Md.: Johns Hopkins University Press, 1994), pp. 53–75.

69. Charles R. Babcock, "Israel's Backers Maximize Political Clout," *Washington Post*, September 26, 1991, p. A21.

70. Yossi Shain, "Ethnic Diasporas and U.S. Foreign Policy," *Political Science Quarterly* 109 (Winter 1994–1995), p. 814.

71. Paul Watanabe, *Ethnic Groups, Congress, and American Foreign Policy: The Politics of the Turkish Arms Embargo* (Westport, Conn.: Greenwood Press, 1984), pp. 49, 58.

72. Dan Morgan, "Abortion Fight Blocks U.S. Aid to Israel; Officials Say Bond Rating at Risk," *Washington Post*, December 19, 1995, p. A4.

73. American Israel Public Affairs Committee, "What Is AIPAC?" Washington, D.C., n.d., mimeographed.

74. Some, such as former Congressman Paul Findlay (R-Ill.), have described AIPAC as the "King of the Hill." See Findlay, *They Dare Speak Out: People and Institutions Confront Israel's Lobby* (Westport, Conn.: Lawrence Hill, 1985), p. 25.

75. John T. Tierney, "Interest Group Involvement in Congressional Foreign and Defense Policy," in Randall B. Ripley and James M. Lindsay, eds., *Congress Resurgent: Foreign and Defense Policy on Capitol Hill* (Ann Arbor: University of Michigan Press, 1993), p. 94.

76. Congressional Quarterly, *The Washington Lobby* (Washington, D.C.: Congressional Quarterly, 1974), p. 117; Mitchell Geoffrey Bard, "The Influence of Ethnic Interest Groups on American Middle East Policy," in Eugene R. Wittkopf, ed., *The Domestic Sources of American Foreign Policy* (New York: St. Martin's Press, 1994), pp. 59–63; Shain, "Ethnic Diasporas," p. 817; Mahoney and Wallace, "The Domestic Constituencies of the Security Assistance Program," p. 146.

77. On AHI and Greek lobbying, see Christopher Madison, "Effective Lobbying, Ethnic Politics, Preserve U.S. Military Aid for Greece," *National Journal* 18 (May 4, 1985), pp. 961–65.

78. Watanabe, *Ethnic Groups*, p. 146.

79. Steven Pressman, "Countries Turn to Professionals for Lobbying," *Congressional Quarterly Weekly Report* (December 15, 1984), pp. 3104–5.

80. William M. LeoGrande and Philip Brenner, "The House Divided: Ideological Polarization over Aid to the Nicaraguan 'Contras,' " *Legislative Studies Quarterly* 18 (February 1993), pp. 110–11.

81. The Dayton Accord contained the pledge of an unspecified amount of U.S. military assistance to help arm and train the Bosnian military. See Michael Dobbs, "U.S. Starts Process of Army Aid," *Washington Post*, December 21, 1995, p. A35; Dana Priest, "U.S. May Send $100 Million in Arms, Equipment to Bosnia," *Washington Post*, February 8, 1996, p. A21.

82. See, for instance, Paul Taylor, "Mandela Complains That U.S. Aid to South Africa Is 'Peanuts,' " *Washington Post*, November 19, 1994, p. A20.

83. Dick Kirschten, "Ethnics Resurging," *National Journal* 8 (February 25, 1995), p. 484.

84. Central and East European Coalition Factsheet, Washington, D.C., 1995, p. 1 (mimeographed).

85. Brenner et al., *The Value of Foreign Aid*, pp. 1, 4; AIPAC, "Why Foreign Aid? We Can't Afford Not To," Washington, D.C., n.d., p. 3; Johnson, "What the U.S. Gains by Arms Transfers," p. 12.

86. Barry Blechman argues that the aerospace lobby has made "hardly a ripple in Washington" and has "apparently even had trouble persuading defense companies to support its efforts to loosen export controls." See Blechman, *The Politics of National Security: Congress and U.S. Defense Policy* (New York: Oxford University Press, 1990), p. 127.

87. Mahoney and Wallace, "The Domestic Constituencies of the Security Assistance Program," pp. 143–44.

88. Caleb Rossiter, "Financing Military Exports," in CDI, *Conventional Arms*, p. 47.

89. Mahoney and Wallace, "The Domestic Constituencies of the Security Assistance Program," p. 127.

90. J. J. Goldberg, *Jewish Power: Inside the American Jewish Establishment* (New York: Addison-Wesley, 1996), pp. 266–77.

91. Obey and Lancaster, "Funding Foreign Aid," p. 146.

92. John Felton, "Boosters of Overseas Programs Get a Hand in House Budget," *Congressional Quarterly Weekly Report* (April 28, 1990), p. 1279.

6

Base-Rights Countries

Aid to base-rights countries is addressed throughout the book because of its historically prominent stature in the overall U.S. security assistance effort.[1] Here these programs are examined more critically and prescriptively. Particular attention is paid to the recent past and to the future, although the chapter is set in a historical context. While base-rights aid is being phased out in the post–Cold War era, it played a crucial role in the post–World War II U.S. strategy that relied consistently on forward presence, crisis response, and overseas engagement. Overseas military facilities remain important for the United States, but security assistance will no longer be a primary instrument for securing access to them.

BASE-RIGHTS AID

In the 1950s, the United States began to provide security assistance to several countries in exchange for access to bases or other military facilities on their territories. Most of this assistance was military aid under the Foreign Military Financing program and economic aid through the Economic Support Fund. From FY 1962 to FY 1992, an annual average of about 10 percent of all U.S. foreign aid went to base-rights countries.

However, following the 1992 U.S. withdrawal from bases in the Philippines, and an effective end to base-rights aid to Portugal in FY 1995, the United States had only two traditional base-rights arrangements: with Greece and Turkey (see Table 6.1).[2] Partly as a result, only 5 percent of the $14.3 billion foreign aid budget for FY 1995 went to base-rights countries. Even this low percentage, however, understated the precipitous decline in base-rights aid because almost all of the $648 million that went to Greece and Turkey that year was in the

Table 6.1
U.S. Aid to Base-Rights Nations, FY 1988–FY 1996 (in millions of dollars)

COUNTRY	FY 88	FY 89	FY 90	FY 91	FY 92	FY 93	FY 94	FY 95	FY 96
Greece	344.1	350.7	349.1	350.6	350.3	315.3	283.6	247.3	250.6
Turkey	526.3	563.5	516.1	804.0	504.9	653.5	406.4	400.5	392.9
Portugal	117.1	152.6	126.6	126.6	142.2	91.0	81.5	0.5	0.8
Philippines	142.6	425.6	273.4	273.4	74.4	42.3	0.9	–	–
TOTAL	1130.1	1492.4	1265.2	1554.6	1071.8	1102.1	772.4	648.3	644.3

Notes: Figures include military assistance (FMF loans and grants, IMET, and counternarcotic aid) and ESF assistance. FY 1996 figures are estimates valid as of March 1996.

Sources: U.S. Agency for International Development; U.S. Department of State; Congressional Research Service.

form of market rate loans, not grants or even concessional (low-interest) loans, as had been the case in most prior years. This downward trend was in line with a sentiment expressed by many members of Congress since at least the late 1980s: that base-rights aid be "phased out as soon as possible."[3] The "end of an era" for traditional American base arrangements abroad was clearly in sight.

In the 1970s and 1980s, certain factors began to undermine U.S. relationships with base-host countries. Questions of compensation became more pressing. Greece and the Philippines, in particular, viewed U.S. compensation for base access as little more than rental payments. Governments threatened eviction if higher rents were not forthcoming. Then, too, some of these governments did not view the Soviet threat with the same concern that Washington did. A third factor was sensitivity about national sovereignty as well as various domestic political considerations within host nations. Finally, by the late 1980s, U.S. budget constraints, shifts in U.S. strategic priorities, and significant congressional actions also came into play.

The Strategic Utility of Overseas Bases

The United States entered World War II with about 100 overseas bases, but in 1946 there were more than 7,000. In 1990 the United States had about 700 overseas bases or major military facilities in twenty-four countries. This number was reduced more than one-third by 1994.[4]

The number of bases is less significant than their locations and capabilities, however. While longer-range aircraft obviated the need for many such bases, fighter aircraft still depend on them. The bases provide key hubs for air and naval forces. Airlift provides transoceanic transport for manpower and other high-priority cargoes. Global airlift operations rely on a network of fourteen key bases, seven in NATO countries and three in East Asia. Naval forces prefer to operate within 1,500 nautical miles of land bases to facilitate delivery of supplies and antisubmarine protection by land-based aircraft. Some of the overseas facilities also permit naval forces to reach crisis areas more rapidly.[5]

Overseas bases have been integral to the U.S. approach to the world since 1945 and an essential element of American globalism. A U.S. defense strategy, premised in large part on forward presence and crisis response, sees the bases and other military facilities as key elements for global power projection.

During the Cold War, the placement of overseas bases was designed principally to contain Soviet power in Europe, Asia, and the Middle East. Thus, U.S. policy held that these bases served to protect both the United States and host countries from the Soviet threat. Increasingly, though, host countries began to weigh the strategic utility of these American bases differently.

Most U.S. bases overseas have been located in Germany, Great Britain, Italy, Japan, and South Korea, nations whose governments did not question their strategic utility, at least until quite recently. In the 1970s and 1980s, however, some base-host nations challenged the assumption that U.S. bases provided protection from external threats. Instead, they claimed, the bases served only American interests. In the 1980s, Greece charged that the bases offered no protection against Turkey, its main adversary, while the Corazon Aquino government in Manila declared that it saw no external threat to the Philippines.

These perspectives inclined Greece and the Philippines to treat base compensation as rent and to demand increased payments. Through the early Bush administration, Washington continued to maintain that the bases protected host states from the Soviet threat. But retrenchment of Soviet power and, then, the dissolution of the Soviet Union forced a complete rethinking of this proposition. A reevaluation was also mandatory because budgetary pressures required that support infrastructure be tailored to match smaller forces.

Nevertheless, both the Bush and Clinton administrations stated that overseas bases and U.S. access to various foreign facilities would continue to play a major role in America's global presence. The 1991 and 1994 national security strategy statements, for instance, cited forward presence and crisis response as two of the four key security requirements in the post–Cold War era. These statements asserted, among other things, that crisis response capability and the forward presence of U.S. military forces often buttress alliances, deter aggression, and preserve regional balances.[6]

The Gulf War. Long before the 1991 Persian Gulf War, strategic planners were acutely aware of the importance that European and Pacific bases had for Gulf contingencies. Indeed, the crisis initiated by Iraq's August 1990 invasion of Kuwait demonstrated the utility of many of these bases. For instance, Turkey permitted the United States to use its air bases, Greece allowed the use of its Souda Bay facilities for the transshipment and storage of supplies to Saudi Arabia, and Portugal granted the United States overflight rights and permission to use Lajes Air Base in the Azores. The Philippines played a lesser role, acting as a staging area for amphibious marine units, a logistical center in support of Diego Garcia, and a point of support for many of the blockade ships in the Gulf.

This episode provided at least a partial rationale and justification for a future overseas basing system. However, the system in place by the mid-1990s differed substantially from that which existed in 1990.

FOREIGN POLICY IMPLICATIONS

Base agreements raise several sets of foreign policy issues for host governments. First, by the 1970s or 1980s, the agreements were increasingly seen by many as vestiges of an outdated patron-client relationship. This sentiment was especially evident in the Philippines and Greece. Host governments felt it necessary to demonstrate their independence from the United States.

These governments also sometimes feared that American forces stationed on their territories might interfere in domestic politics. U.S. military actions to aid President Aquino during the December 1989 attempted coup against her government fostered the appearance that she needed to be propped up by Washington, presumably with the quid pro quo of continued U.S. use of Philippine bases. And in 1975 the United States held discussions with separatist elements in the Azores with an eye toward retaining base access there, should communists come to power in Portugal.[7]

The perceived association of a particular government, often a repressive one, with American bases further complicated matters. Political factions often defined themselves as for or against these bases. U.S. base-support aid to the Ferdinand Marcos regime in the Philippines, for example, actually undermined long-term political stability.[8]

Beyond these ramifications, U.S. aid money paid to maintain the bases sometimes affects internal regional relationships or civil-military relations within host nations. Thus, when the United States eliminated ESF aid to Portugal for use of the Azores facilities in FY 1993, Lisbon had to consider directing more budget resources to the islands in order to honor its internal agreement with them. In the Philippines, loss of U.S. bases and a diminution of close, long-standing ties to the U.S. military were sources of considerable concern to the Philippine armed forces.[9]

Another set of foreign policy issues concerns the uneasiness of host governments about becoming entangled in international disputes that may jeopardize their national interests. All base-rights agreements between the United States and base-host countries specify that the latter must be consulted before any U.S. action is undertaken outside the scope of these agreements. Host countries are adamant about this. Just three of many examples illustrate the problem.

First, only Great Britain permitted use of its bases for the 1986 U.S. bombing attack on Libya, while Spain and Portugal expressly denied permission. Likewise, in the Persian Gulf War, both Turks and Greeks worried that allied attacks on Iraq could invite retaliation against their bases. Had Turkey forbidden use of its installations, prosecution of the air war against Iraq in 1991 would have been seriously complicated. Finally, the American commitment to Israel has strained U.S.-host relationships because all of these countries maintain important ties with Arab countries. Only Portugal allowed the United States to use its territory to resupply Israel in the 1973 Arab-Israeli conflict, and Lisbon stated subsequently that it would deny future U.S. requests for such purposes.[10]

Sometimes a reverse danger exists: that the United States might become entangled in disputes that the host state has with third parties. In the early 1980s, the Philippines reportedly attempted, unsuccessfully, to use U.S. base agreements to bolster its claim to the Spratley Islands, claimed by the People's Republic of China. Likewise, Greece won a U.S. promise in 1990 to guarantee Greek territory against an attack from any hostile power, including Turkey.[11]

Lastly, many base-host nations have been concerned about transit and storage of nuclear weapons on and through their territories. Following the 1966 crash in Spain of a U.S. nuclear-armed bomber, for instance, a 1976 U.S.-Spanish defense agreement restricted the storage of nuclear weapons on Spanish territory.

U.S. policy, however, is that Washington will not confirm or deny the presence of nuclear weapons on American ships, aircraft, or bases, and this has created problems with host countries. Thus, Article 8 of the 1987 Philippine constitution bans nuclear weapons from the country's territory, and in 1988, the United States agreed not to store nuclear weapons in the Philippines. But a subsequent dispute over nuclear weapons in transit at Subic Bay Naval Base could not be resolved and contributed to the U.S. military's withdrawal from that country.[12] However, President Bush's 1991 decision to remove all sea-based tactical nuclear weapons and sea-launched cruise missiles from U.S. surface ships and attack submarines made most American overseas bases virtually nuclear free by July 1992.

Foreign Assistance: Budgetary Implications

Early U.S. postwar relations with all base-rights countries involved direct or implied promises of aid. Congress came to accept this practice as a general element of U.S. policy as early as the 1953 basing agreement with Spain. Even the House Appropriations Committee, usually critical of foreign aid under Congressman Otto Passman (D-La.), agreed that security assistance was needed to "assure the maintenance of U.S. military bases abroad."[13] In a spirit of collective defense and comparative advantage, Washington provided military aid, and in return, these nations offered the United States base access.

The notion of paying for this access did not become acutely divisive until the late 1970s when host countries began demanding much more compensation. Annual base-rights payments then increased, especially during the first Reagan administration, although they leveled off at about $1.4 billion in the late 1980s. And while most base-rights aid in FY 1980 was in the form of loans, it was almost all in grant form by the late 1980s, with a small percentage in concessional loans. Base-rights aid remained at this level through the early Bush administration, but only because of the Persian Gulf conflict. It plunged subsequently, as mentioned above.[14]

During the 1980s, base-rights nations acquired a fine-tuned, if inflated, sense of what Washington would pay for the bases. The financial benefit derived from the bases became a key consideration in deciding whether they should remain. However, as the overall foreign aid budget leveled off and then declined, and with fiscal constraints and competing priorities within the foreign aid budget itself, congressional criticism of these programs grew. The demise of the Soviet Union raised the distinct possibility that Congress would end base-rights aid altogether.

Although largely moot by the mid-1990s, two other budget-related issues arose. First, should these aid payments be considered strictly as rent paid for use of foreign bases? As time passed, this became the position of most host nations. The U.S. government, however, never officially adopted this view. Instead, Washington asserted that the bases furthered both American and host country interests. Therefore, they should stand apart from the aid issue. The second issue was whether this aid should come from the Pentagon's budget, especially considering its direct impact on U.S. overseas defense posture. However, despite reasoned arguments for doing this, dating from at least the Fairless Commission report in 1957, base-rights aid remained within the foreign assistance budget.[15]

Executive-Legislative Relations

The executive branch is traditionally uneasy about congressional questioning of painstakingly negotiated international agreements, but today Congress carefully reviews base and facilities agreements and associated undertakings, including promises of aid. The original treaties with base-host countries were negotiated in the 1950s during the Cold War. Subsequent executive branch promises of aid to these countries under the legal penumbra of the early accords were often made without adequate prior consultation with Congress. This would be unthinkable today. The Senate Appropriations Committee in 1988 "strongly reminded" base-rights countries that the president has no constitutional authority to "commit this Committee or the U.S. Congress to pay or obligate 1 cent to them in order to ensure that the U.S. obtains or retains access to foreign military bases."[16] And when the Cold War ended, the House Appropriations Committee urged "graduating" European base-rights nations from the FMF program.[17]

By 1992, executive-legislative tension in this area eased considerably for several reasons:

- Many overseas bases lost their value after the Cold War and were closed.
- The Gulf War demonstrated the utility of *some* overseas basing system to many members of Congress.
- Base payments leveled off, then fell; most base-host countries accepted this, albeit reluctantly.
- The United States withdrew completely from the Philippines in 1992, and a 1990 agreement with Greece reduced American presence in that country.
- Military equipment made "surplus" when the Cold War ended was used as a partial substitute for base aid.
- Burden-sharing arrangements were pursued more actively with Turkey.

BASE-RIGHTS COUNTRIES: ASIA

With the explosion of Mt. Pinatubo in 1991 that rendered Clark Air Base unviable, the collapse of negotiations that fall between Washington and Manila, and the navy's subsequent withdrawal from Subic Bay Naval Base in 1992, the United States moved toward alternative facilities arrangements in the region.[18] The Philippines agreed to resume U.S. Navy ship calls and joint military exercises in 1993, and in 1995, Manila once again tried to invoke a now-much-diluted security tie with Washington in its dispute with China over the Spratley Islands.[19] But the character of American military presence in the Pacific Basin had changed permanently. The U.S. basing system in the Pacific today consists of a combination of various facilities access agreements, commercial relationships, enhanced use of U.S. and allied facilities, and an overall reduction in Pacific fleet forces from Cold War levels.

Arrangements with Singapore typify much of current U.S. posture. Worried about the balance of forces in Asia in a post–Cold War environment, Singapore courted Washington assiduously in an attempt to ensure a continued strong American presence in the region. In November 1990, Singapore agreed to allow American access to its facilities on a nonrental basis. That agreement, supplemented by another in 1992, permits the United States to operate resupply ships from Singapore, repair ships in the country's commercial shipyards, and rotate U.S. Air Force squadrons into a Singapore air base for one month at a time. Singapore also hosts the Seventh Fleet's logistical command task force. The United States does not pay for using the facilities. However, the designation of Singapore as one of only two worldwide ''regional contracting centers'' for the U.S. Navy (the other is in Naples) brings substantial business to the country. Washington also agreed to increase training programs for Singapore's military.[20] The no-cost facilities relationship the United States has enjoyed with Bahrain since the 1950s seems to have been a model of sorts for this more recent relationship with Singapore. Malaysia, Thailand, Indonesia, and Brunei now have analogous access arrangements with the United States.[21] These access arrangements involve neither U.S. aid nor the thorny sovereignty and legal problems associated with traditional base agreements. Moreover, virtually all countries in Southeast Asia, including Vietnam, welcome a U.S. regional presence.

U.S. forces in the Asia-Pacific region were reduced from 135,000 in 1990 to about 100,000 in 1994. Facilities long utilized by the navy, such as those on Guam, received renewed attention, and the security of Japan and South Korea continued to be primary American interests; and these interests were joined by concern about the proliferation of weapons of mass destruction and the rapid rise in Chinese power. Because of its ability to accommodate large deck ships, the Yokosuka Shipyard in Japan is a particularly important facility. By 1996, Japan had agreed to spend about $4 billion annually to host U.S. forces and installations, and it incurred another $1 billion in indirect costs. Indeed, it was less expensive for the U.S. taxpayer to maintain American forces in Japan (and South Korea) than in the United States.[22]

In April 1996, President Clinton and Japanese Prime Minister Ryutaro Hashimoto signed a sweeping new joint declaration on security. The United States agreed to return to Japan all or part of eleven military installations in Okinawa, although Japan would pay for these base closures, and all of the 47,000 U.S. troops in Japan would remain in that nation. Just weeks earlier, the USS *Inde-*

pendence—based in Japan—had been dispatched to Taiwan to deter China from continuing its provocative military maneuvers clearly designed to intimidate Taipei. The joint declaration committed the United States to continue its sizable military presence in Asia, while Japan agreed to provide crucial logistical support to U.S. forces in peacetime and to "study" the prospect of a more active role in the event of war.[23]

BASE-RIGHTS COUNTRIES: EUROPE

Bases in Greece and Turkey often have contributed to tense, even stormy relations with Washington. Compared to U.S. ties with most other NATO allies, relations with Athens and Ankara are "thin." That is, the United States does not share the same depth of political, historical, economic, and (in the case of Turkey) cultural linkages with these two nations that it does with, say, the British Isles, Italy, or Scandinavia. Instead, as noted by former U.S. ambassador to Greece, Monteagle Stearns, the United States had, at least until quite recently, "essentially military relationships with Greece and Turkey, the purposes of which [the United States] defines, depending on political expediency, as either more or less than they are."[24] But even after the disintegration of the Soviet Union, Turkey retains strategic value for the United States. Greece, on the other hand, has not had comparable importance; despite unrest in the Balkans, Greece has only modest strategic significance for the United States today.

Turkey's supportive role during Operations Desert Shield and Desert Storm resulted in a substantial increase in U.S. military and economic assistance in FY 1991 and FY 1992. Other rewards were forthcoming, such as a doubling of Turkey's textile quota. But Turkey—and Greece and Portugal, too—soon confronted a different political climate. Congress had long earmarked mandatory minimum funding levels for Greece and Turkey. For FY 1993, however, Congress reduced FMF base-rights aid and imposed ceilings that established maximum FMF funding levels for concessional loans: Turkey ($450 million), Greece ($315 million), and Portugal ($90 million). Through the efforts of Senator Robert Byrd (D-W.Va.), chairman of the appropriations committee and Ankara's principal advocate in Congress, Turkey received a $200 million ESF grant that year. By FY 1995, Turkey's ESF grant fell to $50 million, Portugal received no base-rights aid, FMF loans were at market rates, and FMF loan levels fell to $365 million for Turkey and $247 million for Greece.[25] By 1996, the State Department's requests for FMF to Turkey and Greece (for FY 1997) were only $175 million and $122.5 million, respectively, and Congress was ill-disposed toward granting the full requests. Congressman Benjamin Gilman (R-N.Y.), chairman of the House International Relations Committee, said that Turkey "is an appropriate case . . . where the United States can graduate a country from a foreign assistance program."[26]

Greece

United States–Greece relations were acrimonious throughout most of the 1980s partly because of the political salience within Greece of the American bases. This changed only after the fall of the Andreas Papandreou government and its replacement in April 1990 by a conservative government. The change in governments and the new European security environment, which lessened the importance of Greek bases, paved the way for the signing of the Mutual Defense and Cooperation Agreement in July 1990. Under this accord, the United States retained only its military facilities on Crete: Souda Bay and Iraklion. The politically visible and sensitive Hellenikon base outside Athens was relinquished, as was a base at Nea Makri. The agreement was more generous toward Greece than seemed justified by its strategic significance. Athens was to continue to receive $7 of aid for every $10 of U.S. aid to Turkey (the ratio is discussed below); U.S. facilities were reduced from four to two; Greece received $1 billion in excess U.S. defense articles; and Washington pledged to guarantee Greek territory against an attack by any country, including Turkey.[27] The future of U.S. bases in Greece, by 1996, hinged more on the continued political clout of pro-Greece members of Congress than it did on either an objective assessment of the bases' utility or internal Greek political currents.

Turkey

U.S. military facilities in Turkey are governed by the 1980 Defense and Economic Cooperation Agreement, an accord that is renewed annually and may be terminated on short notice by either party. Relations between Turkey and the United States before 1980 were often strained, but they warmed during the 1980s, aided by the presence of conservative governments in both countries and the Reagan administration's tolerance of the military regime in Ankara.[28] The Reagan, Bush, and Clinton administrations often requested more aid for Turkey than Congress was willing to approve. From FY 1985 through FY 1995, U.S. foreign assistance to Turkey averaged about $550 million annually, but it fell sharply after that time.

The appropriate level of U.S. aid is a perennial source of tension. Three sets of factors affect this issue: Turkey's determination to modernize its defense forces, congressional insistence on the 7:10 ratio between Greece and Turkey, and the requirement for the United States to weigh growing fiscal and political pressures on the overall foreign aid budget against an assessment of Turkey's strategic importance and its need for aid.

Since much of Turkey's military equipment was outdated, defense modernization became a high priority. Turkey instituted a ten-year force modernization program in 1986, and other major programs were subsequently also undertaken to upgrade the armed forces. Even with a reduction in the size of the Turkish Army, the cost of all these programs has far exceeded U.S. aid levels.[29] Ongoing military modernization, nonetheless, gives Ankara a strong incentive to seek close ties with and maximum assistance from the United States.

Turkey has long been unhappy about the congressionally mandated linkage of aid between itself and Greece. The Turks rightly emphasize their far greater strategic importance to the United States and NATO, much larger military contribution, more urgent military and economic requirements, and multiple external and internal threats. Ankara has some levers of influence in Washington: the consistent backing of successive administrations, skilled professional lobbyists, and the support of a few key members of Congress like Senator Byrd. Moreover, the Israeli government has worked quietly with the Israel lobby since the mid-1980s to further some key Turkish interests.[30] Indeed, in February 1996, Israel and Turkey signed an unprecedented military accord, the first such agreement ever reached by the Jewish state with an Islamic country.[31]

Turkey, however, lacks a powerful Turkish-American lobby with the political clout of Greek-American interest groups. Like the Israel lobby, Greek Americans have been a uniquely successful ethnic group in exerting their political influence for the benefit of a foreign country. Many of the more than 3 million Americans of Greek descent are prosperous and politically active; organizations like the American Hellenic Institute have lobbied effectively for aid to Greece; and Greece has powerful patrons in Congress. The Greek lobby's first major victory came in 1974 with the imposition by Congress of a Turkish aid embargo in reaction to Turkey's invasion of Cyprus.[32] Thereafter, Congress accorded Greece favored treatment, often over executive branch objections. Among other things, Congress has variously given Greece earmarked annual foreign aid allotments, liberal concessional loans, and a guaranteed $30 million grant in military aid whenever Turkey received any grant in military aid.

No privilege accorded Greece was more significant than the 7:10 aid ratio. A 1978 amendment to the Foreign Assistance Act of 1961 (PL 95–384) stipulated that aid to Turkey and Greece should "be designed to insure that the present balance of military strength among countries in the region . . . is preserved." The Greek government determined that balance would be met when Greece received 70 percent of whatever amount of military aid was approved for Turkey. A majority of Congress, led by members with substantial Greek-American constituencies, agreed with Athens. Consequently, the 7:10 ratio has become the de facto definition of the Aegean military balance since 1979. The executive branch persistently resisted this formula, arguing that Turkey's strategic importance far exceeds Greece's and that much of the Greek allotment should go to Turkey. Nonetheless, the 7:10 ratio was maintained rigidly by Congress.[33] However, Turkey's aid package was qualitatively superior: For instance, only Turkey received ESF grants, and in the last years of the Cold War, 90 percent of Turkey's total aid was in grant form, while 90 percent of aid to Greece was in concessional loans. Ankara complained bitterly (and Athens rejoiced) when all FMF aid to Turkey and Greece was put on a concessional loan basis in FY 1993.[34]

From 1946 through 1993, U.S. military aid alone totaled over $8.2 billion to Greece and $12.5 billion to Turkey.[35] After 1993, budgetary pressures and Congress's aversion to foreign aid caused aid levels to drop sharply. This frustrated Turkey, but it was a fact of life to which Ankara had to adjust. Post–Cold War aid to Turkey depended also on judgments about Turkey's strategic value. Ankara's continued significance seemed evident in the 1990–1991 Persian Gulf conflict. President Turgut Ozal cooperated fully with the U.S.-led coalition: He terminated the flow of petroleum from Iraqi pipelines, he opened Incirlik Air Base to U.S. military aircraft, and he deployed 100,000 Turkish troops near the Iraqi border. These actions cost Turkey at least $5.6 billion. Much, but not all, of this amount was offset by aid from the United States, Japan, Saudi Arabia, Kuwait, and others. But the economic burden was not the only cost incurred. The Ozal government was criticized bitterly at home for its role in the anti-Iraq coalition, and terrorist attacks were directed at Turkish and American officials.[36]

Domestic political developments within Turkey could well affect its future relationship with the United States and other countries. Indeed, partly because of domestic politics, the United States can expect less cooperation on non-NATO issues. The Turkish military seized control of the government in 1960, 1971, and 1980. While democracy seems less fragile today, the Turkish government is increasingly critical of American use of its air bases for overflights of Iraq carried out under Operation Provide Comfort, established in 1991 in the wake of the Persian Gulf War.[37] Turkey's poor human rights record also troubles Washington. While successive administrations have not let this upset established relationships, Ankara's use of American and European weapons against Kurdish civilians in Turkey and Iraq has strained its relations with Germany and France and triggered criticism from some members of Congress.[38] Finally, Islamic fundamentalism may someday present a challenge to Turkey's secular government. The first Islamist-led government in 73 years came to power in July 1996 when Necmettin Erbakan became prime minister and his Welfare Party, with more seats in Parliament than any other political party, formed a coalition with the party of former Prime Minister Tansu Ciller. Although, before assuming office, Erbakan had been critical of, among other things, the Israel-Turkey military relationship and U.S. use of Turkish air bases for Operation Provide Comfort, neither he nor the Welfare Party was systematically anti-American or anti-Western. Upon taking office, Erbakan reaffirmed Turkey's status as a ''democratic, secular and social state of law'' and said that Turkey would retain its ties to the West while developing relations with Islamic countries.[39]

However, as a DOD official supportive of continued U.S. aid to Turkey remarked in 1992: ''[W]ith the Soviet Union gone and an independent Armenia next door, to say nothing of the Kurdish problem, Turkey might become a liability rather than an asset.''[40] Ongoing regional conflict could spread, raising the possibility of Turkish military involvement in the Transcaucasus or elsewhere. Turkey reacted vehemently to a military cooperation accord signed in May 1996 between Russia and Armenia, and Ankara expressed harsh opposition to proposed security pacts by Russia with Georgia and Azerbaijan.[41] Prime Minister Ciller warned in 1995 that should Greece extend its territorial waters in the Aegean Sea from six to twelve miles, it would be a "cause of war";[42] only heavy diplomatic pressure from the United States brought Turkey and Greece away from the brink of war in January 1996 in a dispute over the sovereignty of a few islets in the Aegean; and Athens announced a $10 billion armaments program that was designed to keep pace with Turkey's weapons modernization.[43] And Turkish forces moved into northern Iraq in 1992, 1995, and 1996. All of these developments clearly concerned regional states, European members of NATO, Russia, and the United States.

Still, the United States and Turkey should continue to share many common interests. Ankara will pursue an independent course—but within the framework of NATO and the U.S. commitment. To sever these ties exposes Turkey to regional threats, ensures the loss of foreign aid and advantageous military relations with the United States, and distances Turkey economically from the European Union. For the United States, Turkey is strategically positioned to facilitate U.S. political, military, intelligence, and economic interests in the Middle East and Black Sea regions and with the 45 million ethnic Turkic peoples in the former Soviet Central Asian republics. Indeed, Turkey is crucial to a spectrum of issues of importance to the United States, including the future of NATO, peacekeeping in the Balkans (Turkey has trained Bosnian Muslim troops), stability in the Aegean, sanctions against Iraq, relations with the former Soviet republics, peace and stability in the Middle East (Turkey has strained relations with Syria and Iran), and transit routes for Central Asian oil and gas.[44] The enduring U.S. interest in Turkey was well phrased by former U.S. ambassador to Turkey, Morton Abramowitz, as "the need to maintain a stable, secular democracy in a Muslim country in an area of turbulence, poverty, and religious radicalism."[45]

Portugal

Portugal signed its first base-rights treaty with the United States in 1951 to afford Washington access to its military facilities at Lajes Air Base in the Azores. Over the years, Portugal received more than $1.7 billion in military aid and $900 million in ESF before security assistance was ended in FY 1995. The treaty was renewed in 1995 for a five-year period when the United States offered Portugal $173 million in excess defense articles.[46] Unlike Greece and Turkey, Portugal's base relationship with the United States has been relatively free of domestic political controversy. The Lajes Air Base retains utility as a transit point facilitating U.S. strategic mobility in various European and non-European contingencies, although the United States has reduced the size of the base. While Portugal may deny the United States access to Lajes for most Arab-Israeli conflicts, the base's continued value was evident during the Persian Gulf War when

U.S. forces conducted refueling operations there. Portugal granted permission for use of Lajes and for mainland overflights.[47]

BASE-RIGHTS COUNTRIES: THE MIDDLE EAST

American forces have been engaged in combat in the Middle East more often than anywhere else in the world since the 1970s, yet the United States has not used security assistance for the purpose of securing permanent military bases in the region. Before the Iranian revolution of 1979, U.S. forces had access to only one country in the Persian Gulf—Bahrain—and this involved only two or three destroyers and a U.S. Navy command ship. Washington began to negotiate facilities agreements with some Gulf states that year, but before Iraq's 1990 invasion of Kuwait, U.S. access to, and overt presence in, the Persian Gulf states was modest. Since the Gulf War, however, the United States has commonly had 20,000 military personnel, twenty ships, and numerous land-based aircraft in the Gulf region at any one time. Regimes whose survival could hinge on American forward presence in the Persian Gulf region now welcome that presence. The United States currently has access to military facilities in all six moderate Gulf states, it joins in combined exercises with the forces of the Gulf Cooperation Council, it prepositions large quantities of military equipment in the region, and—as in October 1994—Washington responds rapidly to threatening moves by Iraq or Iran.[48] Except for very modest aid under the International Military Education and Training program and the transfer of some surplus military equipment, none of this formidable U.S. posture involves security assistance.

An Israeli Option?

Except for substantial quantities of prepositioned military equipment, the United States maintains no significant military facilities in Israel.[49] However, in 1993, over the opposition of the U.S. Navy and the rest of DOD, AIPAC and pro-Israel legislators like Senator Daniel Inouye (D-Hawaii) urged that elements of the Sixth Fleet be home-ported in Haifa, Israel.[50] Inouye's proposal was not acted upon, but other members of Congress are likely to endorse comparable moves in the future. Advocates of such proposals argue, among other things, that this would stretch U.S. forward presence capabilities, tangibly symbolize Washington's commitment to Israel, and aid Israel's economy. The following are just some of the reasons why home-porting in Haifa, or similar actions, would be inadvisable.[51]

Military Factors. Navy home-porting facilities in Italy and Sicily are satisfactory, and Haifa would not meaningfully extend forward presence. Israel is far from the vital Persian Gulf region—where the United States already has adequate actual and potential presence. Substantial U.S. forces in a small, conflict-prone country like Israel would also be especially vulnerable to attack.

Moreover, there is no persuasive reason for yet another indicator of the deep U.S. commitment to and strategic cooperation with Israel.

Diplomatic Factors. American and Israeli interests in the Middle East often differ. While the two countries interact in many security areas, Washington has been traditionally hesitant about open operational collaboration for fear of upsetting key Arab countries. The future of strategic cooperation with Israel relates importantly to the conclusion of a comprehensive Arab-Israeli peace settlement, one that proves to be stable *over time.* The absence of such a settlement affects the American public's attitude toward Israel, encourages the proliferation of weapons of mass destruction in the region, and subjects U.S. ties with much of the Arab world to constant tension. Home-porting Sixth Fleet ships in Israel, if *ever* advisable, should follow, not precede, such a peace agreement. Beyond this, many Israelis, especially Israeli Defense Force officers, have long opposed a permanent physical presence by American forces on Israeli soil. Israel is dependent on the United States for its survival, but the Jewish state takes justifiable pride in defending itself. American bases would be seen as impugning Israeli sovereignty.

Political Factors. By the late 1980s, for the first time since 1948, much of the American public turned against Israel on several human rights and foreign assistance issues. Military aid, for instance, is particularly unpopular, and Israel-Egypt received almost all U.S. security assistance by the mid-1990s. Moreover, a 1992 survey found that while anti-Semitic beliefs among Americans declined notably from 1962 levels, "stereotypes about Jewish power in the U.S. and American Jewish loyalty to Israel have become more prominent."[52] When U.S. overseas forces fall from Cold War levels, and Americans lose jobs because of military base closings at home, it would be politically imprudent to put foreigners to work by basing elements of the Sixth Fleet in Israel—a developed country that already receives a huge portion of all U.S. foreign aid.

CONCLUSION

Payment of security assistance to foreign nations for the use of their military facilities was a low-profile issue by the mid-1990s. It could soon become a no-profile issue. By 1995, the United States had withdrawn from bases in the Philippines and hundreds of other military installations worldwide, security assistance to Portugal had ceased, the Soviet threat was long gone, and only Greece and Turkey remained as traditional (now, low-cost) base-rights countries. Washington enjoyed cordial relations with the democratic governments in Athens and Ankara and shared substantial strategic interests with the latter. For years, the Greek bases were considered expendable, but aid to Greece was sustained by pro-Greece members of Congress. To a much lesser degree, Turkey also benefited from ethnic politics, even if its sometime benefactor was AIPAC. Ankara was distressed by the declining level and quality of U.S. aid but had reluctantly accepted the situation.

The end of the Cold War demands a persuasive rationale for the continuance of any form of overseas basing system. Operations Desert Shield and Desert Storm indicated both that bases abroad have continued value and that America's friends and allies would allow base usage for purposes deemed beneficial to both parties. Employment of major elements of the U.S. armed forces outside the Western Hemisphere since the Gulf War—whether in deterring Iraq and China or in peacekeeping in the Balkans—has generally reflected some variant of this 1990–1991 experience. That is, U.S. forces (air and ground units, in particular) are often employable overseas only with the full political, military, and financial cooperation of countries that also stand to gain from such employment.

Most Asian, European, and Persian Gulf states want an American military presence in their regions. The facilities access agreement with Singapore symbolizes a healthy turn of events. From Washington's perspective, this form of agreement is attractive since Singapore and other countries in Asia and the Middle East receive no U.S. aid for providing base access. The commercial aspect of the Singapore type of arrangement is notable. Instead of huge, politically awkward American government military facilities, U.S. armed forces rely heavily on in-country commercial contractors.

Base-related security assistance, however, may soon be of only historical interest. A critical Congress and constraints on the federal budget could overcome the traditional reluctance of the executive branch to phase out the remaining two programs. Indeed, the posture of the executive branch was changing: Internal FY 1997 State Department planning documents initially zeroed out base-rights aid to Greece and Turkey.[53] While these two countries will continue to receive excess U.S. defense articles and get preferred treatment in commercial sales of advanced weaponry, the end of an era is in sight.

NOTES

1. Portions of this chapter draw from Duncan L. Clarke and Daniel O'Connor, "U.S. Base-Rights Payments after the Cold War," *Orbis* 37 (Summer 1993), pp. 441–57.

2. In 1988, the United States and Spain concluded a new base accord that closed the American base at Torrejon but allowed other facilities to remain without compensation. This brought the Spanish base relationship into line with U.S. base relationships with other major developed NATO allies such as Germany and Great Britain.

3. U.S. Congress, House, Committee on Appropriations, *Foreign Operations, Export Financing, and Related Programs Appropriations Bills, 1993*, 102d Cong., 2d sess., 1992, Rpt. 102–585, p. 6.

4. Craig M. Brandt, "U.S. Military Bases Overseas: Military Expediency and Political Dilemmas," in Craig M. Brandt, ed., *Military Assistance and Foreign Policy* (Wright-Patterson Air Force Base, Ohio: Air Force Institute of Technology, 1990), p. 185; "Pentagon Adds 83 Bases to Europe Cutbacks," *Washington Post*, January 31, 1992, p. A6; U.S. General Accounting Office [hereafter, GAO], *European Drawdown*, NSIAD-94–195BR, Washington, D.C., June 1994.

5. See James R. Blaker, *United States Overseas Basing: An Anatomy of the Dilemma* (New York: Praeger Publishers, 1990), pp. 29, 63, 68; GAO, *Strategic Air Lift: Further Air Base Reductions in Europe Could Jeopardize Capability*, NSIAD-94–138, Washington, D.C., June 1994.

6. *National Security Strategy of the United States* (Washington, D.C.: Government Printing Office [hereafter, GPO], 1991), pp. 25, 27–29; *A National Security Strategy of Engagement and Enlargement* (Washington, D.C.: GPO, 1994), pp. 7–8.

7. Sheila Coronel, "The Lost Revolution," *Foreign Policy* 84 (Fall 1991), pp. 177–78; Brandt, "U.S. Military Bases Overseas," p. 196.

8. Stanton H. Burnett, *Investing in Security: Economic Aid for Noneconomic Purposes* (Washington, D.C.: Center for Strategic and International Studies, 1992), pp. 53–54.

9. William Branigan, "Philippine Military, Bucking Senators, Urges Retention of U.S. Naval Base," *Washington Post*, August 19, 1991, p. A11.

10. See Richard F. Grimmett, *Current Issues with the "Base Rights" Countries and Their Implications*, Congressional Research Service, Washington, D.C., 1988, p. 4; Brandt, "U.S. Military Bases Overseas," p. 196.

11. William E. Berry, *U.S. Bases in the Philippines: The Evolution of the Special Relationship* (Boulder, Colo.: Westview Press, 1989), pp. 237–38; "U.S.-Greece Sign Agreement on Military Bases," *Washington Post*, July 9, 1990, p. A16.

12. Grimmett, *Current Issues*, pp. 11, 13; "Given One Year's Notice, U.S. Begins to Pull Out of Subic Base," *Washington Post*, December 28, 1991, p. A15.

13. U.S. Congress, House, Committee on Appropriations, *Mutual Security Appropriations Bill for 1958*, 85th Cong., 1st sess., 1957, Rpt. 1172, p. 5.

14. U.S. Agency for International Development [hereafter, AID], *U.S. Overseas Loans and Grants: July 1, 1945–September 30, 1993*, Washington, D.C., 1994.

15. For an extended discussion of these issues, see Clarke and O'Connor, "U.S. Base-Rights Payments," pp. 445–49.

16. U.S. Congress, Senate, Committee on Appropriations, *Foreign Operations, Export Financing, and Related Programs Appropriations Bill, 1989*, 100th Cong., 1st sess., 1988, Rpt. 100–395, p. 179.

17. House Committee, *Foreign Operations . . . 1993*, p. 10.

18. The tight relationship between U.S. economic aid and military bases contributed greatly both to the limited effectiveness of the overall aid program to the Philippines and to political instability. See Ernest H. Preeg, *Neither Fish nor Fowl: U.S. Economic Aid to the Philippines for Noneconomic Objectives* (Washington, D.C.: Center for Strategic and International Studies, 1991); Robert F. Zimmerman, *Dollars, Diplomacy & Dependency: Dilemmas of U.S. Economic Aid* (Boulder, Colo.: Lynne Reinner, 1993), p. 116.

19. Keith Richburg, "Dispute Over Islands and China's Gunboats Roiling Asian Waters," *Washington Post*, June 5, 1995, p. A14; William Branigan, "U.S., Russia in Race to Sell Arms in Asia," *Washington Post*, July 31, 1993, p. A17.

20. John Yang, "Singapore Agrees to Host Navy Unit," *Washington Post*, January 4, 1992, p. A13; Steven Erlanger, "The Search for a New Security Umbrella," *New York Times*, May 12, 1991, p. E2.

21. U.S. Department of Defense [hereafter, DOD], Office of International Security Affairs, *United States Security Strategy for the East Asia–Pacific Region*, Washington, D.C., 1995, p. 29; David B. H. Denoon, *Real Reciprocity: Balancing U.S. Economic and*

Security Policy in the Pacific Basin (New York: Council on Foreign Relations, 1993), pp. 38, 41.

22. DOD, *United States Security Strategy for the East Asia–Pacific Region*, pp. 23–25; Joseph S. Nye, Jr., "U.S. Presence: Oxygen for Asia," *Washington Post*, December 8, 1995, p. A27.

23. Kevin Sullivan and John Harris, "Clinton Hails Partnership With Japan," *Washington Post*, April 18, 1996, p. A1; Kevin Sullivan and Mary Jordan, "U.S. to Trim 11 Bases on Okinawa," *Washington Post*, April 16, 1996, p. A1.

24. Monteagle Stearns, *Entangled Allies: U.S. Policy toward Greece, Turkey, and Cyprus* (New York: Council on Foreign Relations, 1992), p. 23.

25. AID, *U.S. Overseas Loans and Grants*, pp. 163, 173, 181; U.S. Department of State, *Congressional Presentation for Foreign Operations, Fiscal Year 1996*, Washington, D.C., 1996, pp. 315, 348, 364.

26. Philip Finnegan, "U.S. Budget Battle Brews over Aid to Turkey, Greece," *Defense News*, April 1–7, 1996, p. 10; idem, "U.S. House Panel Cuts Aid to Turkey, Greece," *Defense News*, June 3–9, 1996, p. 6.

27. "U.S.-Greece Sign Agreement," p. A16; "Greece and U.S. Sign 8 Year Pact Exchanging Arms Aid for Extended Use of Bases," *New York Times*, July 9, 1990, p. A8.

28. Bruce Kuniholm, "Turkey and NATO: Past, Present, and Future," *Orbis* 27 (Summer 1983), p. 431.

29. David Silverberg, "Turkey Seeks Sleeker Force through 1990s," *Defense News*, February 24, 1992, p. 14; "Turkey's Armed Forces: A Modernizing Military," *DISAM Journal* 17 (Spring 1995), pp. 1–33.

30. Philip Robins, *Turkey and the Middle East* (New York: Council on Foreign Relations, 1991), p. 84; Steve Pressman, "Countries Turn to Professionals for Lobbying," *Congressional Quarterly Weekly Report* (December 15, 1984), pp. 3104–5.

31. Turkey and Israel had significant, if quiet, strategic ties before 1996. See Andrew Mango, *Turkey: The Challenge of a New Role* (Washington, D.C.: Center for Strategic and International Studies, 1994), pp. 116–17; Barbara Opall, "Israel, Turkey Establish Strategic Relations," *Defense News*, April 25–May 1, 1994, p. 1. The sweeping 1996 agreement covered, among other things, joint military training and exercises in Turkey and Israel, transfers of sensitive defense technologies, and intelligence sharing. While some lauded the agreement, pointing to shared strategic interests and other commonalities between the two countries, it is fraught with risks for Turkey. The Turkish military—a primary defender of a secular Turkey, if not always of democracy—was the driving force behind the accord. The agreement was soon denounced by Egypt, Syria, Iran, and Iraq and, more ominously, by powerful Islamist forces within Turkey itself, including the man who became prime minister in 1996: Necmettin Erbakan. Moreover, Turkey sent its first ambassador to Israel only after the 1993 Israeli-Palestinian peace accord; a reversal of the Arab-Israeli peace process could make the 1996 military agreement a political albatross for Ankara. See Gil Sedan, "New Turkish Prime Minister Critical of Israeli Alliance," *Washington Jewish Week*, July 4, 1996, p. 16; John Pomfret, "Turkey Strengthens Ties to Israel," *Washington Post*, June 2, 1996, p. A24.

32. See Paul Watanabe, *Ethnic Groups, Congress, and American Foreign Policy: The Politics of the Turkish Arms Embargo* (Westport, Conn.: Greenwood Press, 1984); Thomas Franck and Edward Weisband, *Foreign Policy by Congress* (New York: Oxford

University Press, 1979), pp. 35–45; Neil A. Lewis, "Greece and Turkey, the Local War," *New York Times*, March 26, 1987, p. B8.

33. Stearns, *Entangled Allies*, pp. 40–50. Unlike most analysts, Stearns finds merit in the 7:10 ratio.

34. AID, *U.S. Overseas Loans and Grants*, pp. 163, 181.

35. Ibid.

36. Bruce Kuniholm, "Turkey and the West," *Foreign Affairs* 70 (Spring 1991), pp. 35–38; Sabri Sayari, "Turkey: The Changing European Security Environment and the Gulf Crisis," *Middle East Journal* 46 (Winter 1992), pp. 13–14.

37. Just months before he became prime minister in 1996, Necmettin Erbakan declared, "When we come to power, the first thing we will do will be to ask this force to kindly leave Turkey." Umit Enginsoy, "Kurd Debate Underscores U.S.-Turkish Relations," *Defense News*, July 15–21, 1996, p. 4.

38. John Pomfret, "Turkish Premier Assails Kurdish Attack's Critics," *Washington Post*, April 5, 1995, p. A21; Thomas W. Lippman, "Turkey Catches Flak in Congress," *Washington Post*, March 23, 1995, p. A24.

39. Kelley Courtier, "Islamic Leader Wins Approval Vote in Turkey," *Washington Post*, July 9, 1996, p. A10; Eric Rouleau, "Turkey: Beyond Ataturk," *Foreign Policy* 103 (Summer 1996), pp. 76–80.

40. Interview of DOD official by Duncan L. Clarke, Washington, D.C., March 1992.

41. Umit Enginsoy, "Turkish-Russian Contretemps Could Thwart NATO Expansion," *Defense News*, May 13–19, 1996, p. 1; Shireen Hunter, "The Muslim Republics of the Former Soviet Union: Policy Challenges for the United States," *Washington Quarterly* 15 (Summer 1992), pp. 66–69.

42. D. G. Kousouolas, "The Aegean as 'a Greek Lake,' " *Washington Post*, July 16, 1996, p. A15.

43. Ibid.

44. Thomas Lippman, "End of Cold War Enhances Turkey's Standing in West," *Washington Post*, March 29, 1996, p. A30; Ziya Onis, "Turkey in the Post–Cold War Era: In Search of Identity," *Middle East Journal* 49 (Winter 1995), pp. 57–62.

45. Morton I. Abramowitz, "Turkey after Ozal," *Foreign Policy* 91 (Summer 1993), p. 181.

46. AID, *U.S. Overseas Loans and Grants*, p. 173; Col. Jesse M. Perez, "Portugal," *DISAM Journal* 18 (Fall 1995), p. 7.

47. GAO, *Strategic Airlift*; U.S. Congress, House, Subcommittee on Europe and the Middle East, Committee on Foreign Affairs, *Hearings and Markup: Foreign Assistance Legislation for Fiscal Years 1992–93*, 102d Cong., 1st sess., 1991, pt. 3, pp. 54–55.

48. DOD, Office of International Security Affairs, *United States Security Strategy for the Middle East*, Washington, D.C., May 1995, pp. 1–3, 29.

49. The U.S. armed forces have never been enthusiastic about stocking such large quantities of military supplies in Israel. Israel's friends in Congress, not the U.S. military, are primary advocates of the prepositioning. See Shai Feldman, *The Future of U.S.-Israel Strategic Cooperation* (Washington, D.C.: Washington Institute for Near East Policy, 1996), pp. 45–46.

50. Richard Sia, "U.S. Considers Building Navy Base at Israeli Port," *Houston Chronicle*, February 18, 1993, p. A18.

51. Interview by Duncan L. Clarke with White House official, Washington, D.C., March 1993; Karen L. Puschel, *U.S.-Israeli Strategic Cooperation in the Post–Cold War*

Era: An American Perspective (Boulder, Colo.: Westview Press, 1992), pp. 145–62; David Makovsky, "Pentagon Wary of Enhanced Cooperation with Israel," *Jerusalem Post*, March 18, 1993, p. A1; William H. Rowden and Andrew Dallas, *Port of Haifa Study: Summary Report* (Alexandria, Va.: Center for Naval Analysis, May 1993); Feldman, *The Future of U.S.-Israel Strategic Cooperation*, pp. 45–46. These remarks are not directed at the separate issue of stationing of American troops in the Golan as part of a peace settlement with Syria.

52. Anti-Defamation League of B'nai B'rith, *Highlights from an Anti-Defamation League Study on Anti-Semitism and Prejudice in America*, New York, November 16, 1992, pp. 14, 18–19.

53. Interview of senior State Department official by Jason Ellis, Washington D.C., June 1996.

7

The Lion's Share: Egypt and Israel

From the late 1970s through FY 1997, Israel annually received at least $3 billion in security assistance: $1.8 billion in military aid under the Foreign Military Financing program and $1.2 billion in economic aid under the Economic Support Fund. Egypt commonly received yearly amounts of about $2.1 billion in security aid: $1.3 billion in FMF and $815 million in ESF.[1] Annual U.S. aid to Israel and Egypt throughout this period constituted between 33 and 43 percent of the entire foreign assistance budget. These two countries dominated the security assistance program, and their prominence within that program accelerated after the Cold War. About 92 percent of all security assistance went to Israel-Egypt in FY 1997. Total reported U.S. aid (loans and grants) to Egypt by that time stood at $49 billion, 75 percent of which was security assistance. Total U.S. aid to Israel (excluding $9.8 billion in housing loan guarantees) was more than $71 billion, about 90 percent of which was security assistance.[2] Moreover, 30 percent of the entire U.S. foreign affairs budget (function 150 account)—which funds, among other things, all forms of foreign aid, the State Department and three other foreign affairs agencies, the Peace Corps, and contributions to the United Nations and other international organizations—is currently consumed by aid to Egypt and Israel.[3]

As stunning as these amounts are, they substantially understate the magnitude of assistance. This is because these figures are in current, not constant, dollars (i.e., inflation is not taken into account) and because they do not reflect the numerous special privileges accorded to Israel. When the value of these privileges is computed, an average of at least $500 million annually is generally added to the $3 billion–plus in officially reported yearly aid to Israel since FY 1985.[4]

Since the 1970s, the U.S. government's rationale for aid to Israel and Egypt has become a virtual mantra, repeated by successive administrations. Declaratory U.S. policy asserts that the aid is designed primarily to secure "a just and lasting comprehensive peace" between Israel and its neighbors, especially Egypt; re-affirm the U.S. commitment to a democratic Israel; promote regional stability by helping Egypt modernize its armed forces; and encourage sustainable development and a market-oriented economy in Egypt.[5] U.S. government publications proclaim an "unshakable" U.S. commitment to Israel "for historic, political, and moral reasons."[6]

Historic, moral, and strategic reasons are certainly factors in America's commitment to Israel. Fundamentally, however, this relationship is driven and sustained by domestic political forces in the United States. Egypt receives a high level of aid because those forces, and administration officials, rightly view peace between Egypt and Israel as vital to the security of the Jewish state. Aid to Egypt (and to Jordan and the Palestinian Authority) is largely derivative of aid to Israel. The unabashed political purposes of aid to Egypt were, and remain, to reward Cairo for making and maintaining peace with Israel; to build mass support within Egypt for the peace treaty with Israel by using ESF aid, development assistance, and PL 480 food aid to create a link between peace and a more open, prosperous society; and to secure a strategic relationship between Egypt and the United States.

EGYPT

The key political objectives of U.S. aid to Egypt were realized. The aid almost certainly helped solidify peace between Egypt and Israel; it allowed Egypt to stand apart from the rest of the Arab World after the Camp David Accords. In 1990–1991, Egypt joined the United States, Saudi Arabia, and others in rolling back Saddam Hussein's invasion of Kuwait. Cairo and Washington now have close strategic ties, and Egypt once again has a leading role among Arab states. Moreover, U.S. economic aid has brought some tangible benefits, especially to the country's physical infrastructure; and while hardly a showcase for liberal democracy, Egypt now has a legal political opposition and enjoys one of the freer presses in the Arab World.

Despite these successes, a thorough reassessment of U.S.-Egyptian relations is long overdue, particularly concerning foreign assistance. Egypt's importance for the United States after the Cold War, while substantial, diminished appreciably with the dissolution of the Soviet Union. Moreover, the September 1993 Declaration of Principles with the Palestine Liberation Organization (PLO) initiated a peace process between Israel and key Arab actors, and whatever the eventual outcome of this process, it is increasingly difficult to justify paying Cairo huge sums to do what is, presumably, in Cairo's best interests: remain at peace with Israel. In addition, political and fiscal realities in the United States have taken a toll on the overall foreign aid budget and will likely affect Egypt.

Finally, the aid program with Egypt is so riddled with endemic weaknesses that program results have often been mixed or counterproductive.

While Egypt does not have the level of societal instability of, say, Algeria, it suffers pronounced political, social, and economic debilities. Per capita gross domestic product fell between 1986 and the mid-1990s to a mere $600, unemployment stood at more than 20 percent, and a 1994 report by the United Nations found that Egypt was "in danger of joining the world's list of failed states."[7] Civil strife between Egyptian security forces and Islamic insurrectionists since 1990 has claimed thousands of lives, including those of leading politicians, media figures, and intellectuals. Partly because of this, there have been widespread human rights abuses by the government. Political participation has also been severely restricted. Indeed, President Hosni Mubarak's insistence on personal, centralized control of decision-making has effectively thwarted the emergence of a representative political class. Moreover, although the military and security forces are privileged elements in a sea of poverty and U.S. military aid pays more than 50 percent of Egypt's defense budget, this segment of society has not escaped a variety of afflictions. Included among them is a widening social and political gap between officers and enlisted men and penetration of the security forces by Islamist radicals, especially in southern Egypt.[8]

The absence of vigorous, reliable Egyptian advocates of the United States is particularly striking. American-trained Egyptian military officers and civilians often find their careers sidetracked; there is no sizable core of secular, educated, moderate, U.S.-supportive political activists; almost all opposition parties, in varying degrees, are anti-American; and some of these parties, as well as some Egyptian economists, contend that the huge U.S. aid program has cost the country too much of its sovereignty—a view mirrored in a popular (if erroneous) description of the U.S. aid bureaucracy as Egypt's "shadow cabinet."[9]

The economic and military aid programs for Egypt have been repeatedly faulted for mismanagement and inefficiency,[10] but there is a more basic problem. While short-term U.S. political goals have been realized, the highly politicized nature of the program undermines its long-term effectiveness. That is, Egyptian officials have always recognized that this aid is forthcoming because of supposed U.S. strategic interests and, especially, because of entrenched support for Israel in Congress and in successive U.S. administrations. Almost from the program's inception, Egypt viewed the aid as an assured entitlement for having made peace with Israel. As long as Cairo honored the peace treaty and did not upset a Middle East peace process, it *knew* that aid would continue to flow. That is, its aid allotment would not be cut substantially unless Israel's was also reduced.[11] With such an assurance, it was predictable that attempts by Washington to place additional conditions on this aid would be successfully resisted by Egypt, even when they promised to improve program effectiveness. Partly as a consequence, U.S. aid has promoted neither sustainable economic development nor much-needed economic reform. This can only impact negatively on U.S. interests and political objectives.[12]

The overriding political imperatives of encouraging Egypt to remain at peace with Israel and to assist in (or not impede) a peace process between Israel and other Arab actors have usually deterred Congress and the executive branch from vigorously overseeing the program, pressuring Egypt to take corrective measures, or reducing aid levels substantially. An example of this "hands-off" approach (although here Congress also sought to subsidize American wheat farmers) was PL 480 food assistance. Although Egypt was the major recipient of U.S. food aid, and Egyptians were so abundantly supplied with American grain that many farmers fed their cattle loaves of bread made from this grain, until 1992 the State Department and many in Congress resisted cutting the program.[13] Concerning the overall aid package to Egypt, former AID official Robert Zimmerman finds that "No one in the State Department or elsewhere in the U.S. government wants to risk an embarrassing assessment of how aid resources have failed to stimulate the type of economic, social, and political development necessary for self-sustaining peace in the Middle East."[14]

Finally, Egyptian-Israeli relations have rarely been cordial, and most segments of Egyptian society deeply distrust Israel.[15] A December 1994 poll indicated that a majority of Egyptians even opposed maintaining formal ties with Israel.[16] Egypt's defense minister reportedly remarked in 1993 that his country's military modernization was aimed at Iran and Israel, and—partly because of Israel's nuclear weapons capability and Jerusalem's repeated refusals to begin denuclearization talks with Egypt and other Arab states—Cairo has rejected several U.S. attempts to initiate direct channels of communication between the Israeli and Egyptian militaries.[17] Moreover, Egypt reacted harshly to the hard-line Likud government that assumed office in 1996.[18]

ISRAEL

A reassessment of the aid program to Israel is also in order. Threats to Israel's security will surely continue for many years, but prior to Binyamin Netanyahu's 1996 assumption to prime minister, Israel's security was more assured than at any time in its history. The Cold War was over, Israel's security tie with the United States was intimate, the Israeli Defense Force was preeminent militarily in the region, the solid front of hostile Arab states was gradually eroding, and (critically) the peace process was largely on track. Tragically, however, some of the security threats to Israel were aggravated or engendered by Prime Minister Netanyahu's resistive approach to the peace process (discussed below). This had the potential of affecting the flow of American aid.

In addition to the regional security situation, several interrelated factors could affect the future of the largest U.S. foreign aid program. They include strategic considerations, domestic political forces in the United States, American public opinion toward Israel and foreign assistance, the supposed relationship between aid and influence, pressures to balance the federal budget, and Israel's own conception of the continued utility of foreign aid.

The Strategic Relationship

While a full treatment of the subject is beyond the scope of this study, it is evident that strategic and geopolitical considerations rooted in traditional realist assumptions about foreign policy, while germane, tell relatively little about the unique, often-labeled "special relationship" between the United States and Israel. Indeed, it was not until the September 1970 crisis between Jordan and Syria that the White House first saw Israel as having potential strategic utility for the United States—although Israel's influence on the outcome of that crisis was "secondary at best."[19] By at least 1972, however, President Nixon no longer considered Israel to be a source of regional stability; in fact, he came to believe that Israel and its organized American supporters often undermined U.S. interests.[20] Most executive branch officials in 1970, as in the 1980s and today, did not/do not see Israel as a net strategic asset.[21] The attitude of a former Pentagon official is typical: "Israel's strategic value to the United States was always grotesquely exaggerated. When we were drafting contingency plans for the Middle East in the 1980s, we found that the Israelis were of little value to us in 95 percent of the cases."[22]

"Strategic cooperation" between the two countries, first formalized in 1983, was spearheaded by a small band of American supporters of Israel and a handful of senior officials (some of whom later regretted it, including Robert McFarlane, President Reagan's national security adviser) over the opposition of the secretary of defense, joint chiefs of staff, and much of the State Department below the level of the secretary.[23] Secretary of State George Shultz later told AIPAC executive director Thomas Dine that he hoped to make it impossible for a future secretary of state who might be less supportive of Israel "to overcome the bureaucratic relationship between Israel and the U.S." created during the Reagan years.[24] Close security cooperation continues today, although it is even less important to Washington than it was in the past. Only a crisis in the relationship seems likely to weaken this "strategic" tie.

A national interest-based rationale (among others) will continue to be employed publicly by Israel, its American advocates, and the U.S. government to justify the flow of American aid. But while the United States derives some benefits from the relationship—in counterterrorism cooperation and intelligence exchange, for instance—these public assertions are widely discounted in private by many U.S. national security officials.[25] Even some committed American supporters of Israel like Bernard Reich agree that "Israel is of limited military or economic importance to the United States. . . . It is not a strategically vital state."[26] Israeli analyst Shai Feldman concurs: "[T]he strategic dimension of America's motivation for supporting Israel never comprised the core of these relations. Rather . . . 'softer' value-based considerations and the nature of American domestic politics combined to play a much more important role.''[27]

Arab-Israeli Peace Process

One of the major interests continuously central to U.S. Middle East policy from at least the Nixon administration to the present has been the promotion of peace between Israel and its neighbors. A joint statement issued by President Clinton and Israeli Prime Minister Shimon Peres in April 1996 anchored their "strategic partnership" in two main principles: the U.S. commitment to Israel and a mutual determination to achieve a "comprehensive" Middle East peace settlement.[28] Joseph Alpher, former director of the Jaffee Center for Strategic Studies at Tel Aviv University, asserts that a commendable condition for future "American strategic support for Israel" may be one that "*requires* that Israel remain pledged to a workable peace process.''[29] Similarly, the "working premise" of a spring 1996 study by Shai Feldman that projected closer strategic relations between the United States and Israel in the future was that the "current phase of the Arab-Israeli peace process will be completed by the end of this decade, resulting in peace agreements between Israel and Syria and Lebanon.''[30] Should the United States perceive Israel to be largely responsible for disrupting or ending a peace process that had made substantial headway by May 1996, relations between the two countries could cool considerably. In time, this perception might lead to the kind of crisis that would have a corrosive impact on strategic cooperation.[31]

This scenario became less hypothetical when Binyamin Netanyahu defeated Shimon Peres. Netanyahu questioned key assumptions that had undergirded negotiations between Israel and the Palestinian Authority; he also challenged some conditions that were widely seen as necessary for a more comprehensive peace settlement, such as the land-for-peace principle, which is an essential basis for negotiations. Yet Netanyahu deflected Egyptian President Hosni Mubarak's July 1996 warning—that it would be "very dangerous" to discontinue the pursuit of territorial settlements—by reiterating his often-expressed view that this principle was subject to "differing interpretations.''[32] By the fall of 1996 the outlook was bleak. President Mubarak and Jordan's King Hussein (whose domestic base of support for engagement with Israel was fragile) both denounced Netanyahu for the impasse, a summit meeting in Washington to resolve the problem was largely unsuccessful, Israel was a politically polarized country, its Likud government appeared to lack the will to move toward final status negotiations with the Palestinian Authority, and there was virtually no likelihood of a peace treaty between Israel and either Syria or Lebanon.[33]

This gloomy prognosis changed only marginally and fleetingly when Netanyahu, in January 1997, finally decided to honor an agreement struck by his Labor government predecessor to withdraw Israeli troops from 80 percent of the city of Hebron. Israeli-Palestinian negotiations resumed, but U.S. officials confirmed that the scope and timing of future West Bank withdrawals would be determined unilaterally by Israel.[34] Contrary to Secretary of State Warren Christopher, Netanyahu and Yasser Arafat clearly had not "found common cause,"[35] and Israeli settlement and highway construction on the West Bank continued apace.[36] Indeed, Netanyahu's provocative decision to build a huge housing project for Jews in the Har Homa area of East Jerusalem brought the peace process to a complete halt by March 1997 and incurred the wrath of virtually every country in the world. Even the Clinton administration issued tepid criticisms while, at the same time, the United States vetoed an otherwise unanimous U.N. Security Council resolution condemning the housing project as "illegal and a major obstacle to peace."[37]

As early as March 1993, President Clinton had made it clear that his strategy for an Arab-Israeli peace settlement was to provide Israel with such generous military, economic, and political support that it would be confident about taking "risks for peace"—such as withdrawing from the West Bank and the Golan Heights.[38] Indeed, no American president was a more consistently magnanimous benefactor of Israel. Yet Netanyahu's cautious, even obstinate, attitude toward the peace process in 1996, and especially his lifting of the previous government's restraints on expanding Jewish settlements in the West Bank, raised doubts about the wisdom of the strategy pursued by the Clinton administration. While President Clinton did not have the close personal relationship with Netanyahu that he had had with Labor Prime Ministers Yitzhak Rabin and Shimon Peres, neither he nor Congress seemed prepared to exert sustained, meaningful pressure on Israel, let alone withhold foreign aid.[39] Indeed, Netanyahu boldly threatened to "activate" the pro-Israel lobby in America "in order to stand up to pressure" that might come from Washington.[40]

The Domestic Political Process

If strategic importance is a secondary or tertiary consideration in explaining the closeness of America's tie to Israel, the legacy of the Holocaust and Israel's democratic character are central. Yet even they acquire explanatory power only as themes that play out in the context of the domestic American political process. Congress and special interest groups, especially ethnic lobbies, often have a decisive impact on foreign assistance policy (Chapter 5). The influence of Congress and interest groups on U.S. foreign policy is nowhere more evident than with regard to aid to Israel.

Former chairman of the House Committee on Foreign Affairs, Congressman Clement Zablocki (D-Wis.), remarked in 1976 that "Congress is too responsive to the lobbies of ethnic and special interests in the U.S. to be able to take the lead in foreign policymaking without endangering the national interest."[41] Congress does, indeed, appear to be particularly responsive to select ethnic lobbies.[42] This is certainly so concerning Congress's interrelationship with AIPAC, easily the most successful of such lobbies. Many Jewish-American groups and individuals (and others) seek to influence Congress and, often, the administration on matters of Middle East policy, but AIPAC is a registered lobby working to advance Israel's interests. (AIPAC maintains that it furthers American national interests by encouraging close, mutually beneficial U.S.-Israel ties.)[43] Some strong defenders of Israel and AIPAC, like Steven Spiegel, downplay the impact of the Israel lobby and contend that most policy decisions affecting Israel are made on the basis of objective U.S. national interests "unrelated to domestic politics."[44] However, few scholars, independent observers, U.S. government officials, informed Israelis, or even committed American partisans of Israel agree with Spiegel.[45] For instance, Orthodox rabbi Dov Zakheim, a former Pentagon official with close personal ties to Israel, relates: "Virtually all informed Israelis recognized that congressional pliability on . . . any policy relating to Israel did not necessarily connote sincere agreement with that policy. It was as much a reflection of domestic U.S. politics, most notably of deference to AIPAC and to Israel's other Washington allies on all matters relating to Israel."[46]

As with the above treatment of strategic cooperation, this study is not an appropriate locus for a thorough analysis of AIPAC and associated groups. Still, a central focus of the lobby, perhaps its primary mission, has been to maintain or expand Israel's annual foreign aid allocation. The realization of this objective hinges critically on the effectiveness of the lobby and its allies in influencing the U.S. government's most reliable backer of Israel: the U.S. Congress. What follows is a summary of some of the factors that appear to explain the clout of this interest group in Congress.

Seymour Martin Lipset and Earl Raab find that the factors explaining "the political influence of the Jews" include "heavy financial contributions, their disproportionate presence in opinion-making professions (such as journalism and academia), extraordinary levels of activism and voting, an extensive organization network, and . . . sizable blocs of Jewish voters in key states."[47] Equally important, there is only one weighty interest group in the domestic political game to affect U.S. Middle East policy: the organized Jewish community. That is, there is no effective countervailing political force to deflect congressional responsiveness to this group. Arab Americans, for instance, are insignificant players.[48]

Members of Congress who seek reelection, as most do, place a special premium on two things: votes and money. When foreign assistance is at stake, the Israel lobby has demonstrated repeatedly that it can deliver both. An extraordinary indicator of the potential political leverage of the American Jewish community (2.3 percent of the nation's population) on this and other issues is that it commonly contributes between 25 and 33 percent of *all* funds collected by major political campaigns in the United States.[49] Because of huge political contributions, Jewish activists broadly agree that "[w]e have access [to political leaders] far beyond our numbers."[50] This may also be one reason why pro-Israel forces win well over 90 percent of the roll call votes affecting Israel and why they get their way on ESF and other economic aid to Israel 82 percent of the time—even over presidential opposition.[51] It is not surprising, therefore, that both the former editor of AIPAC's newsletter and an outspoken critic of AIPAC can agree that while its influence is not limitless, the Israel lobby substantially "shapes" U.S. Middle East policy.[52]

Another factor in AIPAC's success is a close-knit network of congressional staff members who serve variously as aides, informants, decisionmakers, and whistle-blowers. Morris Amitay, former executive director of AIPAC, remarked that there are many congressional staff members "who happen to be Jewish, who are willing . . . to look at certain issues in terms of their Jewishness, and this is what has made this thing go effectively. . . . [They] are in a position to make the decisions in these areas for senators."[53] Most of AIPAC's lobbyists have served on congressional staffs, and many well-placed congressional staff members are former AIPAC employees. The political intelligence network is the envy of other lobbies.[54] Former AIPAC legislative director Douglas Bloomfield states frankly that AIPAC lobbyists "are treated as colleagues by our former colleagues, as tutors by the younger staffers and as equals by members of Congress themselves. . . . One aide frequently would tip off AIPAC of unfriendly plans hatched by his boss."[55] That AIPAC has clout on foreign assistance legislation and most other issues relating to Israel's welfare is virtually axiomatic in Washington, especially in Congress. Concerning aid to Israel, a senior staff member on a Senate committee said, "It is very difficult to even ask questions on this topic because of fear of firing up the pro-Israel lobby."[56]

There are countless instances, and some detailed case studies, of the influence of the lobby and of other Jewish organizations or individuals on Israel-related issues. AIPAC, for instance, is substantially responsible for the United States paying most of the research and development costs of Israel's largest defense program, the Arrow missile, despite severe criticism of the program by the U.S. General Accounting Office and opposition from the U.S. Army and most of the rest of the national security bureaucracy. Indeed, AIPAC was wholly responsible for defeating major proposed *domestic* legislation that threatened funding for the Arrow.[57] Friends of Israel, working through Congress, have been regularly successful in channeling U.S. foreign assistance to Israel and Israelis.[58]

AIPAC's clout was evident during the 1995–1996 debates over the foreign assistance budget when a Republican-controlled Congress slashed most major aid programs except those for the untouchables, Israel and Egypt. The lobby's influence was apparent in May 1995 when President Clinton, accompanied by Israeli Prime Minister Yitzhak Rabin, addressed AIPAC's annual conference. The president, who had been unusually solicitous of Israel's welfare, asked for AIPAC's customary support for the entire administration foreign aid package.[59] Yet AIPAC shocked the administration and its staunchest congressional allies by supporting the much-smaller Republican foreign aid bill.[60] The Republicans, after all, were in the majority, and the bill contained guaranteed full funding for Israel-Egypt. The lobby's standing with the administration was untarnished, however, partly because AIPAC and the Israeli government successfully lobbied

Congress for two high-priority administration programs: aid to Jordan and the Palestinian Authority.[61] Many conservative members of Congress normally critical of foreign aid ultimately voted for the leaner FY 1996 bill (42 percent of which went to Israel-Egypt) so as not to impede an ongoing Arab-Israeli peace process and to avoid antagonizing AIPAC and other Jewish groups. Referring to Congress's fear of AIPAC, Congressman Tim Valentine (D-N.C.) remarked: "[I]n private conversations, many members" support cutting aid to Israel, but "in public they won't even breathe that."[62]

Fear of AIPAC and allied groups and, for some members, a genuine personal attachment to Israel are among the reasons why Congress has exercised virtually no oversight of U.S. aid to the Jewish state. Moreover, through both direct and indirect means, Congress often has deterred the executive branch from carefully monitoring the program. As a consequence, the largest foreign assistance program in history—larger than the Marshall Plan, even in constant dollars—goes unmonitored by Congress and is only loosely monitored by the executive. This has meant, among other things, that despite numerous instances of improper and illegal Israeli uses of U.S. aid, there are virtually no congressional oversight hearings on these matters;[63] Congress has never acted on any of the several State Department reports mandated by the Arms Export Control Act (PL 90–629) concerning Israel's unauthorized retransfers of U.S. technology; there has never been a comprehensive, systematic audit of Israel's FMF account—by far the largest U.S. military aid program; and executive branch officials who uncover improprieties by the Israelis, such as former State Department Inspector General Sherman Funk, risk congressional retribution.[64]

Public Opinion

Possible circumstantial evidence of the influence of AIPAC and associated groups may be suggested by polling data on public opinion about U.S. aid to Israel. That is, especially since the end of the Cold War, there has been a wide gap between, on the one hand, the public's critical attitudes about aid to Israel and Egypt and, on the other hand, consistently high levels of foreign assistance to these two nations. Hence, there must be some explanation other than public opinion for this generous aid, such as special interest group influence and/or a conviction by members of Congress that Israel and Egypt are vital U.S. interests and are, therefore, uniquely deserving.

The government of Israel and American Jewish organizations make prodigious efforts to influence American public opinion, particularly leadership (elite) opinion. For instance, the Israeli Foreign Ministry alone, at its own expense, annually brings 400 to 500 American opinion-makers—local politicians, mayors, union leaders, clergy, journalists, and others—to Israel for tours and briefings.[65] Nonetheless, public and leadership support for assistance to Israel has been generally eroding since at least 1990.[66] By the mid-1990s, public support for aid to Israel and Egypt had become very soft. A 1994 poll by the Chicago

Council on Foreign Relations found that 44 percent of the public and 50 percent of the leaders would decrease or stop aid to Israel, while only 9 percent of the public and 4 percent of the leaders would increase it. The same survey reported comparable findings for U.S. aid to Egypt.[67] Another poll that year by the Wirthlin Group, one that first informed respondents about the amount of aid Israel had already received from the United States, found that 69 percent of the public wanted to reduce or stop aid to Israel.[68] A 1995 survey by the Program on International Policy Attitudes at the University of Maryland found less public support for aid to Israel-Egypt than for any other U.S. foreign assistance program: 56 percent wanted this aid reduced, while just 4 percent would increase it.[69]

DE FACTO ENTITLEMENTS

Security assistance has traditionally been viewed as a tool of U.S. foreign policy—that is, as one of several means available to policymakers for advancing national interests. However, since at least the early 1980s, this functional-instrumental depiction of security assistance has not been an entirely accurate characterization of U.S. aid to Israel and Egypt. As a rule (to which there are exceptions), a tool for the implementation of policy is maximally effective when its wielder has, and is seen by others as having, a reasonable degree of freedom of action in its employment. This is not the case with aid to Israel-Egypt.

On the contrary, because Washington has designated these two nations as strategic assets deserving of generous allotments of aid even long after the Cold War has ended, they have come to view the aid as an entitlement. That is, aid is seen by them as a quid pro quo for their real or supposed strategic importance to the United States. This perception has been reinforced and legitimated by the Congress in yearly foreign assistance appropriations. A common, if tactlessly expressed, Israeli viewpoint was evident in a 1981 remark by Israel's deputy minister of finance: U.S. aid "is a narcotic and we are hooked. . . . This [aid] elevator will go down when we tell you. You won't tell us."[70] He was proven correct, of course (discussed below). Yet when the aid spigot is locked in the "on" position, the president has minimal ability to flexibly employ this instrument to promote American interests. Aid continues to flow at customary levels despite gross misexpenditures of funds and frequent contraventions of U.S. laws and policies.[71]

CONCLUSION

Defense News, usually sensitive to Israel's interests, urged in 1996 that Israel be weaned "off the dole" by phasing out FMF aid over a ten-year period. It found that U.S. subsidies and special privileges to Israel contributed to the loss of American defense jobs and business.[72] However, *military* aid will continue, partly because even an unlikely near-term peace with Syria will not eliminate potential threats to the Jewish state.[73] In keeping with past practices, continued military aid to Israel would likely be accompanied by substantial military aid to Egypt.

Economic Support Fund aid to Egypt and Israel, however, could and should decline. Even some American supporters of Israel who oppose any reduction of aid acknowledge Israel's declining need for economic aid;[74] other partisans of Israel are concerned that the aid package to Israel-Egypt will be vulnerable politically if ESF is *not* cut as the overall foreign assistance budget falls.[75] A commission composed largely of past and present U.S. government officials, all strongly supportive of Israel, also agreed in 1997 that "weaning Israel off U.S. economic assistance is long overdue."[76]

Moreover, a growing number of Israeli and American economists and government officials view ESF aid and huge U.S. housing loan guarantees as harmful to Israel's economy. They find that the aid distorts market incentives, impairs the country's competitiveness, and invites irresponsible public expenditures.[77] Jack Kemp, a staunch Israel supporter, declared shortly before becoming Bob Dole's vice presidential running mate in 1996 that continued U.S. aid was "counterproductive" for the Jewish state,[78] and the Jerusalem-based Institute for Advanced Strategic and Political Studies urged an end to all foreign aid by mid-1998 because aid "feeds the overgrown bureaucracy and perpetuates a cycle of dependency."[79] Likewise, Joel Bainerman, publisher of *Tel Aviv Business*, believed that an Israel with a per capita income of $16,000 would prosper from the complete loss of U.S. economic aid.[80] As economic aid to Israel declines, ESF and other nonmilitary aid to Egypt will also fall. ESF aid to Egypt served short-range U.S. political objectives, but this infusion of economic assistance— the largest in history to a single country (Israel excepted)—"has not enabled the people of Egypt to experience measurable, sustained progress in the areas that most affect their daily lives."[81] Indeed, an internal State Department report prepared for Secretary of State Warren Christopher in 1996 recommended reducing ESF aid to Egypt in the late 1990s.[82]

Concerned that aid to Israel-Egypt was crowding out development and humanitarian aid to needy nations, a coalition of eleven charitable and religious organizations sought in 1995 to stimulate congressional interest in restructuring foreign assistance allocations. As in the past, however, they lacked political leverage, and a representative of one of these groups, Bread for the World, lamented: "Nobody wants to touch it."[83] And nobody did. For instance, Congressman Sonny Callahan (R-Ala.) (who chaired the foreign operations subcommittee of the committee on appropriations and had never in his long career voted for a foreign aid bill) first expressed his concern about the "sacred cow" of aid to Israel and Egypt, then joined his colleagues in appropriating funds to continue feeding the cow.[84] And Congressman Michael Forbes (R-N.Y.) reiterated what has been a political verity in Washington since the 1970s: "Aid to Egypt and Israel is untouchable."[85]

The economic portion of the aid package to Israel became "touchable," politically, only after Prime Minister Netanyahu's speech to a wildly cheering joint session of Congress in July 1996. Even then, Netanyahu's conditional, self-assured remarks made it evident that he was confident that Congress would take its cue from Israel as to the pace and level of possible cuts in aid: "In the next *four* years, we will *begin* the *long-term process* of *gradually* reducing the level of your generous *economic* assistance."[86] And AIPAC soon "clarified" Netanyahu's remarks by reasserting Israel's alleged ongoing need for large-scale U.S. subsidies in order to, among other things, "enable Israel to make economic reforms."[87]

A persuasive case can be made for reducing security assistance, especially ESF, to Israel and Egypt. If it had not been linked with aid to Israel, aid to Egypt would have been cut years ago. Reducing ESF aid will have no appreciable impact on the peace process. That process was in jeopardy by 1996, well before any cuts had occurred. Moreover, reductions in economic assistance will be gradual, and military aid will continue to flow. Indeed, Egypt and Israel have understood for some time that American aid was likely to decrease.

However, aid to Israel is unlikely to be reduced significantly, if at all, unless Congress alters its habitual posture on this matter. The prospects for such a change in disposition were better in 1996–1997 than at any time in the prior 25 years. Yet aid reductions will depend much more on Israel's acquiescence to them and on Congress's sympathetic identification with supposed Israeli needs— as articulated by AIPAC and its allies—than they will, for instance, on fiscal considerations, public opinion, or (probably) a collapse in the peace process— even one attributed largely to Israel's actions.

NOTES

An earlier, substantially abbreviated version of this chapter appeared as Duncan L. Clarke, "U.S. Security Assistance to Egypt and Israel: Politically Untouchable?" *Middle East Journal* 50 (Spring 1997).

1. See U.S. Department of State, *Congressional Presentation for Foreign Operations, Fiscal Year 1997*, Washington, D.C., 1996, pp. 422, 424, 489, 495; U.S. Agency for International Development [hereafter, AID], *U.S. Overseas Loans and Grants: July 1, 1945–September 30, 1994*, Washington, D.C., 1995, pp. 4, 10, 13. All FMF and ESF to Israel and Egypt since the mid-1980s have been in grant form.

2. Clyde R. Mark, *Israel: U.S. Foreign Assistance*, CRS Issue Brief, Congressional Research Service, Washington, D.C., October 18, 1996, pp. 3, 11, 14–15; U.S. Department of State, *Congressional Presentation*, pp. 422, 424; AID, *U.S. Overseas Loans and Grants*, pp. 4, 10, 13. Cf. Shawn L. Twing, "A Comprehensive Guide to U.S. Aid to Israel," *Washington Report on Middle East Affairs* 14 (April 1996), pp. 7, 49–52.

3. Casimir A. Yost and Mary Locke, *U.S. Foreign Affairs Resources: Budget Cuts and Consequences*, Occasional Paper (Washington, D.C.: Georgetown University, Institute for the Study of Diplomacy, 1996), pp. 8, 26.

4. The $3 billion–plus figure excludes U.S. housing loan guarantees to Israel. For a partial listing of these privileges, see Mark, *Israel: U.S. Foreign Assistance*, pp. 2–8;

Colin Campbell, "U.S. Devises Many Ways to Help Its Friend Israel," *Atlanta Constitution*, January 21, 1990, p. A1; Twing, "A Comprehensive Guide to U.S. Aid to Israel,"
pp. 49–52. For sharply contrasting views on the costs and benefits of the U.S.-Israel
relationship in the context of foreign aid, see George W. Ball and Douglas B. Ball, *The
Passionate Attachment: America's Involvement with Israel, 1947 to the Present* (New
York: W. W. Norton, 1992), esp. pp. 255–82; and A. F. K. Organski, *The $36 Billion
Bargain: Strategy and Politics in U.S. Assistance to Israel* (New York: Columbia
University Press, 1990).

  5. U.S. Department of State, *Congressional Presentation*, pp. 416–17.

  6. U.S. Department of Defense [hereafter, DOD], *United States Security Strategy in
the Middle East*, Washington, D.C., May 1995, p. 7.

  7. Paul Lewis, "UN Lists Four Nations at Risk of Wide Income Gaps," *New York
Times*, June 2, 1994; World Bank, *World Development Report*, Washington, D.C., 1993,
p. 238.

  8. Cassandra [pseudonym], "The Impending Crisis in Egypt," *Middle East Journal*
49 (Winter 1995), pp. 15–24; John Lancaster, "Praised Abroad, Egypt's Ruler Faltering
at Home," *Washington Post*, March 13, 1995, p. A1.

  9. Cassandra, "The Impending Crisis in Egypt," pp. 25–26; John Lancaster, "U.S.
Aid Has Yet to Lift Most Egyptians," *Washington Post*, April 5, 1995, p. A1.

  10. See, for instance, U.S. General Accounting Office [hereafter, GAO], *Military Aid
to Egypt: Tank Coproduction Raised Costs and May Not Meet Many Program Goals*,
NSIAD-93-203, Washington, D.C., July 1993; GAO, *Foreign Assistance: AID Strategic
Direction and Continued Management Improvements Needed*, NSIAD-93-106, Washington, D.C., June 1993, pp. 34–36.

  11. Douglas M. Bloomfield, "Foreign Aid Cuts No Mirage This Time," *Washington
Jewish Week*, July 11, 1996, p. 17.

  12. Robert F. Zimmerman, *Dollars, Diplomacy, and Dependency* (Boulder, Colo.:
Lynne Rienner, 1993), pp. 85–86. Zimmerman is a retired foreign service officer with
years of experience with AID. His book focuses particular attention on Egypt. See also
Lancaster, "U.S. Aid Has Yet to Lift Most Egyptians," p. A1; GAO, *Egypt's Capacity
to Absorb and Use Economic Assistance Effectively*, ID-77-33, Washington, D.C., September 1977, p. 1.

  13. Zimmerman, *Dollars, Diplomacy, and Dependency*, p. 180.

  14. Ibid., p. 93. See also Vernon W. Ruttan, *United States Assistance Policy: The
Domestic Politics of Foreign Economic Aid* (Baltimore, Md.: Johns Hopkins University
Press, 1996), p. 301.

  15. Fawaz A. Gerges, "Egyptian-Israeli Relations Turn Sour," *Foreign Affairs* 74
(May-June 1995), pp. 73–75; interview of Alfred Leroy Atherton (1990), in Stephanie
Hoffman, ed., *Egypt: Country Collection*, Foreign Affairs Oral History Program (Arling-
ton, Va.: Association for Diplomatic Studies and Training, 1996), pp. Atherton 24–25.

  16. Gerges, "Egyptian-Israeli Relations," p. 74.

  17. Eric Rozenman, "Their Eyes on Egypt," *Washington Jewish Week*, February 11,
1993, p. 5; Barbara Opall, "Israel Seeks to Warm Cold Peace," *Defense News*, July 29–
August 4, 1996, p. 3. See also Caroline Faraj and Steve Rodan, "Israel Downplays
Egyptian Exercise," *Defense News*, September 30–October 6, 1996, p. 50; "Egypt Re-
ceived Scud Missile Parts from North Korea, Report Says," *Arms Control Today* 26
(July 1996), p. 25.

18. John Lancaster, "Mubarak, Netanyahu Affirm Views in 'Cordial' Talks," *Washington Post*, July 19, 1996, p. A3.

19. Alan Dowty, *Middle East Crisis: Decision-Making in 1958, 1970, and 1973* (Berkeley: University of California Press, 1984), p. 177.

20. William B. Quandt, *American Diplomacy and the Arab-Israeli Conflict since 1967* (Washington, D.C.: Brookings Institution, 1993), p. 426; Henry Kissinger, *Years of Upheaval* (New York: Little, Brown, 1982), pp. 202–3, 212, 1205; Anatoly Dobrynin, *In Confidence: Moscow's Ambassador to America's Six Cold War Presidents (1962–1986)* (New York: Times Books, 1995), pp. 303–4. For a contrasting view, see Adam M. Garfinkle, "U.S. Decision Making in the Jordan Crisis: Correcting the Record," *Political Science Quarterly* 100 (Spring 1985), p. 137.

21. This is especially so of the U.S. armed forces and most civilians in DOD. See Shai Feldman, *The Future of U.S.-Israel Strategic Cooperation* (Washington, D.C.: Washington Institute for Near East Policy, 1996), pp. 7, 16, 21, 46.

22. Interview by Duncan L. Clarke, former DOD official, Washington, D.C., December 1993. Similar views were expressed by numerous past and present government officials.

23. Robert C. McFarlane, *Special Trust* (New York: Cadell & Davies, 1994), pp. 187–88; Howard Teicher and Gayle R. Teicher, *Twin Pillars to Desert Storm: America's Flawed Vision in the Middle East from Nixon to Bush* (New York: William Morrow, 1993), pp. 91–93, 141, 222, 271–74, 357; Karen Puschel, *U.S.-Israeli Strategic Cooperation in the Post–Cold War Era: An American Perspective* (Boulder, Colo.: Westview Press, 1992), pp. 73–77; Helena Cobban, *The Superpowers and the Syrian-Israeli Conflict: Beyond Crisis Management?* (New York: Praeger Publishers, 1991), pp. 78–103. Secretary of State George Shultz, a principal architect of strategic cooperation, never mentions the subject in his lengthy memoirs except to regret his support for the U.S. funding of Israel's canceled Lavi fighter. George P. Shultz, *Turmoil and Triumph: My Years as Secretary of State* (New York: Charles Scribner's Sons, 1993), p. 143.

24. Thomas A. Dine, "The Revolution in U.S.-Israel Relations," 1986 (typescript/mimeographed).

25. Numerous interviews of U.S. government officials by Duncan L. Clarke, 1990–1995; Duncan L. Clarke, "The Arrow Missile: The United States, Israel and Strategic Cooperation," *Middle East Journal* 48 (Summer 1994), pp. 475–91; Cobban, *The Superpowers and the Syrian-Israeli Conflict*, pp. 83–111; Andrew Cockburn and Leslie Cockburn, *Dangerous Liaison: The Inside Story of the U.S.-Israeli Covert Relationship* (New York: HarperCollins, 1991); Seymour M. Hersh, *The Samson Option: Israel's Nuclear Arsenal and American Foreign Policy* (New York: Random House, 1991). Former director of the Office of Egyptian Affairs in the U.S. Department of State, Edward L. Peck, says: "My concern with the Arab-Israeli question is that we always—or so often—wound up doing things which may have been good for Israel but were clearly not good for us." Interview of Edward L. Peck (1989), in Hoffman, *Egypt*, p. Peck-6.

26. Bernard Reich, *Securing the Covenant: United States–Israel Relations after the Cold War* (Westport, Conn.: Praeger, 1995), p. 123.

27. Feldman, *The Future of U.S.-Israel Strategic Cooperation*, pp. 6–7.

28. Thomas W. Lippman, "Anti-Terrorism Accord Signed," *Washington Post*, May 1, 1996, p. A23.

29. Emphasis added. Joseph Alpher, "Israel: The Challenges of Peace," *Foreign Policy* 101 (Winter 1995–1996), pp. 142–43.

30. Feldman, *The Future of U.S.-Israel Strategic Cooperation*, pp. 3, 23.

31. Ibid., pp. 61–62.

32. John Lancaster, "Mubarak to Netanyahu: Help Me, I'll Help You," *Washington Post*, July 23, 1996, p. A12; Thomas W. Lippman, "Netanyahu Affirms His Hard-line Image," *Washington Post*, July 10, 1996, p. A13.

33. Richard N. Haas, "The Middle East: No More Treaties," *Foreign Affairs* 75 (October 1996), pp. 53–63; Michael Dobbs and Nora Boustany, "Summit Concludes with Little Progress," *Washington Post*, October 3, 1996, p. A1; Caroline Faraj and Barbara Opall, "Questions, Recriminations Haunt Middle East Prospects for Peace," *Defense News*, October 21–27, 1996, p. 4.

34. Jim Hoagland, "The Hebron Pawn," *Washington Post*, January 19, 1997, p. C7.

35. Ibid.

36. David Makovsky, "Netanyahu Okays Housing Near Jerusalem," *Washington Jewish Week*, February 20, 1997, p. 18.

37. John M. Goshko, "U.S. Vetoes Move to Block Israel Housing," *Washington Post*, March 8, 1997, p. A1.

38. Feldman, *The Future of U.S.-Israel Strategic Cooperation*, p. 31; Lippman, "Netanyahu Affirms His Hard-line Image," p. A13.

39. See Douglas Bloomfield, "Time for a Serious Netanyahu Commitment," *Washington Jewish Week*, October 3, 1996, p. 25; Barton Gellman, "Limits Lifted on West Bank Settlements," *Washington Post*, August 3, 1996, p. A1.

40. Bloomfield, "Time for a Serious Netanyahu Commitment," p. 25; Neal Sher, "Testing the Prime Minister's Political Skills," *Washington Jewish Week*, October 3, 1996, p. 25. American partisans of Israel opposed even "the threat of punitive measures against Israel." Report of the Presidential Study Group, *Building for Security & Peace in the Middle East* (Washington, D.C.: Washington Institute for Near East Policy, 1997), p. 54.

41. Quoted in Thomas M. Franck and Edward Weisband, *Foreign Policy by Congress* (New York: Oxford University Press, 1979), p. 165.

42. See Yossi Shain, "Ethnic Diasporas and U.S. Foreign Policy," *Political Science Quarterly* 109 (Winter 1994–1995), pp. 811–41.

43. See Raphael Danziger and Bradley Gordon, "End American Aid to Israel? No, It Remains Vital," *Middle East Quarterly* 2 (September 1995), pp. 13–21. The authors are AIPAC officers.

44. Steven L. Spiegel, *The Other Arab-Israeli Conflict* (Chicago: University of Chicago Press, 1985), p. 160.

45. For example, see Mitchell Geoffrey Bard, *The Water's Edge and Beyond: Defining the Limits to Domestic Influence on United States Middle East Policy* (New Brunswick, N.J.: Transaction Publishers, 1991); Reich, *Securing the Covenant*, pp. 65–90; Edward Tivnan, *The Lobby: Jewish Political Power and American Foreign Policy* (New York: Simon & Schuster, 1987); Alpher, "Israel: The Challenges of Peace," p. 142; J. J. Goldberg, *Jewish Power: Inside the American Jewish Establishment* (New York: Addison-Wesley, 1996), esp. pp. 251–78.

46. Dov S. Zakheim, *Flight of the Lavi: Inside a U.S.-Israeli Crisis* (Washington, D.C.: Brassey's, 1996), p. 216. See also pp. 133, 165–66.

47. Seymour Martin Lipset and Earl Raab, *Jews and the New American Scene* (Cambridge, Mass.: Harvard University Press, 1995), pp. 145–46.

48. Ibid., p. 145; Bard, *The Water's Edge and Beyond*, p. 22.

49. Matthew Dorf, "Jews and White House Access," *Washington Jewish Week*, March 13, 1997, p. 26.

50. Lipset and Raab, *Jews and the New American Scene*, p. 138; Goldberg, *Jewish Power*, pp. 275–77.

51. Bard, *The Water's Edge and Beyond*, pp. 24, 277, 280–81, 286.

52. Ibid., p. 5; Donald Neff, *Fallen Pillars: U.S. Policy towards Palestine and Israel since 1945* (Washington, D.C.: Institute for Palestine Studies, 1995), p. 4.

53. Quoted in Stephen Isaacs, *Jews and American Politics* (New York: Doubleday, 1974), p. 34.

54. Dan Raviv and Yossi Melman, *Friends in Deed: Inside the U.S.-Israeli Alliance* (New York: Hyperion, 1994), pp. 318–20; Douglas M. Bloomfield, "Israel's Standing in the Congress: Will Foreign Aid Be Spared?" in Nimrod Novick, ed., *Israel in U.S. Foreign and Security Policies* (Tel Aviv, Israel: Jaffee Center for Strategic Studies, Tel Aviv University, 1983), pp. 19, 21. See also Zakheim, *Flight of the Lavi*, p. 9.

55. Bloomfield, "Israel's Standing in the Congress," pp. 21–22.

56. Interview by Duncan L. Clarke, U.S. Senate staff member, Washington, D.C., November 1993.

57. Clarke, "The Arrow Missile," esp. pp. 488–90; GAO, *U.S.-Israel Arrow/ACES Program: Cost, Technical Proliferation, and Management Concerns*, NSIAD-93-254, Washington, D.C., August 1993.

58. See, for instance, Bard, *The Water's Edge and Beyond*; Duncan L. Clarke and Alan S. Cohen, "The United States, Israel and the Lavi Fighter," *Middle East Journal* 40 (Winter 1986), pp. 16–32. The United States even subsidizes *Israel's* foreign aid to developing countries. See Duncan L. Clarke, "U.S.-Israeli Cooperative Development Programs: The Berman Amendment," *Middle East Journal* 45 (Spring 1991), pp. 265–76.

59. "Remarks by the President to AIPAC Policy Conference," White House, Washington, D.C., May 7, 1995 (transcript/mimeographed).

60. None of the twenty Jewish House Democrats supported the bill because, said Congressman Howard Berman (D-Calif.), it "sets Israel up for the fall in the future because when they want more cuts, there will be nowhere else to take them." Douglas M. Bloomfield, "Democrats Boiling over Aid," *Washington Jewish Week*, May 25, 1995, p. 15; Ann Devroy, "Veto Aimed at Foreign Policy Bill," *Washington Post*, May 25, 1995, p. A1.

61. Caroline Faraj and Philip Finnegan, "Israel Lobbies White House for Military Aid to Jordan," *Defense News*, December 18–24, 1995, p. 1; Lally Weymouth, "Unfair Standards of Compliance," *Washington Post*, October 16, 1995, p. A21; Douglas M. Bloomfield, "Lobbying for Hussein," *Washington Jewish Week*, March 16, 1995, p. 23.

62. Thomas W. Lippman, "Mideast Aid Survives Budget Ax," *Washington Post*, October 23, 1995, p. A6.

63. Hearings held in 1992 and 1993 by a subcommittee that rarely deals with foreign aid constitute a unique exception. The subcommittee was chaired by Congressman John Dingell (D-Mich.), whose congressional district contains one of the largest concentrations of Arab Americans in the country. U.S. Congress, House, Subcommittee on Oversight and Investigations, Committee on Energy and Commerce, *Hearing: Illegal Military Assistance to Israel*, 103d Cong., 1st sess., 1993; and 102d Cong., 2d sess., 1992.

64. These and other matters are addressed in Duncan L. Clarke, "Israel's Unauthorized Arms Transfers," *Foreign Policy* 99 (Summer 1995), pp. 89–109. See also U.S.

Department of State, Office of the Inspector General, *Report of Audit: Department of State Defense Trade Controls*, Washington, D.C., March 1992, pp. 1–2, 4, 17–18, 25; GAO, *Export Controls: License Screening and Compliance Procedures Need Strengthening*, NSIAD-94–178, Washington, D.C., June 1994, pp. 2–13, 19; idem, *Military Sales to Israel and Egypt: DOD Needs Stronger Controls over U.S.-Financed Procurements*, NSIAD-93–184, Washington, D.C., July 1993, pp. 25, 32, 36, 39–40; Bill Gertz, "Israelis Face Query on Sales to China," *Washington Times*, June 19, 1996. ESF aid to Israel is largely unmonitored. A former State Department official says of ESF: The United States "for political reasons" gives Israel a "blank check. They could, if they wanted to, order ... four shiploads of pornographic movies. We'd pay for that. Because there are no restrictions." Interview of Edward L. Peck, in Hoffman, *Egypt*, p. Peck 5.

65. Thomas L. Friedman, *From Beirut to Jerusalem* (New York: Farrar, Straus & Giroux, 1989), p. 441.

66. For early post–Cold War surveys, see Benjamin Ginsberg, *The Fatal Embrace: Jews and the State* (Chicago: University of Chicago Press, 1993), p. 220; B'nai B'rith Anti-Defamation League poll, April 28–May 1, 1992, Roper Center, Conn., 1992; John E. Reilly, ed., *American Public Opinion and U.S. Foreign Policy: 1995* (Chicago, Ill.: Chicago Council on Foreign Relations, 1995), p. 32.

67. Reilly, *American Public Opinion*, p. 32.

68. Ella Bancroft, "Americans Disapprove Present Israel Aid Level by Three to One," *Washington Report on Middle East Affairs* 14 (July-August 1995), p. 86.

69. Steven Kull, *Americans and Foreign Aid: A Study of American Public Attitudes*, Program on International Policy Attitudes, University of Maryland, March 1, 1995, pp. 11–12.

70. Quoted in Zimmerman, *Dollars, Diplomacy, and Dependency*, p. 150. For a similar episode, one involving an Israeli defense official, see Zakheim, *Flight of the Lavi*, pp. 176–77.

71. See, for instance, Zimmerman, *Dollars, Diplomacy, and Dependency*, pp. 57–58, 143, 147; Clarke, "Israel's Unauthorized Arms Transfers"; GAO, *Defense Industrial Security: Weaknesses in U.S. Security Arrangements with Foreign-Owned Defense Contractors*, NSIAD-96–24, Washington, D.C., February 1996, pp. 22–23. Zimmerman (pp. 58, 140–42) finds that ESF aid has *aggravated* tensions between Egypt and Israel and within Israel.

72. "Time for Self-Reliance," *Defense News*, August 26–September 1, 1996, p. 20. See also Shawn L. Twing, "Funding the Competition: Aid to Israel Returns to Haunt U.S. Industry," *Defense News*, March 3–9, 1997, p. 19.

73. Peace could be costly for the United States. Israeli officials apparently concluded in 1995 that a peace with Syria could cost Washington a lump-sum payment of $12 billion to Israel in military and nonmilitary aid, a sum that former DOD official Dov Zakheim denounced as setting "new standards for chutzpah." Dov Zakheim, "Peace with a Price Tag," *Washington Times*, January 5, 1996. See also Yost and Locke, *U.S. Foreign Affairs Resources*, p. 27.

74. Reich, *Securing the Covenant*, pp. 105, 107.

75. Congressman Howard Berman (D-Calif.) said, "If Israel and Egypt are untouched and all else is cut, soon aid to Israel will take a whack. [The] argument for foreign aid falls off if just one country is left." Douglas M. Bloomfield, "Foreign Aid Wedge," *Washington Jewish Week*, March 30, 1995, p. 27; idem, "Aid Cuts Require Planning," *Washington Jewish Week*, July 6, 1995, p. 17.

76. Presidential Study Group, *Building for Security & Peace in the Middle East* (Washington, D.C.: Washington Institute for Near East Policy, 1997), p. 55.

77. Howard Rosen, "Economic Relations between Israel and the United States," in Robert O. Freedman, ed., *Israel Under Rabin* (Boulder, Colo.: Westview Press, 1995), p. 208; Joel Bainerman, "End U.S. Aid to Israel? Yes, It Does Harm," *Middle East Quarterly* 2 (September 1995), pp. 3–12.

78. *The Jubilee Plan for Economic Freedom in Israel* (Jerusalem: Institute for Advanced Strategic and Political Studies, July 1996), p. 5.

79. Ibid., pp. 11, 31–32.

80. Bainerman, "End U.S. Aid to Israel?" pp. 3–12.

81. Zimmerman, *Dollars, Diplomacy, and Dependency*, pp. 104–6.

82. At Secretary Christopher's behest, a U.S. delegation visited Cairo in April 1996 to assess the implications of reduced security assistance to Egypt. Interviews by Jason Ellis, State Department officials, Washington, D.C., 1996.

83. Lippman, "Mideast Aid Survives Budget Ax," p. A6.

84. Ibid.

85. Ibid.

86. Emphases added. Netanyahu lauded Congress: "If I could only get the *Knesset* to vote like [the U.S. Congress]." Shawn Cohen, "Netanyahu Wows Congress, Not U.S. Arab Group," *Washington Jewish Week*, July 18, 1996, p. 12.

87. "Aid to Israel," American Israel Public Affairs Committee, Washington, D.C., October 21, 1996, (mimeographed); E. V. Kontorovich, "Time to Cut Aid to Israel," *Wall Street Journal*, August 8, 1996, p. A10.

8

Conclusion: Toward a New Consensus on Security Assistance?

The end of the Cold War sounded a death knell for the long-standing anti-Soviet rationale of the U.S. security assistance program. While the program's record during the Cold War era was decidedly "mixed" in many respects, it was an instrumental factor, nonetheless, in checking the Soviet Union and its allies and in helping governments allied to the United States defend themselves against external and internal foes. The core Soviet containment justification for security aid was supplemented with other objectives in the 1970s: underwriting a Middle East peace process, combating international terrorism and narcotics trafficking, and funding some voluntary U.S. peacekeeping operations. To these aims, others were added following the 1991 collapse of the Soviet Union: stemming nuclear proliferation, international law enforcement cooperation, and facilitating NATO expansion. Indeed, as a percentage of foreign aid spending, security assistance generally increased after the Cold War period. This chapter provides a cautious overview of what may be an emerging, if tacit, consensus on the role of security assistance in contemporary U.S. foreign policy, and it sketches the program's new dimensions.

THE U.S. GLOBAL ROLE: COMPETING VISIONS

The United States lost its defining foreign policy focus with the demise of the Soviet Union. Some disorientation as to future missions, goals, and priorities was understandable and probably inevitable in the aftermath of the decades-long struggle that had so gripped the nation. By 1996, however, it could no longer be so confidently claimed that the United States had moved "from containment to confusion"[1] or that Washington might be "self-deterred"[2] from playing an international leadership role in the absence of a superpower adversary. On the contrary, the Clinton administration, albeit belatedly, opted for continued, if tempered, American activism on a global scale. This was evident not only in foreign economic policy and the promotion of democracy but also in such areas as countering the proliferation of weapons of mass destruction, expanding NATO eastward, sending troops into Bosnia and Haiti, renewing vital security accords with Japan, assertively deterring threats against Kuwait and Taiwan, and reacting vigorously to domestic and international terrorism. The United States is not going to be a stay-at-home power, at least for the foreseeable future. Neo-isolationists[3] and libertarians[4] appear to have lost the debate over the post–Cold War U.S. global role, if not necessarily on the substantive merits of the issues, surely in practice.

However, the future role of the United States in world affairs is not yet wholly defined, and what seems to be an emerging, discernible consensus on the place of security aid in U.S. foreign policy must await further clarification of America's larger world role. Given the reasonable presumption that the United States will be an international actor of consequence, two large, recurring questions are: How should America apportion/balance its enormous energies between external and internal affairs? How, when, and to what degree should the United States concern itself with global security issues?

Some—including much of the general public and both the author of the containment doctrine, George Kennan, and longtime critic of U.S. overseas military interventions, Ronald Steel—hold that it is time for the United States to play a sharply reduced role on the world stage and focus on the principal threats to the nation's welfare: the multitude of festering domestic problems afflicting American society.[5] Even some internationalists who would have the United States play a far more active global role than would Kennan or Steel agree that domestic problems should be accorded top priority.[6] Others, including many (certainly not all) liberal and conservative/neoconservative internationalists, urge a continued, or even augmented, world role for the United States.[7] Both groups today generally back the active promotion of democracy abroad, although the former tend to prefer pursuing this goal through such means as sustainable development and human rights, while the latter generally opts for greater sensitivity to traditional security interests. There is broad agreement on the need to counter nuclear proliferation and international terrorism, and some modern Wilsonian liberals are outspoken advocates of U.S. military intervention (preferably through collective, rather than unilateral, action) for "higher" humanitarian purposes—such as curtailing genocide in Africa or the Balkans.

SURVIVAL OF SECURITY ASSISTANCE

For security assistance generally, the end of the Cold War clearly illuminated the program's scope and significance in terms not colored by an anti-Soviet mantra. To some extent, warfare in the Persian Gulf and, later, in southeastern

Europe and elsewhere seemed to slow the decline in congressional support for security aid. Military conflicts were obviously not obsolete, and the need for multilateral cooperation in warfare became readily apparent. Moreover, high-profile developments such as the incessant flow of illicit drugs into the United States and dramatic terrorist incidents in the United Kingdom, Israel, and—with disturbing frequency—against American forces overseas and in the United States itself reminded policy officials, Congress, and the general public that security concerns intersected the domestic and international realms. At the same time, a widely held view that the promotion of democracy tended to make for a more peaceful world seemed to provide at least a partial rationale for some forms of assistance and for an activist U.S. international posture.

The defense budget fell in real terms every year from FY 1985 to FY 1995, but the so-called peace dividend never materialized, and the steady decline in defense spending leveled off somewhat in FY 1996. That year, too, Congress passed the lowest foreign aid budget since the earliest years of the program. An alarmed Clinton administration mounted a full-court press in support of international affairs spending, arguing that "it is the United States that stands the most to lose if we retreat" from the international stage.[8] While downward pressure on the international affairs budget continued, a tacit and ad hoc export-development–security-based alliance of administration officials, private organizations, and various legislators increasingly began to view these expenditures—particularly in the security assistance realm—as important to the U.S. international role. They voiced their collective concern that an emaciated international affairs budget (which, of course, also includes funding for, among other things, the State Department, the Agency for International Development, and the U.S. contribution to the United Nations) was harming America's security and economic interests abroad.[9]

Some Clinton administration officials predicted that FY 1996 would mark the low point in international affairs funding.[10] To the chagrin of much of the Republican majority in Congress, the Clinton administration—which argued that it was necessary to protect American interests—raided the Pentagon's budget for a variety of international affairs projects, including arms sales to Jordan, anti-terrorism assistance to Israel, and the peace operation in Bosnia.[11] However, even former Senator and 1996 Republican presidential nominee Bob Dole, while not uncritical of elements of the foreign aid program, did not question the need for or desirability of foreign assistance.[12] Moreover, most Republican legislators continued to be much more sympathetic to providing assistance for security purposes than, for example, for economic development. Many members of Congress by 1996 seemed to identify with the view of Ambassador Craig Johnstone: namely, that cutting foreign aid further in the name of budget balancing was self-defeating; not only was that well "dry," but "if we do not exert . . . leadership we . . . will pay an enormous price later on."[13]

Program Structure and Composition

There is little prospect at present for a comprehensive reform of the foreign assistance program, despite considerable agreement that the 1961 Foreign Assistance Act is in dire need of a sweeping overhaul. Nevertheless, the security assistance program has proven to be more dynamic and adaptable than it might appear to the casual observer. Although Congress, for instance, has not authorized the program since 1985, the legislature has often employed special legislation to fill this void—for example, its passage of the Freedom Support Act.

From a programmatic standpoint, long before the end of the Cold War, most security aid went to "advance peace" in the Middle East, not to counter supposed Soviet proxies in the Third World. Indeed, only rarely was security aid arguably substantial enough in itself to result in victory by U.S.-supported forces over those who identified with the Soviet Union or its allies. However, the program has had a certain constancy from the Truman administration through the present, with continuous emphases on such strategic objectives as maintaining an adequate overseas presence and crisis response capability; enhancing the effectiveness of coalition operations through joint training and improved interoperability of friendly forces; and helping allies defend themselves while at the same time working cooperatively to preclude threats to regional stability antithetical to U.S. interests.[14] Under this rubric, security assistance has been variously used as a complement to or substitute for a robust foreign policy.

At the same time, particularly in the post-Soviet era, the security assistance program has been partly reinvented, with the prospect of further changes to come. As Chapters 6 and 7 indicated, major program changes have either already occurred or are probable for, respectively, base-rights countries and Egypt-Israel. Concerning the former, aid to such long-standing recipients as Portugal, Spain, and the Philippines has been phased out, while assistance to the two remaining base-rights recipient states, Greece and Turkey, has become increasingly tenuous. Indeed, internal State Department deliberations in 1996 on the FY 1997 foreign operations account saw security assistance to both Greece and Turkey initially zeroed out.[15] While Greece retains relatively little strategic value for the United States, its linkage with aid to Turkey remains intact. By the same token, assistance to Turkey was seen by the Clinton administration as proving its worth in such areas as the Bosnian "equip-and-train" program, even as Congress escalated its criticism of Turkish military maneuvers against the Kurdish population in eastern Turkey and human rights abuses generally.[16] Indeed, a senior administration official testified in 1996 that Turkey's obvious geostrategic importance and continued security cooperation make it "hard to overstate the importance of Turkey as a U.S. ally."[17]

As for Egypt-Israel, senior Clinton administration officials were divided between those who viewed this aid as sacrosanct even years after the 1979 Camp David Accords and those who wanted a reduction in at least *economic* aid to these two countries. However, the Clinton administration maintained the status quo, at least through 1996. Even as Congressman Sonny Callahan (R-Ala.), chairman of the House Appropriations Committee's Foreign Operations Subcommittee, lamented a special, election-year administration request in 1996 for $100 million in anti-terrorism assistance for Israel, Congress remained committed to these annual grants.[18]

Moreover, Israeli Prime Minister Benyamin Netanyahu indicated in July 1996 remarks before Congress an apparent, if qualified, willingness to engage in a long-term process of weaning Israel from the $1.2 billion annual ESF subsidy, while maintaining the $1.8 billion FMF support indefinitely.[19] This followed on the heels of Jordanian criticism of perceived low levels of U.S. assistance despite compliance with the peace process; internal concern in the State Department over the relatively small amount of aid to the Palestinian National Authority; an April 1996 U.S. delegation's visit to Egypt at Secretary of State Warren Christopher's behest to assess the implications of reduced security assistance to Cairo; and a general sentiment in the executive branch that the Egypt-Israel aid linkage remain intact through the proposed process of aid reduction for FY 1999 and beyond.[20]

While the exact scope and pace of possible alterations in these programs remain unclear, the likely evolution of other elements of the security assistance program is somewhat more evident. Rather than pursuing exclusively a "pivotal states strategy" of "rigorously discriminate assistance"[21] to a handful of countries, the executive branch has had some success in persuading Congress to appropriate some funds for important "regional accounts." Hence, Egypt, Israel, Greece, and Turkey were joined by the mid-1990s by such recipients as Bosnia, Haiti, and Jordan, while a small, yet growing, portion of the annual ESF and FMF request was being set aside for regional contingencies. In Africa, for instance, ESF allotments for the African Regional Democracy Fund increased for three successive years—to $8 million in FY 1996; and this was complemented by separate appropriations for regional peacekeeping.[22]

ESF and FMF funds have also been tapped for a variety of functional purposes, both within a given regional theater of operation and globally. For example, in Central and Eastern Europe, $60 million in foreign operations money (plus $40 million from the Department of Defense) was spent in FY 1996 and requested again the following year to ensure that Partnership for Peace (PFP) countries "seeking to join NATO are ready to share all military, political, and economic burdens of NATO membership when the Alliance decides to admit new members."[23] Specifically, allocated funds sought to improve interoperability of forces; train Central and East European militaries for an enhanced peacekeeping role and further participation in NATO/PFP exercises; facilitate the democratic consolidation of defense forces; prepare and equip national forces dedicated to participating in PFP exercises; and enhance the transparency of national defense planning and budgetary processes throughout the former East bloc. These endeavors are substantively complemented by funds provided under the IMET program and the Pentagon's military-to-military contacts initiative, which focused considerable attention on this region after the fall of the Berlin Wall.

Other functional issues have also garnered an increasing percentage of scarce security assistance resources in the post–Cold War era. The Anti-Terrorism Assistance (ATA) program showed modest increases, and the voluntary peacekeeping operation account was up considerably from Cold War levels despite the painful U.S. experience in Somalia. One of the real "winners," however, was the International Narcotics and Law Enforcement Affairs (INL) account. INL received only $101 million in FY 1994, but concern over international narcotics trafficking and organized crime, which the U.S. government declared to be two of the "most serious threats to the security and vital interests of the United States,"[24] translated into a $187.9 million appropriation in FY 1995 and a $213 million FY 1997 request. Counternarcotics objectives included reducing the size and scope of the international drug trade by strengthening the ability of law enforcement and judicial institutions to investigate and prosecute major narcotics organizations. INL funds were targeted at stemming the explosion of transnational organized crime and thwarting its "corrosive impact" on the nascent free market economies of central and Eastern Europe and the NIS. These funds focused especially on developing training and information-sharing programs to combat money laundering and other financial crimes and the international smuggling of contraband.[25]

Washington's post–Cold War concern about nuclear proliferation was also addressed partly through the international affairs budget. For instance, to help counter North Korea's nuclear weapons program, the United States negotiated an accord whereby Pyongyang agreed to eventually dismantle this program in exchange for heavy fuel oil and international financing and construction of two light-water reactors. Toward this end, the Korean Energy Development Organization (KEDO) was created in 1994 to facilitate the process and take the lead on reactor construction. While the project retained Clinton administration support, Congress balked at "rewarding" a nuclear proliferant and, therefore, at funding KEDO's work.[26] Although it approved a total of $14 million for FY 1994–FY 1995, the House of Representatives cut the administration's $25 million FY 1997 request almost in half despite administration warnings that "without the funding, KEDO will not be able to . . . carry out its objectives, thereby weakening the credibility of U.S. leadership . . . and contributing to rising security tensions on the Korean peninsula."[27]

Similarly, the Nonproliferation and Disarmament Fund, while somewhat more secure by 1996, also faced intense scrutiny by the Republican-dominated 104th Congress. In FY 1994, the NDF emphasized the destruction of weapons and the safeguarding of their components, but its mission expanded in FY 1996 to include export control assistance and countering nuclear smuggling. NDF resources then doubled from an initial $10 million to $20 million in FY 1996. Still, program needs outpaced allocated funds. Despite proclaiming the importance of nuclear nonproliferation objectives, Congress funded the program at 20 percent below the administration's FY 1996 request, even as it also reduced the Defense Department's share of the antiproliferation Cooperative Threat Reduction program from $371 million to $298 million. At the Senate's insistence, however, CTR gained more prominence in the FY 1997 deliberations when it was reauthorized, amply funded, and given an expanded mandate that included attention to domestic preparedness for nuclear, biological, or chemical emergencies.[28] Nuclear nonproliferation promised to remain a key focus of U.S. foreign policy. Defense and foreign assistance programs to achieve this objective will be in place for the foreseeable future.

CONCLUSION

Perhaps surprisingly, even after the Cold War, security assistance remains an important tool for U.S. policymakers. Several traditional program elements were intact; others were changing or, sometimes, disappearing; and still others addressed problems of increasing salience: anti-terrorism, nuclear nonproliferation, counternarcotics, and others.

While moving unquestionably beyond containment, U.S. foreign policy continued to rely on the security assistance program and foreign aid generally as policy instruments for engagement abroad. These instruments of American diplomacy seemed likely to be retained, in modified form, for some time to come. However, despite some unsuccessful attempts, there was no sweeping reform of foreign assistance institutions or legislation; moreover, the availability of sufficient resources to conduct an active foreign policy remained very much of an open question. There did seem to be a growing sense that U.S. leadership required adequate resources. But it was by no means evident that, for instance, money "saved" by reductions in the base-rights and Egypt-Israel accounts would be "reinvested" in other foreign assistance program accounts where identifiable needs existed. All things considered, securing U.S. global leadership through vision, political will, and resources would appear to be the real challenge of the post–Cold War era. Indeed, international stability and American interests require nothing less.

NOTES

1. Richard N. Haass, "Paradigm Lost," *Foreign Affairs* 74 (January–February 1995), p. 43.

2. Stanley R. Sloan, *The United States and the Use of Force in the Post–Cold War World: Toward Self-Deterrence?* Congressional Research Service Report for Congress, Washington, D.C., July 20, 1994, pp. 1, 5, 29.

3. Eric Nordlinger, *Isolationism Reconfigured: American Foreign Policy for a New Century* (Princeton, N.J.: Princeton University Press, 1995).

4. Ted Galen Carpenter, *A Search for Enemies: America's Alliances after the Cold War* (Washington, D.C.: The Cato Institute, 1992).

5. George F. Kennan, *Around the Cragged Hill* (New York: Norton, 1993); Ronald Steel, *Temptations of a Superpower* (Cambridge, Mass.: Harvard University Press, 1995).

6. Zbigniew Brzezinski, *Out of Control: Global Turmoil on the Eve of the 21st Century* (New York: Charles Scribner's Sons, 1993).

7. See Morton H. Halperin and David J. Scheffer, *Self-Determination in the New World Order* (Washington, D.C.: Carnegie Endowment for International Peace, 1992); David Callahan, *Between Two Worlds* (New York: HarperCollins, 1994); Henry Kissinger, *Diplomacy* (New York: Simon A. Schuster, 1994); Joshua Muravchik, *The Imperative of American Leadership* (Washington, D.C.: American Enterprise Institute, 1996).

8. Warren Christopher, "America's Leadership, America's Opportunity," *Foreign Policy* 98 (Spring 1995), p. 7.

9. Casimir A. Yost and Mary Locke, *U.S. Foreign Affairs Resources: Budget Cuts and Consequences*, ISD Occasional Paper, Institute for the Study of Diplomacy, Georgetown University, Washington, D.C., June 5 1996; Thomas W. Lippman, "U.S. Diplomacy's Presence Shrinking," *Washington Post*, June 3, 1996, p. A1; William C. Harrop and Robert J. McCloskey, "Diplomacy on the Cheap," *Washington Post*, June 18, 1996, p. A13.

10. Interview of senior State Department official by Jason Ellis, Washington, D.C., July 1996. At the same time, long-term Republican budget-balancing plans called for the entire International Affairs budget to fall to a mere $12.5 billion by 2002.

11. Thomas W. Lippman, "Aircraft Deal with Jordan Arouses GOP Complaints," *Washington Post*, February 14, 1996, p. A25; John F. Harris, "Israel to Get $100 Million in U.S. Anti-Terrorism Aid," *Washington Post*, March 15, 1996, p. A22; Carroll J. Doherty and Pat Towell, "Clinton Plan to Tap Pentagon for Aid Program Draws Fire," *Congressional Quarterly Weekly Report* (February 10, 1996), p. 361.

12. Bob Dole, "Shaping America's Global Future," *Foreign Policy* 98 (Spring 1995), pp. 38–39; John McCain, "Imagery or Purpose? The Choice in November," *Foreign Policy* 103 (Summer 1996), p. 34.

13. Craig Johnstone, "Foreign Policy on the Cheap: You Get What You Pay For," *U.S. Department of State Dispatch* 6 (October 16, 1995), p. 743.

14. White House, *A National Security Strategy of Engagement and Enlargement*, Washington, D.C., February 1996, pp. 14–15; U.S. Department of State, *Congressional Presentation for Foreign Operations: Fiscal Year 1996* [hereafter, *CPD . . . FY 1996*] (Washington, D.C.: Government Printing Office [hereafter, GPO], 1995), pp. 7–8.

15. Interview of senior State Department official by Jason Ellis, Washington, D.C., June 1996.

16. John Pomfret, "U.S. Operation in Turkey Seeks to Train, Unite Croats and Muslims," *Washington Post*, June 6, 1996, p. A21; Michael Dobbs, "Clinton Announces Start of Long-Delayed Bosnian Equip-and-Train Program," *Washington Post*, July 10, 1996, p. A13; U.S. Department of State, *Congressional Presentation for Foreign Operations: Fiscal Year 1997* [hereafter, *CPD . . . FY 1997*] (Washington, D.C.: GPO, 1996), pp. 314–15.

17. Statement by Undersecretary of State Lynn E. Davis before the House Appropriations Subcommittee on Foreign Operations, 104th Cong., 2d sess., April 30, 1996, p. 10 (mimeographed).

18. Chairman Sonny Callahan sardonically suggested at the FY 1997 foreign operations bill markup that the "President start giving out gifts such as *Forrest Gump* rather than these hundred million dollars that he commits because they give me heartburn."

See unofficial transcript of remarks at the House Appropriations Subcommittee on Foreign Operations hearing on *Foreign Assistance Programs for Fiscal Year 1997*, 104th Cong., 2d sess., March 27, 1996, p. 1 (mimeographed).

19. Federal News Service, "Netanyahu Promises to Try for Lasting Peace," *Washington Times*, July 11, 1996, p. A11.

20. Interview of State Department officials by Jason Ellis, Washington, D.C., June and July 1996.

21. Robert S. Chase, Emily B. Hill, and Paul Kennedy, "Pivotal States and U.S. Strategy," *Foreign Affairs* 75 (January–February 1996), p. 35.

22. *CPD . . . FY 1996*, pp. 209–14.

23. *CPD . . . FY 1997*, pp. 299–300.

24. Ibid., p. 72.

25. Ibid., pp. 72–74.

26. Robert A. Manning and James Przystup, "Starve North Korea—or Save It? Right Now We're Doing Both," *Washington Post*, June 23, 1996, p. C4; Michael J. Mazarr, *North Korea and the Bomb: A Case Study in Nonproliferation* (New York: St. Martin's Press, 1995), pp. 173–80.

27. Cf. Davis testimony, p. 17.

28. Jason D. Ellis, "Nunn-Lugar's Mid-Life Crisis," *Survival* 39 (Spring 1997), pp. 84–110.

Bibliographic Essay

Over the years, congressional committees, U.S. government-sanctioned commissions, the Congressional Research Service (especially Larry Nowels), and the U.S. General Accounting Office have examined various elements of the security assistance program. Annual government publications also provide essential data on the program: U.S. Agency for International Development, *U.S. Overseas Loans and Grants and Assistance from International Organizations: Obligations and Loan Authorizations*; U.S. Defense Security Assistance Agency, *Foreign Military Sales, Foreign Military Construction Sales and Military Assistance Facts*; and U.S. Department of State, *Congressional Presentation for Foreign Operations* (formerly *Congressional Presentation Document for Security Assistance*). Useful (if uncritical) official information can be obtained in the *DISAM Journal*, which is a quarterly publication of the Defense Institute of Security Assistance Management at Wright-Patterson Air Force Base, Ohio.

While there is a huge, ever-expanding literature on such subjects as conventional arms transfers and economic development assistance, there is a paucity of scholarly work on security assistance as an element of the overall foreign aid program. *Send Guns and Money* is the only comprehensive, authored treatment of the subject.

There are two edited books on aspects of the program. Ernest Graves and Steven Hildreth's *U.S. Security Assistance: The Political Process* (1985) has aged gracefully.[1] Particularly well done are chapters by Richard Grimmett on the history of the program, by Steven Hildreth on perceptions of the program from 1959 to 1983, and by Franklin Kramer on government decision making. Craig Brandt's *Military Assistance and Foreign Policy* (1990) also retains considerable value.[2] This is especially so for the contributions of Brandt on U.S. overseas bases, of Joseph Burke on the policy process for U.S. arms sales to the Middle East, and of Larry Mortsolf and Louis Samelson on Congress and military aid.

Neither of the edited volumes, nor any other book, treats the security assistance program in its entirety.[3] A particularly glaring omission is the absence of any extended treatment of the largest U.S. economic aid program—the Economic Support Fund.[4] A partial exception, however, is Robert Zimmerman's outstanding *Dollars, Diplomacy, and Dependency* (1993).[5]

Many of the studies that have dealt, in varying degrees, with security assistance as foreign aid focus on U.S. military assistance within a defined historical period. For example, the early Cold War period is examined by William Brown, Jr., and Redvers Opie in *American Foreign Assistance* (1953);[6] by John Holcombe and Alan Berg in *Map for Security* (1957);[7] and by Chester Pach in *Arming the Free World* (1991).[8] The Eisenhower administration is covered by Charles Wolfe, Jr., in *Foreign Aid: Theory and Practice in Southern Asia* (1960)[9] and by John Montgomery in *The Politics of Foreign Aid* (1962).[10] Similarly, Lewis Sorley's *Arms Transfers under Nixon* (1983)[11] deals with the Nixon years; Harold Hovey's *United States Military Assistance* (1966)[12] covers the period through the early Johnson administration; and the Carter administration is examined by Joanna Spear in *Carter and Arms Sales* (1995).[13]

Finally, there are other books of interest that bear variously on security assistance as foreign aid. These include Harold Hovey and Harold Clem's *Collective Defense and Foreign Assistance* (1968);[14] Stephanie Neuman and Robert Harkavy's *Arms Transfers in the Modern World* (1979);[15] Andrew Pierre's *Arms Transfers and American Foreign Policy* (1979);[16] Andrew Pierre's *The Global Politics of Arms Sales* (1982);[17] Paul Hammond, David Louscher, Michael Salomone, and Norman Graham's *The Reluctant Supplier* (1983);[18] David Louscher and Michael Salomone's *Marketing Security Assistance* (1987);[19] and Cynthia Arnson's *Crossroads: Congress, the Reagan Administration, and Central America* (1989).[20]

NOTES

1. Ernest Graves and Steven A. Hildreth, eds., *U.S. Security Assistance: The Political Process* (Lexington, Mass.: Lexington Books, 1985).

2. Craig M. Brandt, ed., *Military Assistance and Foreign Policy* (Wright-Patterson Air Force Base, Ohio: Air Force Institute of Technology, 1990).

3. See, however, U.S. Congress, House, Committee on Foreign Affairs, *Report of the Task Force on Foreign Assistance*, 101st Cong., 1st sess., Rpt. 101–32, 1989; idem, *Background Materials on Foreign Assistance*, 101st Cong., 1st sess., 1989; Duncan L. Clarke and Steven Woehrel, "Reforming United States Security Assistance," *American University Journal of International Law and Policy* 6 (Winter 1991), pp. 217–49.

4. A solid, if unpublished, paper was done by Congressional Research Service analyst Larry Nowels, "Economic Security Assistance as a Tool of American Foreign Policy," Research Report, National War College, Washington, D.C., 1987.

5. Robert F. Zimmerman, *Dollars, Diplomacy, and Dependency: Dilemmas of U.S. Economic Aid* (Boulder, Colo.: Lynne Rienner, 1993).

6. William A. Brown, Jr., and Redvers Opie, *American Foreign Assistance* (Washington, D.C.: Brookings Institution, 1953).

7. John L. Holcombe and Alan Berg, *Map for Security* (Columbia: University of South Carolina School of Business Administration, 1957).

8. Chester A. Pach, *Arming the Free World: The Origins of the Military Assistance Program, 1945–1950* (Chapel Hill: University of North Carolina Press, 1991).

9. Charles Wolf, Jr., *Foreign Aid: Theory and Practice in Southern Asia* (Princeton, N.J.: Princeton University Press, 1960).

10. John D. Montgomery, *The Politics of Foreign Aid* (New York: Praeger Publishers, 1962).

11. Lewis Sorley, *Arms Transfers under Nixon: A Policy Analysis* (Lexington: University of Kentucky Press, 1983).

12. Harold A. Hovey, *United States Military Assistance: A Study of Policies and Practice* (New York: Praeger Publishers, 1966).

13. Joanna Spear, *Carter and Arms Sales: Implementing the Carter Administration's Arms Transfer Restraint Policy* (New York: St. Martin's Press, 1995).

14. Harold A. Hovey and Harold J. Clem, *Collective Defense and Foreign Assistance* (Washington, D.C.: Industrial College of the Armed Forces, 1968).

15. Stephanie G. Neuman and Robert E. Harkavy, eds., *Arms Transfers in the Modern World* (New York: Praeger Publishers, 1979).

16. Andrew J. Pierre, ed., *Arms Transfers and American Foreign Policy* (New York: New York University Press, 1979).

17. Andrew J. Pierre, *The Global Politics of Arms Sales* (Princeton, N.J.: Princeton University Press, 1982).

18. Paul Hammond, David Louscher, Michael Salomone, and Norman Graham, *The Reluctant Supplier: U.S. Decisionmaking for Arms Sales* (Cambridge, Mass.: Oelgeschlager, Gunn and Hain, 1983).

19. David Louscher and Michael Salomone, *Marketing Security Assistance: New Perspectives on Arms Sales* (Lexington, Mass.: Lexington Books, 1987).

20. Cynthia J. Arnson, *Crossroads: Congress, the Reagan Administration, and Central America* (New York: Pantheon Books, 1989).

Index

Erbakan, Necmettin, 160, 166n
Ethiopia, 71
Europe. *See* Eastern Europe; Western Europe; New Independent States
European Community, 129
Excess Defense Articles (EDAs), 15, 24, 35, 41, 127, 158, 164
Export-Import Bank, 52, 103

F-4 Phantom aircraft, 49
Facsell, Dante, 115
Fairless Commission, 155
Farabundo Marti National Liberation Front (FMLN). *See* El Salvador
Feldman, Shai, 173–74
Findlay, Paul, 146n
Fish, Howard, 129
Forbes, Michael, 180
Ford, Gerald, administration of, 53–60, 104, 127
Foreign Affairs, 7
Foreign Assistance Act, 1n, 10, 15–16, 48–49, 54, 59, 81, 123n, 159; reform of, 2–3, 86, 89–90, 104, 112–14, 117, 121, 132, 192
Foreign Military Financing (FMF), 13, 15–16, 26, 68, 75, 80–81, 89, 92, 179; and base-rights states, 149, 157, 193; and Camp David recipients, 18, 169, 193. *See also* Foreign Military Sales
Foreign Military Sales (FMS), 9–10, 15–16, 46, 48–49, 66, 68, 73, 112, 119. *See also* Foreign Military Financing
Foreign Military Sales Act, 10–11, 52, 108
Foreign Operations Administration, 44
Forward defense/presence, 7, 34. *See also* Base-rights
France, 54, 160. *See also* Indochina
Freedom Support Act, 25, 83, 89, 192
Fulbright, J. William, 52
Funk, Sherman, 178

General Accounting Office (GAO), 21–22, 24, 26, 95, 100n
Georgia, 161
Germany, 45, 53, 151, 160, 164n
Gilman, Benjamin, 86, 115, 157

Goldring, Natalie, 144n
Gorbachev, Mikhail, 72
Gorman Commission/Report, 128–29
Gramm-Rudman-Hollings. *See* Deficit Reduction Act
Graves, Ernest, 130
Great Britain, 33–34, 40, 45, 153, 164n
Greece, 4, 9, 16, 24, 34–35, 40, 52, 68, 81, 90, 92, 120, 121n, 161; and base-rights aid, 7, 54, 73, 75, 83, 149, 151, 153, 155, 157–59, 164; Congress and the Greek lobby, 4, 59, 75, 139, 163, 193; Greek-Turkish relations and the 7:10 ratio, 75, 159, 161, 163–64, 167n, 192–93
Greek-Turkish Aid Act, 8, 34
Grimmet, Richard F., 142n
Gross National Product (GNP), 27n, 38, 135
Guatemala, 2, 22, 67, 71, 79
Gulf Cooperation Council (GCC), 162
Gulf War, 1, 82–83, 109, 126, 152, 153–55, 160–62, 164, 190–91

Haiti, 22–23, 190
Hamilton, Lee, 86, 112, 115; Hamilton Task Force, 2, 86, 90, 112–13, 132
Hartung, William, 144n
Hashimoto, Ryutaro, 156
Helms, Jesse, 90, 103, 115, 133
Hinckley, Barbara, 101
Holt, Pat, 111
Honduras, 2, 75, 79, 84
House of Representatives, U.S.: House Appropriations Committee, Foreign Operations Subcommittee, 28n, 44, 103, 114, 117–20, 133, 154–55, 180, 193; House Armed Services Committee, 123n; House Budget Committee, 123n; House Committee on Energy and Commerce, Subcommittee on Oversight and Investigations, 185n; House Committee on Government Operations, 44; House Foreign Affairs (or International Relations) Committee, 86, 105, 108, 114–17, 157, 175. *See also* Congress, U.S.; Senate, U.S.
Human rights, 2, 8, 29n, 58, 60, 128–29,

About the Authors

DUNCAN L. CLARKE is Professor of International Relations at the School of International Service, American University.

DANIEL B. O'CONNOR is affiliated with the School of International Service, American University.

JASON D. ELLIS is affiliated with the School of International Service, American University.

The authors have published extensively on contemporary foreign affairs issues.

ISBN 0-275-95991-0

HARDCOVER BAR CODE